Forever
Music

Forever
Music

by Edith Schaeffer

A Raven's Ridge Book

BAKER BOOK HOUSE
Grand Rapids, Michigan

Unless noted otherwise, Scripture quotations are from the New King James Version, copyright © 1979, 1980, 1982 by Thomas Nelson, Inc., Publishers.

Scripture quotations marked NIV are from the Holy Bible, New International Version, copyright © 1973, 1978 by International Bible Society. Used by permission of Zondervan Bible Publishers.

Library of Congress Cataloging-in-Publication Data

Schaeffer, Edith
  Forever music.

  Bibliography: p. 247
  1. Schaeffer, Edith.   2. Christian biography.
3. Christian life—1960-   . I. Title.
BR1725.S354A33   1985   267'.13'0924[B]   85-31027

ISBN: 0-8010-8336-2

Second printing, May 1993

Printed in the United States of America

This book is dedicated to
Mary Crowley
who had an idea—
followed by a definite choice—
followed by specific action.

This book would never have been "born" if the Steinway baby grand, Model S 281261, had not arrived precisely in the middle of July 6, 1984! That piano, given in memory of Francis Schaeffer, was Mary's idea—but the piano sparked off a whole succession of ideas and action which resulted in my writing this book. The period of research and writing has been a very new chapter in my own life. Mary is one of those people who actually do a thing "in time" to affect history in relation to what they have been given to do. To act "in time" is something worth talking about, and something needing deep thanks and special recognition. Thank you, Mary!

CONTENTS

Forever Music

A New Start for Two People and One Piano

J uly 6, 1935, was one of those hot muggy Philadelphia summer days with the temperature in the nineties and the humidity the same. Strains of Mendelssohn from the church organ drifted out the door of the little United Presbyterian Church on Wayne Avenue in Germantown. People in the pews temporarily stopped their hand-manipulated fans and moved over a bit, as room had to be made for latecomers. Some of those who had been sitting made movements away from the back of the pew as perspiration seemed to glue their clothing to the wood. The wild flowers looked fresh in spite of a few drooping heads, and those who had picked them that morning smiled with satisfaction at each other. It was precisely four o'clock, and a whole new piece of history was beginning. Francis August Schaeffer, born in 1912 right there in Germantown, and Edith Rachel Seville, born in 1914 in Wenchow, Chekiang Province, China, were about to become the first generation of a new family!

People passing by stopped to listen and to wait for a glimpse of the wedding party. They hummed the tune to the familiar "wedding march." Those in the congregation straining to watch the bridesmaids and then the bride on the arm of her father's professor friend walk up the aisle also thought that this was the "right music" for walking up to the moment of making lifelong vows. A few felt some pride in being able to title the music in their minds as "Incidental Music for the Shakespearean play, A *Midsummer Night's Dream.*"

The father of the bride waited at the front with the bridegroom, watching his youngest daughter come forward to be given away to become, with the bridegroom, a separate family. He quietly prayed he wouldn't be overcome with emotion as he asked the questions as officiating pastor. The organ music played an accompaniment to his mixed feelings of sadness and joy as this would be a new beginning for him too. The mother of the bride and the mother of the bridegroom leaned out into the aisle a bit, one on one side, the other on the opposite, each thinking her separate thoughts set to the music coursing through her brain—thoughts to be remembered the next time she heard the same bars played again.

The bride herself walked properly...step...step...step...with practiced timing and natural grace, not too rapidly, trying to walk as if alone and yet smoothly blending with the professor's more jerky steps. The overwhelming realization hit her that this flower-strewn walk was a farewell walk, one saying good-bye to the family togetherness with her parents in the known pattern, and a titanic step into the beginning of a future life and family with a new pattern. That sudden recognition made it necessary to take her eyes away from her mother's smiling encouragement, and to pin them unswervingly on the bridegroom's face. "Hello," not "good-bye," was all her emotions could stand at that moment. It was "hello to us...we'll be *we* from now on" which was being set to music.

Whatever this music had meant to Mendelssohn when he first heard it inside his own head, it has meant a variety of things to actors and actresses waiting in the wings to take their part in the Shakespearean play. It has meant a variety of other things to generations of brides and grooms, their families, and friends. Brides and bridegrooms have walked or waited nervously, expectantly, fearfully, or excitedly to the same order of notes surging through their ears, brains, and beings.

Theater, drama of all sorts, and films may effectively use music to assist in communication of what is taking place in a story so that the audience will understand. But real life's most dramatic moments are also often accompanied by music in some form, never to be forgotten. Music emphasizes as well as surrounds what is going on. Music underlines and gives impact to what is being said, related, promised for the future. Music blends people together and helps them to feel the same things as well as to think separate thoughts.

No matter what music is being played at a wedding—whether Mendelssohn, Bach, or Handel—it is an introduction to a beginning, an opening of a door and a closing of a door. Present and future are meeting at a narrow bridge, and the music carries them across that bridge. Tears will flow some day when another new beginning comes without choice being involved. When indeed "death do us part" the strains of music will still be fresh on the instrument of the brain's fantastic memory. How incredible is the human brain in playing one instrument—or a full orchestra—in a "playback" heard by that one person alone.

Music lulls the baby to sleep as a loving mother or father sings a lullabye. Music helps the Marines to march in astonishing formation. Music takes proud graduates to the platform to receive diplomas. Music binds a family together as they share a symphony orchestra's concert, or sing folk songs by a piano, or listen to a tape of Schubert's quintet. Music causes people to stand at attention when the president or the queen or king walks in. Music makes people dance or jump in the beauty of different countries' folk customs. Music is essential in skating leaps and twirls as well as in ballet. Music brings freedom to weep as well as to laugh.

Human beings are either performers of music or the audience for others performing. Actually music is essential to human beings even as human beings are essential to music. Verbalized communication, both spoken and written, distinguishes human beings from all else, but so also does the communication of music.

A shepherd plays his sweet flute with haunting notes on a Hungarian hillside and feels as well as hears his own music. Later at a village festival or a city concert hall, that composition is hailed as a magical means of transporting many people in some wonderful way to the hillside surroundings of the composer. The reality of music's communication ranges from gentle rural scenes being sketched to stormy waves crashing on rocks being "seen" in the mind's eye. It includes phalanxes of marching soldiers suddenly coming into view in that same mind as the music changes.

Music is so much more than just sound, so much more than just a means of stirring emotions, so much more than a pleasure that relaxes or sweeps away the nagging problems, so much more than a background for eating and talking, so much more than the necessary inspiration for choreographing dance steps, so much more than the medium through which the words of an opera, a cantata, a hymn may be effectively sung, so much more than the emotionally correct surrounding for the romantic words of a love song or a declaration of loyalty for one's country as the words of a national anthem pour forth. Music is a very basic part of understanding the difference between a human being and all else in the universe. Music is an integral part of who we are. It is a part of being human.

Of course, music also has the power to jangle the nerves, to strike discord within as well as to hurt ears. Despair as well as joy can be expressed. Ugliness as well as beauty can be the object as well as the result of an art work. The communication can be of hopelessness as well as of hope, of discouragement rather than encouragement. Music is a means of real expression, the expression of what is deep in the mind and heart of the composer. Fragmentation as well as the unity of blended instruments can be the result of even the most perfectly tuned instruments being played. The instrument of a beautiful human voice does not insure *what* that voice will bring forth or whether truth or falseness is communicated.

No one could "hear" the ideas racing through minds that day in 1935. Silence filled the church as the soloist's voice stopped its outpouring of words about "oh perfect love," and Dr. Seville's firm voice began to read words from his little, white leather-covered book:

> Dearly beloved, we are assembled here in the presence of God, to join this Man and this Woman in holy marriage; which is instituted of God, regulated by His commandments, blessed by our Lord Jesus Christ, and to be held in honor among all men. Let us therefore reverently remember that God has established and sanctified marriage, for the welfare and happiness of mankind. Our Savior has declared that a man shall forsake his father and mother and cleave unto his wife. By His apostles, He has instructed those who enter into this relation to cherish a mutual esteem and love; to bear with each other's infirmities and weaknesses; to comfort each other in sickness, trouble, and sorrow; in honesty and industry to provide for each other, and for their household, in temporal things; to pray for and encourage each other in the things which pertain to God; and to live together as heirs of the grace of life.

How many were thinking of their own past vows as they listened? To how many were the words a real communication of the reality of lasting marriage? And to how many were the words simply syllables without meaning?

Dr. Seville continued, "Let us pray." A rustle of movement gave evidence of some measure of response. Heads were bowed, most of the fans were still.

> Almighty and ever-blessed God, whose presence is the happiness of every condition, and whose favor sweetens every

Francis and Edith Schaeffer after taking their vows on July 6, 1935.

relation: We beseech Thee to be present and favorable unto these Thy servants, that they may be truly joined in the honorable estate of marriage. As Thou hast brought them together by Thy providence, sanctify them by Thy Spirit, giving them a new frame of heart fit for their new estate; and grant unto them, now in the hour of their affiance and throughout their wedded life, Thy heavenly guidance; through our Lord Jesus Christ. *Amen.*

The little, white leather book after forty-nine years still has the fine handwriting of Dr. Seville where he wrote in the names.

Francis, wilt thou have this Woman to be thy wife, and wilt thou pledge thy troth to her, in all love and honor, in all duty and service, in all faith and tenderness, to live with her and cherish her, according to the ordinance of God, in the holy bond of marriage?

(And the Man shall answer: "I will.")

Edith, wilt thou have this Man to be thy husband, and wilt thou pledge thy troth to him, in all love and honor, in all duty and service, in all faith and tenderness, to live with him and cherish him, according to the ordinance of God, in the holy bond of marriage?

(And the Woman shall answer: "I will.")

Then the father of the bride, who was now becoming father-in-law of the bridegroom, took the right hand of the bridegroom and the right hand of the bride and placed them together asking for the following vows to be repeated:

I, Francis, take thee, Edith, to be my wedded wife; And I do promise and covenant; Before God and these witnesses; To be thy loving and faithful husband; In plenty and in want; In joy and in sorrow; In sickness and in health; As long as we both shall live.

Loosing hands so that there might be a specific taking again of hands for this declaration:

I, Edith, take thee, Francis, to be my wedded husband; And I do promise and covenant; Before God and these witnesses; To be thy loving and faithful wife; In plenty and in want; In joy and in sorrow; In sickness and in health; As long as we both shall live.

The giving of the ring followed this, and further prayer, as well as the formal declaration that they were now husband and wife, according to the ordinance of God and the law of the Commonwealth of Pennsylvania. The final strong utterance followed:

Whom God hath joined together, let no man put asunder.

And the blessing:

The Lord bless you, and keep you:
The Lord make His face shine upon you,
    and be gracious unto you:
The Lord lift up His countenance upon you,
    and give you peace:
Both now and in the life everlasting. *Amen.*

A burst of music, the recessional's glad tones, time for a kiss, and then the walk up the aisle with bridesmaids and groomsmen behind, a bevy of friends pressing around, some never to be seen again as paths were to lead in such geographically distant places. Father Seville greeted friends, shaking hands, as a part of the receiving line, just thirty years after his own wedding had taken place in Shanghai. Mother Seville stood by his side remarking that her wedding dress had been a Chinese gown and remembering her honeymoon on the riverboat going down the river from Shanghai, around the coast, and upriver into Wenchow. Thirty years seems a long time to a twenty-year-old, but it seems to diminish in length as years go on. How rapidly generations overlap. The threads of lives and their creativity and discoveries weave and blend with other lives not only within a generation, but across the generations. Weddings are the starting place for the coming together of new sets of genes, producing scientists, musicians, composers, performers, architects, inventors, farmers. They are the starting place of homes, families, educational inspiration in discussion.

Pianos are numbered. If you know where to look, you can find the number of a concert grand piano, or a studio grand, or a baby grand piano and know where it fits in its "line." If people were also numbered and if you were at the wedding reception nibbling the cake, sipping punch, letting cool raspberry sherbet mingle with the coffee ice cream to cool your throat, you might have said, "Oh yes, Seville number 61,237 has just married Schaeffer 72,961." But could you even begin to trace the backgrounds and heritages of these two human beings, a five-foot-six-inch male and a five-foot-two-inch female, both with brown eyes? How many generations would come from this new beginning in the lifetime of these two? And what change in the sights and sounds, the events and actions, the knowledge and understanding of the next fifty years of history would spring from this new beginning? Would their existence cause a ripple? Would their living and working, thinking and communicating make any difference?

A new start was being made by two people who had no idea of the future ahead of them. Where were they going? "To Michigan to work in a summer camp until seminary begins in the fall" would have been their answer. It was during the Depression. Edith would ingeniously devise ways to earn money during her husband's seminary years by dressmaking and by designing and producing leather belts and buttons. They would run a camp in Michigan and the next summer a camp in New Hampshire.

Had you that day been able to whisper, "You'll be in three different locations after seminary—Grove City, Chester, and St. Louis—and then you will be in Switzerland for thirty-six years," you would have probably received a pitying look for your attempt to foretell the future with wild, impossible guesses. If you had gone on to say, "You'll have forty-nine years together before death parts you, and before Francis dies he will have written twenty-three books to be translated into twenty-seven languages, and he will have made three films and hundreds of tapes," the incredulity would have increased.

Whatever was ahead, July 6, 1935, was only a beginning.

It was the same hot day in Queens, New York. It was during the same Depression! The standard of Steinway had not diminished one iota. A lot of money had been offered to the Steinway brothers to use their name on a lesser product, but it was refused. In spite of the Depression the production of Steinway grand pianos continued with the same artistic carefulness in every detail of craftsmanship. Concert grands, studio grands, drawing room grands were all still being made. A new addition came into the Steinway family of pianos at approximately the same time that this new beginning came to two people in Germantown.

In the Pierce Piano Atlas where the numbers of pianos are recorded, like the names of human beings in a county courthouse record, there is a list of numbers from 1936 making it possible to know what pianos were being made in 1935. You see, it takes nearly one year to make a piano, and so July 6, 1935, would have found baby grand piano number 281261 in the midst of its careful growth under the fingers of four hundred workers, each one doing his or her part as carefully and expertly as possible. Every choice of material, every size and shape of all 12,000 parts, and every decision based on each specialist's knowledge and sensitivity made a difference!

The heat of that July day made the lumberyard uncomfortable as men looked for just the right wood to use for pianos. Wood ages a year in the lumberyard outside the factory. After it has aged long enough, workers load the wood into a kiln to dry—with a temperature of about 160° Fahrenheit. Moisture is removed this way so that the wood won't warp. I guess the outside temperature in the nineties would feel cool after any length of time in that huge drying oven!

Piano 281261 has that lovely graceful curve of the Steinway baby grands. That wonderful curve couldn't be formed with a thick piece of wood, and so twelve sheets (and eighteen sheets for concert grands) of 3/16″ maple veneer are glued together, making a more flexible piece of wood. The last veneer to be glued on is an extra-thin slice of mahogany with the glue being carefully brushed on by hand. Four men carry this long laminated piece of wood to the rim press where it is to be bent into shape. The vises and clamps have to be put into place rapidly so that the short drying period of the glue will not make the shaping impossible! As in so many critical moments in making something beautiful and precise, these strong men work in the silence of concentration, knowing that bending must be exactly as it should be so that the sweeping curve will not be spoiled nor the music marred as it comes forth.

So often in life there is a *time* that is precisely the time to do something. It may not be as short as the twelve-minute drying period for the glue, but there are precise times which, if ignored, will destroy beauty and readiness for the next step. This is true in many creative works...including the creative work of relationships in marriage, in the family, among friends, and with fellow workers on a project.

The wood of the rim of number 281261 was left overnight under the strain of tremendous pressure of the press. There never have been short cuts at any stage. The hurry of getting the laminated boards on the press comes to an end when the beautifully shaped rim is lifted off and carried to the drying room, which is humidity controlled. There it spends ten weeks having the moisture content reduced. Other rims are standing in line there, like a gorgeously silent ballet of wood. When ballerinas curve their arms and point their toes in a fantastic leap or bending movement, they are not "still" unless a camera freezes the movement, but these rims remain a lineup of art-works in

Laminated, shaped rims for grand pianos stand for ten weeks in the drying room at the Steinway factory.

silent motion. The drying of that shape is completed with no fear of the piano turning back into a tree.

During that time the 5-foot-1-inch case that was to become baby grand 281261 might have looked up to the 8-foot-11¾-inch towering height of a concert grand. A conversation might have gone something like this: "We can't see our future homes but I envy the brilliance of the music that will pour forth from you as great pianists play to crowds in great concert halls of big cities." And the concert grand might have replied, "Yes, but there is envy on my part too of the loving care you will be given in a cozy living room and of the warm evenings with people gathered around you to sing or to play instruments together for the sheer joy of making music. You'll be a part of family life in a more intimate way." "That may be true—but I look up to you. I'm glad you can send your clear notes to the top balcony."

A separate identity had begun not only for number 281261, but for every other piano whose rim silently stood drying in 1935. They had forgotten their original shapes as trees and were ready now to be filled with that which would make them all they were to be. Rims. *Well-bent* rims. What had the wedding prayer said? "...giving them a *new* frame of heart for their *new* estate." Is this just romantic rubbish? No, it is a very sharp pointing to reality. The two people making a new start are meant to be bent into a frame that is to give beauty, not ugliness. There is a framework for human beings to have a oneness which is an integral part of who human beings are and of what the universe is. Just any old framework will not fit.

In the summer of 1935, two people and one piano were being formed with a proper framework.

About two months later the rim was taken to the frazing department where each worker did his or her part, sawing, planing, and sanding to prepare it for the cross braces, the key bed, and a pin block. Now the rim had become the case for 281261. Another two months later, lacquer was put on the pianos which were to be black, but 281261 was to have a high polished mahogany finish and so it stood a little apart!

On the second floor of the factory, all the while this was going on, a soundboard was being made. The soundboard amplifies the sound of the piano strings so that as the pianist's fingers hit the keys and the hammers hit the strings, a vibration takes place and the sound can be heard throughout the room or to the farthest corners of a huge concert hall. The wood of the soundboard is an expensive grade of Sitka spruce, which has grown for many years to attain the right grain. It is sawed so that the grain is lengthwise, giving a vibration along the length of the boards. The soundboard is made like that of a violin—but of course much larger—and gives a free and even response throughout the entire scale.

The Steinway soundboards are especially shaped to be eight millimeters thick in the center and five millimeters thick at the edges. This shape causes them to vibrate as one unit. Then ribs of sugar pine are glued to the underside so that the board is pushed up into a slight bow, making the sound waves project more efficiently.

The vibrating area of the five-foot-one-inch grand being made in 1935 was 1,659 square inches of this stable Sitka spruce. It holds up under incredible stress and with an amazing amount of vibration! The strings of the piano are stretched across a bridge made of vertical laminations of hard-rock maple capped with solid hard-rock maple. All this is done by hand, with careful sanding and planing. This method of building pianos has been carefully handed down, with bits of improvement added through the years. The strings of the piano are stretched across the bridge at just the right time, and the vibrations of the strings will travel through the bridge to the soundboard as long as the piano lasts.

The "speaking length" of a string is that portion which can vibrate freely. It is the curved shape and position of the bridge that affects that "speaking length." The length of the string, its thickness, and how tightly it is stretched determine how high or low the note will be.

In the middle of the 1800s Steinway began using a cast-iron plate which permitted much higher string tension than could be borne by pianos with all wood or wood fortified with metal bars. This design added strength and enabled the makers to use thinner strings at higher tension and thus gain more volume. When the cast-iron plate arrives at the Steinway factory, it is a dull gray metal and must be ground, smoothed, painted gold, and buffed to a brasslike gleam, giving dignity to the wood and strings so that the piano is appropriate for a drawing room rather than a boiler factory! The stringing technique permitted by this combination of the cast-iron plate and the placement of the bridge would be technical to describe, but you need to know that the results brought forth the possibility of heavier hammers and a wider control which came to be known as "the Steinway system" or "the American system."

In those months of 1935, both piano 281261 and the family Francis and Edith Schaeffer began to emerge. There was a lot of sanding, rubbing off of rough edges, tempering and gluing together that needed to be done in both instances in order to prepare something that was going to last a long time under great tensions and vibrations of a diversity of sorts! This is not farfetched, but truly a sober comparison. There are less carefully made pianos, slapdash by comparison, and there are less carefully worked on relationships which fall apart, breaking up in a discordant and painful sound, just when the most important moment arrives!

The cast-iron plate supports 240 metal strings, so tightly stretched that altogether they exert about 35,000 pounds of tension per square inch. No wonder everything has to be in order, with rough parts ground smooth first. The person who grinds the plate has to wear ear protectors because the noise made by the grinding against the rough metal is so very penetrating. He also wears safety glasses to protect his eyes from flying particles of the iron.

While piano 281261 was being formed in Queens, New York, Edith and Fran were working at a summer camp in Michigan. Edith was having a frustrating time trying to cut Fran's hair so it looked as if a barber had cut it, and trying to wash his shirts and other clothing in a bucket, hoping to produce perfectly beautiful ironed and starched shirts on a wobbly old ironing board with an iron that wouldn't behave. Time was going by as they returned to Philadelphia and Fran began to dig in on Hebrew, Greek, and church history while Edith made leather belts and did dressmaking to make it possible to have three years of seminary during the Depression!

The Steinway Specifications Table lists the tuning pins next and describes them as "premium blued steel with rust-resistant, nickeled heads." You can read a much more detailed description of all this in *The Atlantic Monthly* article "The Quality of the Instrument,"[1] but we need know only that the tuning pins will be anchored in a heavy block of wood called the pinblock which is behind the keyboard. Two hundred forty holes have to be drilled into the cast-iron plate so that the tuning pins can come up through the plate from the pinblock underneath. Carefully the plate is lowered into the piano where it is positioned right over the precious soundboard, but not touching it at all. The building of a Steinway piano requires precise measuring and exact and sensitive work by the hands of craftsmen who are real artists.

Now for the strings. Again let me quote from the Steinway

1. Michael Lenehan, "The Quality of the Instrument," *The Atlantic Monthly*, August, 1982.

specifications: "TREBLE: Twelve whole and one-half sizes from high-tensile Swedish steel. BASS: Swedish steel core wire wound with pure copper." The thin silver-colored steel strings vibrate more rapidly, making the treble notes. The thicker copper-covered strings vibrate more slowly and make the bass notes.

What a difference each string makes and how impossible would be the playing of Liszt or Chopin if even one string were missing, let alone several. The craftsman threading the strings into their proper places needs dexterous as well as strong fingers. These fingers need protection from being cut by the piano wire, however, and so they are wrapped with the proper sort of tape. The stringer puts on 201 treble strings first, three for each treble note. Like threading many needles, he threads the wire through the holes in the tuning pins and then twists or wraps the wire in its proper place around the pin. One by one, he stretches the wire across the plate, around one of the hitchpins, and back to the next tuning pin, where it is threaded and twisted again. In that way one piece of wire makes two treble strings.

Like a weaver making a tapestry, the stringer reaches for one of the thirty-nine thick copper-wrapped bass strings, using one or two for each bass note. One end of the string is attached to a hitchpin; the other is put through a tuning pin and coiled around that pin. The bass strings are placed above the treble strings so that they cross at the center of the soundboard where they can be amplified properly. This is a beautiful economy of space, allowing the piano to be smaller than it otherwise would have to be. But it also is a thing of beauty. There is a harmony of line, as one looks at the stringing with the top off of the piano, as well as harmony of sound if a skillful pianist is playing a harmonious work.

If this were as far as piano 281261 had ever come, it might be a thing of interest to the eyes, but it could not be heard by anyone's ears. Action is needed.

Have you ever watched a movie being made? Cameras are ready, the sound man has his equipment running perfectly, the actors have their lines in their heads, the lights are exactly where they should be with the right intensity or softness. The operative word is "ACTION," screamed or spoken softly by the director, and the reply needed is "rolling." Everything is ready for the drama to be enacted and to be recorded on film. In some people's lives and relationships, when God calls "ACTION," the reply of "rolling" does not come. The Lord says, "I called you, but you did not answer" (Jer. 7:13).

In life, the "action" is what affects history, makes an impact on

The craftsman stringer threads each of the 240 wires through a hole in the tuning pin and then wraps it around the hitchpin.

other people, adds or subtracts something from other people's lives. In the pattern taking shape in the togetherness of two people, there is an ingredient that could be paralleled to the action parts needed by the piano before it can be heard. Music cannot come forth without the movable, constantly changing portions which respond to the hands of the pianist.

In quite another part of the factory, the action parts of the Steinway are being made. The sound that is going to be amplified by the soundboard comes from the strings, of course, but the strings don't send forth a sound to be amplified unless they are hit! Hammers strike the strings to make the sound. The hammer consists of a core of wood covered with dark felt and then another layer of shaped white felt of just the proper thickness. Each of the eighty-eight hammers—one for each key—is glued to a hammer shank, a five-inch-long piece of wood. When these hammers are ready they are all mounted on the action frame, to be installed in the piano case behind the keyboard. Here is a frame within the frame! The action gives firm control, comfortable limitations, an essential form for the freedom of music. There never is true freedom without form. Freedom without form is chaos!

The action parts are joined by miniscule metal pins. Each pin has a crucial place in the action of the piano, and therefore in the music itself! Each pin constitutes a hinge, or an action center, around which the parts must move freely. The human cry is so often "What difference do I make? What significance do I have in history? Am I only a chance particle in the midst of chaos?" It would be good to gaze at an individual action part in a model of one key and all that goes into its movement. It might also be good to read carefully the Steinway specifications concerning action and identify your own importance in relation to these essential parts of the whole. Read with excitement and imagination because in doing so you'll catch a glimpse of something you might have missed about what is going wrong with your own human relationships.

> White, quarter-sawn maple parts are bushed with specially treated wool action cloth for freedom from friction. Parts are anchored in hard maple dowels housed in inflexible seamless brass tubing to assure precise and stable regulation. Exclusive single, combination phosphor bronze repetition and fly spring provides constant, crisp touch response. Specially designed to respond 14 percent faster fortissimo and 6 percent faster pianissimo by using

an exclusive combination of half-round balance rail bearings and strategically placed key leads.

"Freedom from friction" needs special preparation and care ahead of time. "Precise and stable regulation" is needed in life, and attention needs to be paid to its source. There has to be a base that is inflexible in this action unit for the piano. Human beings also need a base that is "inflexible"—not to curtail freedom, but to make freedom have true meaning.

When the action parts are placed in the piano, things begin to come together, but not without much testing to the satisfaction of the experts in each area. In 1935 the keys were made of ivory, although in 1950 Steinway switched to plastic. The ivory of S 281261 covered keys constructed of sugar pine. When they arrived at the factory they were placed on a key frame one by one to make a keyboard. If you walked in at just that time, you would have seen a keyboard without any action that could make music. It has to *be* all together to work together.

Before the keys are placed into the piano, however, the action of each key is carefully tested to make sure that the keys will respond evenly to the fingers of the pianist. This testing is called the "weigh-off." A woman or man sits patiently placing lead weights on the keys, one by one, one by one. Does the key move too rapidly, too loosely? Is the key too stiff? The worker watches to see just how far and how fast each key moves when the weight is put on it and then makes the necessary adjustment. Patience is needed, but also an understanding of the importance of this preciseness to the pianist who will need eighty-eight keys responding to his or her fingers with the correct sensitivity.

Now the keyboard and the action are put into the case which is the framework for which it has all been made. It fits, and it can do in that framework what it has been prepared to do!

The damper man does his work next. Blocks with felt pads that rest on the strings and "dampen" the sound are called dampers. These are necessary to stop vibration in the longer strings, and can be controlled by the pedals. It is the action of the dampers which makes it possible to have longer or shorter sounds, and so the damper man's work is very important for bringing the variations of the music to the ears of the audience. As he works to adjust the dampers until they rest on the strings with an equal amount of pressure, moving up and down, up and down with an even speed, he must sometimes feel discouraged. "Is it important?" But during a concert at Carnegie Hall, he would feel satisfaction as the pianist used the dampers, audibly giving a perfect variation at just the proper places. "My dampers" would be an unspoken phrase, but a satisfying one. "*My* dampers."

Soft restraint. A damper is a soft restraint of a sound that would be too sharp without it. Let your imagination work on the possibility of "soft restraint" among the human sounds that rise to too sharp a pitch. But such dampering can't take place without someone's clever ideas of how to gently and evenly stop the "vibration." It takes work to bring about results that show up, work that can seem like discouraging drudgery. What so many people don't understand is that great works of art don't come about by chance—work is involved. Human relationships are indeed works of art worth working on for a lifetime. Soft restraint needs *someone's* patient work.

But piano 281261 is not finished yet. The tone regulator has to do his skillful specialized work. The quality of the piano's "voice" or sound depends upon his sensitive adjustments of the hammers. He files each hammer with a piece of sandpaper wrapped around a piece of wood. These hammers have just been made, but now they are to be shaped into an egg shape. The shape of the hammers makes all the difference as to how they will strike the strings, and the sound of each note depends on this split second of time when the hammer strikes the string at dead center. The tone regulator uses a little gadget with needles in it to jab at the outer part of the felt—with an exquisite perfection of touch—to make the hammers more resilient and to change the sound. His ear is able to distinguish the delicate changes of sound—whether the full deep sounds of the bass or the clear bright sounds of the treble. The tone regulator spends about twenty-five hours on each piano before it is ready for the piano tuner.

Next the tuner must work in a place where he is shut away from distracting sounds or people. He is alone with the piano. He listens to his tuning fork which vibrates at 440 vibrations per second, and then plays A on the piano and listens carefully. Because of his highly trained ears he knows precisely when the sound is correct. If the note is too low, that means the string is vibrating too slowly, and so he tightens the string with a tool made for that purpose by turning the tuning pin. He loosens the string if the note is too high. These adjustments must be very tiny, a wee bit at a time, and he works over and over again until he is satisfied that each of the eighty-eight notes is in tune.

It is almost 1936 by now, and Steinway piano 281261 is ready for the final polishing of the beautiful curves of its case, the lid, the music rack, the legs...and then for its careful packing into a case for the journey to the display room in the store which had ordered it.

When Edith and Francis Schaeffer had finished the first year of seminary in Philadelphia, they drove in a Model A Ford through Massachusetts into the White Mountains to Rumney, New Hampshire, where they were to run a boys camp called "Camp Richard Webber Oliver." It was a new kind of togetherness, with a different set of strains and stresses as well as an introduction to mountain climbing and breathtaking views. They cared for a range of little boys—taught them, hiked with them, read them stories at night, prayed with them, tied their shoelaces, put mercurochrome on their cuts and ice on their bruises, scolded them for playing with matches, and loved them. It was a kind of tuning and toning, a time of getting ready for another generation to be introduced to a rich, family life. It was both things at once. It was a part of life that was complete in the present, and it was a preparation for a new start—and a series of new starts!

It was very early in 1936 that this one piano, cozily encased in its protective wrappings and box, was traveling in another direction on its way to Minnesota. Who would buy it? Where would the first home be for Steinway 281261? As the unwrapping took place in Boutells music store in Minneapolis, the gleaming mahogany caught rays of sunshine, not dimmed by the Depression! A new start, a continuity, and forty-eight years later there was a recognition that there was to be a connection between the two people and this one piano.

CHAPTER 2

From 1936 to 1984

A new year has a mysterious appeal. To an optimist, any exciting thing might be just around the corner. To a pessimist, dark clouds of trouble wait to cast a shadow on the next chapter of life. The unknown of what is ahead seems to be bound up in those two words "new year," and people say a bit too loudly, "Happy New Year," feeling that verbalizing the wish itself will give birth to happiness.

In spite of the Depression, 1936 was no exception. Edith and Fran hugged each other and simultaneously said, "Happy New Year." It was their first new year as married people. Although they had been married in July and this was the beginning of a new six months, it was a new *year*. What an incredible mark of time a new calendar is. Up goes a new calendar with another number on it. Another year among the ones to be counted in a lifetime. If the years of a life are to be lined up, how many will there be for two people? How many years will there be for one piano?

In January 1936, the *Minneapolis Tribune* was full of headlines concerning the questioning of Bruno Hauptmann in the "Lindy Kidnapping" case as well as of King George V's bronchial ailment, which was becoming more serious in conjunction with his poor circulation. Headlines spoke of the cost of living going up in the Twin Cities, of the sit-down strike staged at the General Motors plant in Flint, Michigan, and of some bill President Roosevelt wanted passed.

The Tuesday, January 14, 1936, *Minneapolis Tribune* had an advertisement on page 5, with a picture of a Steinway baby grand piano. This was followed by an invitation to a concert Tuesday evening at 8:30. "Steinway and Boutells invite you to hear" a pianist, a

The January 14, 1936, Minneapolis Tribune advertisement of a new selection of Steinway grand pianos at Boutells.

violinist, and a cellist as well as a male chorus. Between 7:30 and 8:30 people were invited to inspect the piano salon.

Steinway pianos are all carefully listed in a notebook which has been preserved through the years. The identity of the piano comes in its number. The number first indicates just where that piano fits into history. A human being's birth is supposed to be listed with a proper birth certificate and a record in the county courthouse. People who believe that a spiritual birth takes place at another time in life find meaning in a hymn that asks, "Is my name written there?" singing of a fact put forth in the Bible that a book exists with everyone's name written at the date of his or her spiritual birth. The importance of records is central—if truth matters at all.

At the Steinway building on 57th Street in New York, the notebook resides. Piano number 281261 is precisely recorded between piano 281260 and piano 281262. Not one is missing! You can also discover that piano 281261 was mahogany and on just what date it was sold and to whom. You can trace an individual piano because of this book's interest in details. The book of which the Bible speaks is called "The Lamb's Book of Life." It is a book that gives importance to the detail of human choice and human individuals who make choices. "The Lamb" is spoken of from early in the Old Testament to the end of the New Testament and is known also as "The Messiah." This Book of Life keeps a record which some day can be seen.

Look at the Steinway book (reproduced on pages 36 and 37) and notice that the large number which identifies this piano, 281261, is followed by a lovely handwritten script with a description "Grd S 5'1" Mah." We know 281261 is a model S baby grand that measures five feet, one inch in length and is made of mahogany. The record continues on the other side of the page. Do look, read, and become excited! Please don't be blasé. Let the prickles go up and down your spine! Because of a careful preservation of newspapers in the Minneapolis Public Library and because of a carefully recorded book at Steinway, we *know* just exactly what happened to 281261, and when! When the piano was finished, it was shipped from the factory to Boutells in Minneapolis. We know that a lovely salon had been prepared for a display of Steinways as a first of its kind "in the Northwest" because the newspaper tells us about it. The excitement comes with the *dates!* The record book dates the sale of each piano, as well as telling the place where it was sold. Re-read the date of that concert and presentation of the Steinway collection—it was January 14, 1936. Now read the date of the sale of 281261. It was January 15, 1936.

It was sold the next day, and so we can picture a great deal of

281256 Grd S 51" am wal Jan 16/36 (O984) Lac Na
281257 Grd S 51" am wal Jan 13/36 (O933) " "
281258 Grd S 51" am wal Jan 13/36 (O983) " . "
281259 Grd S 51" mah Jan 13/36 (O650) Lac Na
281260 Grd S 51" mah Jan 14/36 (O661) " "
281261 Grd S 51" mah Jan 17/36 (O711) hac Na
281262 Grd S 51" mah Jan 13/36 (O909) hac Na
281263 Grd S 51" mah Jan 20/36 (O609) " "
281264 Grd S 51" mah Feb 13/36 (O620) " "
281265 Grd S 51" mah Jan 20/36 (O784) " . "
281266 Grd S 51" mah Jan 13/36 (O917) hac Na
281267 Grd S 51" mah Jan 17/36 (O931) " "
281268 Grd S 51" am wal Jan 16/36 (O988) " "
281269 Grd S 51" mah Jan 17/36 (O579) " "
281270 Grd S 51" mah Feb 7/36 (O619) " "
281271 Grd S 51" mah Jan 17/36 (O677) " "
281272 Grd S 51" mah Jan 20/36 (O859) " "
281273 Grd S 51" mah Jan 20/36 (O893) " "
281274 Grd S 51" mah Jan 17/36 (O930) " "
281275 Grd S 51" mah Jan 13/36 (O946) " "
281276 Grd S 51" mah Jan 17/36 (O634) " "
281277 Grd S 51" mah Jan 20/36 (O642) " "
281278 Grd S 51" mah Jan 20/36 (O903) " "
281279 Grd S 51" am wal Jan 20/36 (O985) " "

Steinway log book recording the description and date of sale of Model S baby grand 281261.

anell Bros Detroit Mich	Jan 16	1936	
nr Healy Inc Chicago Ill	Jan 18	1936	
" " " " Music House Inc Great Falls Mont Oct 19 38	Jan 18	1936	
s Piano House Great Falls Mont	Jan 15	1936	
n H. Roze Piano Co Fort Worth Tex sh 1/14/36	Aug 25	1936	
itell Brothers Inc Minneapolis Minn	Jan 15	1936	
Grau's Inc Cincinnati Ohio sh 1/15/36	Mar 2	1936	
ny Mildred White 86 West 49 St Brooklyn NY	Feb 11	1936	
Wilma P. Herrlin 27-19 Pitman Blvd Astoria, L.I. Ny	Feb 15	1936	
le Bros Co Cleveland Ohio	Jan 20	1936	
f Brodt Music Co Madison Wisc	Jan 15	1936	
Porter Son Co. Lima, Ohio	Jan 17	1936	
nell Bros Detroit Mich	Jan 16	1936	
tkins Bros Inc Hartford Conn	Jan 21	1936	
ward J. Rodenbeck 45 Christopher St	Feb 18	1936	
nothy Clarkson Wright Inc Burlington Vt	Jan 17	1936	
le Bros Co Cleveland Ohio	Jan 18	1936	
	Jan 18	1936	
B. Keaton Columbus Ohio sh 1/17/36	Apr 23	1936	
nr Healy Inc Chicago Ill	Jan 18	1936	
y Piano Store Providence R.I.	Jan 17	1936	
fith Piano Co Newark N.J.	Jan 21	1936	
le Music Co San Diego Cal	Jan 22	1936	
hmoller & Mueller Piano Co Omaha Nebr	Jan 22	1936	

what happened, as well as know when the choice was made which gave this piano a home, a house prepared especially for it.

We need to go back to the turn of the century to find that a girl born in Iowa studied at St. Olaf College, and then at the McPhail Conservatory of Music in Minneapolis. Early in the 1900s she was teaching music in North Dakota, but in 1904 she married an engineer and became Mrs. Henry Loomis. Lu and Henry had one daughter, who had piano lessons at a very early age from her skillful teacher-mother. By the age of ten she was turned over to an "outside teacher" who made her practice more and developed her repertoire of classical music. This father with German, Polish, English, and Scottish blood and mother from pure Norwegian stock must have longed for their daughter to become a very special musician. Theirs was an ordinary piano, but they determined to give a gift someday of a Steinway to this "only child"—a gift at some special and perfect moment of life!

In 1933 that little girl, Bernice Loomis, became Mrs. Eugene Lehman. The same Depression was going on in Minneapolis as in Philadelphia and New York. While Edith and Fran were writing letters every day from their colleges (Francis at Hampden-Sydney in Virginia, Edith at Beaver College in Jenkintown, Pennsylvania), Bernice and Eugene were being married and choosing a place to live in Minneapolis where they would struggle along on a low salary until they could afford a larger house on Arthur Street.

Did the two couples know anything about each other? No. Did their lives touch each other's lives? Not until two widows met forty-eight years later. During the thirties there was absolutely no mingling of the history of these people. But, it was the same *period* of history. Philadelphia papers were also carrying news of King George's serious illness and of the trials of Bruno Hauptmann connected with the Lindbergh kidnapping. When the piano was going through its nine months of being built in 1935, the seminary couple were living in a third floor rear apartment near the Philadelphia art museum and Bernice and Eugene Lehman were searching for a house that would be big enough finally to have Dad's wedding gift.

The little first home had no place for a Steinway baby grand which was to be the wedding gift to Henry Loomis's only daughter, and so time needed to go by while Eugene's salary increased enough to afford the proper home for the Steinway.

Can't you just picture the delight of Bernice as she had at last prepared a house for her wedding gift and would be able to choose it in person? Don't you suppose these two arrived at Boutells at 7:30 sharp to walk through the lovely shiny collection of eleven different models of Steinways? Don't you suppose they looked at them, and Bernice tried to discern between the voice of one and then another with an excited response to the clear tones? And then came the concert at 8:30. It must have been lovely to enjoy a free concert, but how much more delight than a concert to realize that the marvelous deep bass and the delicate treble notes of the wedding gift would fill their own house at last. A gift that is promised only becomes a reality when it is taken.

A choice was involved in the taking of this gift. The gift had been provided by the father's promise a long time before, but now was the moment of delight to both the giver and the receiver. A choice had to be made, but the payment was definite and not a problem. "Yes," Bernice said as she touched and stroked the beautiful gleam of the mahogany cover. "Yes," she sighed as she looked at the strings so wonderfully put there by the workers in the Queens factory. "Yes, this is it," she said as she played her favorite bit of Beethoven. "I love it."

The tuning had been perfect, the entire contribution of all four hundred people who had a part had been finished. And now what they had done would go home with her. The gift which had been accepted with love and appreciation would take years to fully treasure and understand. The piano was going to its prepared home, and the home would be affected day by day by the presence of the piano. In a very definite way the four hundred workers in Queens were going to affect that home. In a very specific way the tuners and toners in Queens would affect that home, but so would the Minneapolis tuner. Not one of those people would be without an impact on that home.

What a small illustration of the interweaving of lives and the significant impact of human beings on history. People simply can't live and work without affecting other people, and therefore affecting history. People's ideas and their creativity based on those ideas and their actions based on their ideas affect the history of other people.

Carefully, carefully the movers from Boutells carried the blanket-wrapped piano up the wooden ramp placed on the steps of the house. Gently, gently they turned it on its side and put the legs back in where they belonged. "Where do you want it?" "Right here— okay?" And it was home. The house had become a home with a fresh warmth. The ivory keys and gleam of the wood were not simply beautiful, but were a promise of music and a promise of communication—a third voice in this household of two!

Both Bernice and Eugene played the piano and so they must have had a full evening of music as first one and then the other played a solo and then together they played a duet. This was both audience enough and genius enough to satisfy each other. Talent needs fulfillment of some sort. It is not necessary to have perfection in order to write a poem, arrange flowers, cook a meal, decorate a room, landscape a garden, paint a picture, sing a song, or to play an instrument. It is important to each person not only to have creative ideas hidden in one's mind, or creative talents tingling at the end of one's fingertips, but to express these ideas and to bring forth actively creative things with one's hands. The goal is not to be accepted in an art museum with one's work, nor to be published, nor to be chosen as the interior decorator for a castle, nor to be asked to play for an audience of five thousand, but to do at the level of one's ability what it is possible to do. Psychological frustrations arise from squashing creativity into the dark closet of one's mind, and from never allowing oneself any time or space in life to develop in fresh new areas of creativity.

These two people in Minneapolis began to enjoy their piano alone, with each other, and with friends in a way that enriched their lives through the years. "Enriched" is a word that could be used with several meanings. First of all, the position that Eugene had during the Depression with Brown and Bigelow Company in St. Paul gave him work that interested him in advertising, and in printing calendars, but it didn't make extra money possible for concerts or operas. The possibility of providing a satisfying evening of music day after day not only saved money, but increased skill. Rather than going out for dinner, friends came in for dinner or the evening. One couple came to make an unusual quartet and they had enormous fun. This also enriched their health, since laughter is an excellent medicine and costs nothing!

Let me quote from Bernice herself as she talked to me in 1984.

> We had lots of fun in evenings of music alone, and then in those evenings with our friends. I played classical music as I had been taught through the years, and my husband played jazz. He especially liked playing "Rhapsody in Blue." Oh my, you can't imagine what it sounded like when he played the piano, one friend played the accordion which was a half note lower, and the other friend played a clarinet which was a half note higher.

Bernice, now a widow with many memories, began to laugh as the sound of those four instruments not in tune came back in her mind. She was hearing it so clearly she laughed until the tears came. But were there four instruments? "Oh yes," Bernice said. "I played on the comb when they got going." She could feel the bubbly vibration on her lips in memory too. "The comb, the clarinet, the accordion, and the piano. It sounded awful, I guess, but oh what fun we had. We really enjoyed those evenings as we made our own entertainment."

Is this a waste of a wonderful instrument like the Steinway? Not a bit of it. The piano became the center of that home by giving warmth, togetherness, and the charm of originality. They had no children (a sadness to both of them), but the piano brought a great deal of diversity. Whether one has friends or a family playing string instruments, flutes and recorders to piano accompaniment, or jazz guitar and piano, there are as many original ideas as there are instrument-playing people. There is a togetherness about making music that harmonizes and blends, which can never be accomplished with television as an evening's entertainment. Then there is original composition. Compositions need never to be published to make them a significant part of history.

Family life is a lost art in many places today. People may live in the same house, apartment, cottage, condominium, boat, or cabin, but they have no pattern for a growing life together. Family life needs to have music as a natural outcome of living together. But someone needs to be conscious of providing an atmosphere where music is welcome, accepted with enthusiasm, and appreciated. A home, a family, should provide an appreciative audience for encouragement of drawing, painting, sculpting, smoking meat, cooking, gardening, playing instruments, and composing original music!

How can a home become the birthplace of creativity in the area of music?

A husband and wife are a family even if there are no children. These two who bought piano 281261 were an example of how the sharing of their talents with each other, playing both classical and jazz and popular songs, playing with friends, making music central as a thread of continuity through the years, had much to do with their being such good friends.

However, as you look at other families, you'll see a helpful pattern for family life in their enjoyment together of music. There is father John with his cello, daughter Lisby with her piano, Becky with her violin, and Giandy with his recorder. All born with instruments? No. All staying at one stage of life forever without growing up and marrying and going away? No. But at various stages of growing up, each one has contributed to the other. Mother Prisca has added much with her enthusiasm even though she didn't go on with her piano. Instead she collected records and studied the history of jazz. This same family added another generation of shared music at vacation times in the grandparents' home. Grandfather's violin joined the chamber orchestra and grandmother took over the piano. The purpose was enjoyment and fulfillment in playing and in listening. One family member might curl up in a chair and read a book while others play. Another might embroider a complicated petit point chair seat. The making of music does not stop there but includes listening to recordings of classical composers, talking about their histories, listening to recordings of New Orleans jazz or modern jazz composers and discussing the music or the words. It can include listening to an original composition of a family member or singing a song from grandmother's childhood together. Family life stimulates creativity in music.

What do we see in another home? Little children are gathered up on daddy's knee as he plays the piano and sings Winnie the Pooh songs each night, preceding the reading of stories out loud. "Oh Daddy, please play for me while I do that piece by Telemann on my recorder."

Is there no conflict with music in the home? Often, of course, especially as playmates decide to do an original musical play while another "original" idea is screaming for attention. "Listen to me; I started first."

Family life is not necessarily sweetness and light all the time in order to be good family life. Where originality and creativity are being stimulated, very frequently you have conflict of ideas and so freedom of choice needs to be understood. "Freedom" needs to be defined not in the abstract, but in specific terms. Two people cannot play the piano with two totally different kinds of music at the same time! Two people cannot clash with their drums and flutes or violins and horns playing wildly differing music in the same small living room with the family trying to listen with enjoyment. The meaning of freedom and compassion, of my rights and another person's rights in other areas of life, can be discussed better in the midst of a vivid musical illustration! Music as a part of family life can be used to point out what harmony sounds like and what clashing discord sounds like.

An evening is too short to waste the fun we could have, the beauty we could have, the opportunity to learn something new that we could have by clashing with our instruments and our choices of compositions. Life is too short to spend days, weeks, or months throwing away beauty that is possible by insisting on hedonistic, egotistic, selfish choices which inevitably bring ugliness. Destruction of family life not only kills the beauty of two generations' enjoying and understanding each other's tastes and talents, but it robs people of the richness of three and four generations adding to each other's knowledge and understanding of history (the history of music as well as of other areas of life). Past history can be discovered through the contributions of the very young. Yes—an evening is too short to lose—but "family life" is the tragic loss for those who have thrown it away.

Not only is music a help to family life and to the relationships developing between parents and children, brothers and sisters, cousins, aunts and uncles, and friends, but one generation should be handing down knowledge and love of music very naturally to the next generation.

I was struck by reading an article by R. C. Cole in the June, 1983, *Discover* magazine. It was titled "Living for Beethoven and Quantum Mechanics" and was about Victor Weisskopf who helped make CERN Europe's premier particle research center. This scientist, brilliant in theoretical physics, has a diverse background in the humanities and a cultural appreciation in many areas. He not only cross-country skis, but also turns to playing Mozart as naturally as an English country person would turn for refreshment to a drink of tea by a coal grate! The article points out the impact of one generation upon the next. Victor Weisskopf's great-aunt Tony handed down to him a love of good music without any formal verbalization.

> The grand piano in the living room reminds him of his great-aunt Tony, a concert pianist: "I remember as a little boy sitting under the piano when she played Beethoven, and it came down like water, and I was sitting in the sea of sound." For a while he considered a career in music. Now in the evenings, he likes to go "from rationality to mystery," playing or listening to music with Ellen (his wife). They take their music seriously.[1]

Education does not come in sterile little packages labeled "a course in music appreciation," "a course in appreciating art," "a course in compassion," "a course in recognizing good literature," or "six ways of developing good taste." Education develops in the midst of conversation, reading the classics out loud, lively discussion in wide areas of current events, walks together through art museums, a living room full of art books children grow up spreading out and ab-

---

1. R. C. Cole, "Living for Beethoven and Quantum Mechanics," *Discover,* June, 1983.

sorbing, walks through the woods, and "sitting in a sea of sound" whether under a piano or by a record player!

Just as Victor Weisskopf sat under his Aunt Tony's piano with her wonderful playing of Beethoven sonatas flowing over him like water, giving him an appreciation of music that could never be taken away from him, so little Franky Schaeffer lay on his stomach as a little boy, evening after evening, year after year, watching the flames of the Alpine wood fires burning, while his father answered questions from a diversity of people. Answers to questions concerning philosophy, art, music, science, theology, world affairs, flooded over him and his understanding grew naturally, as further questions came to his own mind and could be asked. It wasn't just floods of information—but warm, intense, caring answers being given to real people with really honest, seeking questions. It was a long, slow preparation giving a base for understanding even as that other young boy was given his unlabeled, unstructured background for music.

The Old Testament in Deuteronomy 6:4-7 gives a strong word from God concerning the information and understanding that is supposed to be relayed from one generation to another. Unhappily the relay has not been faithfully carried out by multitudes of people who have chosen to toss away knowledge and to pass on ignorance instead. Moses said, "Hear, O Israel: The LORD our God, the LORD is one! You shall love the LORD your God with all your heart, with all your soul, and with all your might. And these words which I command you today shall be in your heart; you shall teach them diligently to your children, and shall talk of them when you sit in your house, when you walk by the way, when you lie down, and when you rise up."

The picture Moses gives here as a command of God is of life that is permeated with a natural imparting of truth in conversation during breakfast, during walks, when lying down in a pasture, a garden, or a bed, and sitting at home. Communication with beauty. Later Moses says, "When your son asks you, ... you shall say ..." (Deut. 6:20-24). Questions are anticipated and are to be answered, not brushed off time after time.

Music was a part of this communication. Instrumental music as well as singing was woven into the lives of people as they were told of what had happened generations before, and of what God would have them know. Communication in prose and poetry, communication in writing and talking, communication in art and music were woven together to give understandable information and historic accounts. Education is meant to take place with some measure of excitement as one generation introduces the next to the universe and its form. The search for individual happiness has seemed to erase the sense of responsibility for the next generation. Not only does the drive for individual happiness (so often translated a "convenience") drive out any compassionate attitude for unborn children, but many push aside any striving for imaginative, creative ideas for making a home that would stimulate an interest in all aspects of discovery and knowledge.

Steinway 281261 model S had come into a home that had continuity. Staying in the same house is not of central importance; it is staying in the same family that fulfills a need in human beings and gives stability. After twenty years in Minneapolis Eugene and Bernice Lehman moved to Chatfield, a small town about twenty miles from Rochester, Minnesota. They were surrounded by wonderful Minnesota farms, clusters of houses, a tall silo (or two or three), a red barn, trees planted to protect people and buildings from the winds, all silhouetted against an enormous expanse of blue sky. Chatfield is real, and life there is real, although some people might drive through and think it was just a backdrop for a movie. Small stores and offices are lined up along the main street, with a newspaper office neatly taking its place in the row. As if he were a part of the props for a movie production, an Amish farmer in his wide-brimmed black hat and proper, black clothing carefully brings his horse to a stop in front of the meat store. The carriage has the same boxlike form, with movable flaplike curtains enclosing it, that Amish carriages have had for a hundred years. The horse knows what he is meant to do, and stands still without being tied to any post, for the street is arranged for parking cars, not horses. A wind flaps the flaps and one realizes that there is neither heat in the winter nor air conditioning in the summer within the carriage. Clop, clop—clop, clop—the horse adds a sweet sound to the chugging of a truck motor passing it, and the coughing of a car motor trying to get started as the rest of the residents of Chatfield moved on in 1956 transportation.

American moving trucks are enormous, and moving men have expertise in packing and transporting things from one place to another whatever the distance in between. In England the word used is "removal." You call for a removal company to do the work! Quite descriptive, that! The Lehmans did not move to Chatfield simply to have more sky and distant views of the horizon surrounding them. They had bought the local newspaper, *The Chatfield News*, which still comes out twice a week, bringing local, state, national and international news that would be of interest to residents of two counties.

The Lehmans had removed themselves from the city to a small town, but also from working for a large publishing company to running their own newspaper—an all-absorbing piece of creative work. If anyone has had experience in reporting and gathering news, writing for daily or weekly deadlines, that person knows that "hours for work" and "hours for recreation" are not precisely ticked off by any time clock. Anyone who has started a business for himself, or herself, knows the same thing. Executives or self-employed, creative people discover that sunset blends into moonlight and they need to work both times. The creative urge and inspiration cannot fit into some mechanical schedule. Creative people who do original work do not go out on strike and carry banners against themselves: *"I am unfair to myself. I want shorter working hours and more pay."* I don't care what creative, inventive, or research project anyone is in, when ideas flow and inspiration comes, there is no possibility of fitting it into a prearranged "slot." It is like trying to pack a box or a trunk with too much, so that strings, shirttails, socks, belts, a sleeve are all trailing out from the edges of the lid while you are sitting on it trying to squash it in!

The Lehmans tenderly looked over their Steinway, so expertly moved and set up again, so carefully tuned and ready to be played. Money to go to concerts and operas in Minneapolis was more plentiful by this time, and time for the long evenings around the piano were harder to come by. An effort had to be made to save time for practice, making and sharing music, inviting friends and neighbors in for a musical evening. Although the newspaper took time from the piano, the piano was not only a thing of beauty in the living room that spoke silently of all the memories of those twenty years of marvelous evenings, it also kept on being a voice in the new location as both of the Lehmans played whenever they could fit it in.

Things, material objects, possessions made of wood, brass, fabric, silver, straw, ceramics seem to absorb memories and even the very atmosphere of past events. A book, a painting, a photograph, a quilt, a pair of bookends, shelves, a chair, a pillow, tablecloths, an old stuffed Peter Rabbit, musical instruments bring back whole periods of time, bring back vacations of reading together, evenings of relaxation, times of feverishly working together to make a deadline, nights of sleeplessness caring for a sick child, the sound of an iced drink tinkling in one's left hand as pages rustle from being turned, the smell of a favorite Chinese dish being brought to a three-minute boil while a particular Schubert quintet plays. Continuity is helped by things. A fire, a war, a sudden evacuation, being dragged off to prison camp, or a house or town devastated by war bombs do more to people than interrupt the flow of life during the emergency. Something precious is destroyed, even if *things* are temporary.

As one of the things brought from the Lehmans' life in Minneapolis into the new chapter of their life in the small town, the piano carried with it more continuity than either of them realized. What came forth from that piano in the way of familiar music was as crucial to continuity as the actual instrument.

You or I may never have played an instrument, but we do carry our voices as instruments. We don't need to be opera singers to sing familiar songs out of the past for our own ears, or the ears of our loved ones. Even a hum such as Pooh Bear's hum can bring warm memories, or an undefined sense of being in the presence of familiar sound. A lullaby not heard since childhood can sweep years away and bring a realization that the seventy-year-old me is after all the same person as the seven-year-old me. The total breakdown or breakup of family, of husband-wife oneness, of togetherness in a larger family connection, still leaves that basic continuity of the individual. "It is still me." I may say to myself in the mirror in the quiet of early morning or late night, "No one else may know it, but I am only the same me." How long does a person last? What does "forever" mean practically? Can "forever" be used as a meaningful word?

The Lehmans moved again in 1963 to a larger new house on River Street in the same small town. They worked for the same newspaper and played the same beloved piano. Then in 1970, Eugene Lehman died. The continuity of their married life could then be counted as thirty-seven years—thirty-seven years of talking, writing, and sharing that block of history. For thirty-four years they had shared a piano to bring some other dimension to communication as well as for relaxation. A life together has been condensed to a few paragraphs. A death has been condensed to a sentence. Is there any meaning? What is the human cycle all about? Is a piano more important than a person? What about the life span of a violin? Does a house last longer than the people in it? What about the age of the tree that makes the soundboard of the Steinway?

The history being followed in this chapter is of that piano which started its life in the Queens factory of the Steinway company, and was shipped to Boutells for the first breath-taking northwestern exhibition of a large Steinway collection, and was adopted or bought into a family's life immediately!

Life and death is a central theme of all history, but the theme of this chapter is S model number 281261. What happened to it?

An instrument is silent without a musician, a performer, a human being to play it, either with wonderful skill or with awkward clumsiness. An instrument brings forth the music locked in the brain and the fingers of the maestro. But an instrument also has a life of its own and is needed to open the door for music locked inside a human brain and fingers.

The bugle cannot blow the signal for battle nor the welcome taps bringing a day to its close if there is no bugler. Both the bugle and the bugler affect history whether they are ever awarded a prize or given any recognition.

This model S piano, mahogany in grain and gleam, continued to be played, as well as lovingly polished, now by one person. Bernice Lehman continued to live in the house and to work on the newspaper between 1970 and 1984. Her two trips around the world, including such places as Nepal, Russia, and Japan, indicate an ongoing life as a single person.

Love of music does not dwindle because of being alone. Need of music does not decrease because of being alone. A Hungarian shepherd can play fantastic music for the empty hillside full of stones, grass, scrubby bushes and flowers, with sheep and lambs nibbling in soft chorus. Do no ears hear it? His own ears do. Is he alone in the universe with no other ears to hear? It is important to say for all who find aloneness as a part of life's history that one pair of ears, one rib cage as a sounding board, one person's understanding of music and one person's need to be enveloped in music is reason enough for that one person to play the piano, flute, violin, viola, cello, bass, trumpet, bassoon, harp, sackbut, or whatever. One person's need of being both performer and audience is sufficient to make the playing have value. For those who reach for records to fill the workshop, the kitchen, the garden, the room being plastered or painted, the lonely place of drudgery or creativity, the music that pours forth from that record player is important. Simply because nobody else is around and only one set of ears is listening is no reason to silence the music that is available and needs to be a part of the balance of one's life during each day. One human being alone needs music as much as one human being alone needs water and food.

At the turn of the century an Englishman named James O. Frazier turned away from a rich talent and background for being a successful concert pianist and turned his steps to China, believing truth to exist and being enveloped with a sense of responsibility to make that truth available to people who might never have freedom of choice otherwise. Freedom of choice hinges on knowledge. Without sufficient knowledge of what the choice is, there is no real choice possible. So Frazier sailed to China and went to the most remote places in the high mountains of the Salween district of the Himalayas to climb the rocky Alpine heights, sit by smoky fires, learn a language sufficiently to turn it into written form for people who had never had books before. As this musician walked, rode an ass, or climbed by foot, he was often alone.

A recent book, *Mountain Rain*, written by Frazier's daughter, Eileen Crossman, tells of his spreading out Beethoven concertos and symphonies, Bach concertos, and whatever he had access to, on the back of the animal he was riding. As the notes were seen by his eyes, the rocky, bumpy path disappeared from his notice, his mind was giving a concert to his ears as the notes were translated into the feel of a piano beneath his fingers and the sounds of a symphony orchestra or a chamber music orchestra surrounding him. His brain could so vividly take those black notes on yellowed paper and bring the full, rich tones of a Steinway that he had played in England, the blend of all the proper instruments coming in with perfect timing, that the Lisuland scenery was temporarily blotted out, the clop-clop of the hoofs beneath him was blurred into being no more interruption than a distant plane would make as it flies over a concert hall. Frazier was hearing and being enveloped in full, satisfying music because of his vivid memory plus his complete knowledge and training which translated the notes into the bright language of music.

Another time during a brief vacation his horse brought him over the border of China to the house of missionaries who had a piano. He could not lose time for sleep or eating! His fingers revelled in playing a long repertoire of his beloved classical music. On and on his whole being drank in that music and his hungry fingers devoured the keys. Like a thirsty man coming from a desert journey he drank deeply for the days of drought ahead.

The conscious sacrifice of putting aside his music career did not blot out the love of music. Being alone without the person, or without the whole orchestra full of persons, with whom to play does not erase memory like erasing a tape! Life has different chapters with different geographic surroundings, and different possibilities for search and discovery of some astounding facts about what a human being is. A human being, among other things, thinks and acts and feels, has ideas, can make choices among the ideas, and can communicate verbally and with music.

When Bernice Lehman came to the conclusion that she should move to a small townhouse in Chatfield and give up her work on the newspaper, she decided to sell her piano, not because music no longer mattered, but she no longer had space!

Steinway model S baby grand five-foot-one inch was for sale. Allen Fisher, a piano tuner, living in a nearby town of Dover, fell in love with it when he tuned it! "My two-year-old girl could have it when she grows old enough" was his motive for adding a second piano to his home in a white farmhouse. He loved the voice and tone of this amazingly well-preserved piano. "How could it sound twenty years younger than it is?" he questioned, full of wonder.

It was March 20, 1984, when Bernice said good-bye to her beloved piano as it was driven away, once again carefully wrapped, once again welcomed as a part of a family. Now forty-eight years after having left the Boutells "coming out party" where it was introduced to Minnesota, S model 281261 might have wondered where the concert grand that was made during the same nine months in 1935 was by now. How many more people had heard its voice? Whether it had gone to be in a university music department or to be one of the special collections of concert grands that Steinway keeps for top artists to use in the great halls of the world, it was certain that more people had heard the concert grand than had heard baby grand 281261. Yet the baby grand may have preened a little, and murmured with satisfaction, "I don't suppose concert grand could be in as good a condition as I am."

In the middle of May, Allen Fisher came to a reluctant decision. It wouldn't really be prudent or practical to keep two pianos. His two-year-old daughter was soon to have a baby sister or brother, and the money now tied up in the piano was needed for another use. It would be better to keep the upright piano for his own playing and sell his newly acquired baby grand.

It was therefore sometime in June, 1984, when Steinway baby grand number 281261, which had been so carefully made in 1935, was again for sale. The Fishers had been a kind of foster home for a few weeks during which it had been loved and appreciated, tuned and polished, and prepared for wherever the next, more permanent home would be.

A new chapter of life was ahead. Piano 281261 was going to become very well known indeed.

CHAPTER 3

"Till Death Do Us Part"

I t was to be forty-eight years, ten months, and one week after that July 6 wedding in 1935 that death was to part Francis and Edith. On May 15, 1984, as the grandfather clock struck four, and the Neuchatel clock echoed with a higher note a few moments later, Fran literally breathed his last breath and was immediately absent from his body, absent from Edith, and absent from two daughters sitting with him in the firelight and candlelight of the beauty of that room. Where had he gone? There had been such clear communication such a short time before. How can anyone say death is natural? The natural thing is to have a person be a whole person. The silent body, the unmoving body, the unbreathing lungs are unnatural to family members who have just felt a pressure of the hand (pressure commanded by a brain), who have just heard a communication verbalized (also by a living brain) so short a time before. Death is a part of death. Death is abnormal to a living person; it is not a part of life.

Cancer had been discovered more than five and a half years before. The leaves were a bright yellow that October day in Rochester, Minnesota—too cheerful, too beautiful—as Fran came down from the operating room where the node had been cut from his neck and the news had been given to him within minutes: "malignant." It seemed that the trees outside should have turned grey! Further test results and the program of chemotherapy were outlined carefully and with compassion by Dr. Monty Petitt on the afternoon of October 11, 1978. The next chapter of our lives together was to be in and out of Rochester's Mayo Clinic with a succession of checkups and a continued program of chemotherapy to which I added a careful program

51

of nutrition, hoping it would help his system handle the chemotherapy.

This period of more than five and a half years was not a "grinding to an end," but the beginning of a distinctly new chapter of creativity in living. It was not a time of slowly dying, but of completing fresh and important work. Mathematically figured out, the time between the diagnosis of Fran's cancer and his death was precisely 11.4 percent of our married life. If you add the three years of college preceding our marriage during which we wrote every day and influenced each other's thinking and work, that time of having cancer was exactly 10.7 percent of the time from the day we met to the day of his death.

What is the point of reducing that period Fran had cancer to a statistic? The point is that creativity, productive work, completing a project, making an impact on history are so central to fulfilling a purpose and meaning in a lifetime that one should not easily become a dropout because of limitations, hindrances, handicaps, afflictions, difficulties. I needed to be aware of that statistic to recognize how important it had been to fight on together for the use of time. It is amazing how much can be packed into a short piece of time in the midst of "impossibilities." It is also amazing how easily time is tossed away as unimportant, regarded as simply non-time, a period not to be counted.

In a short space, flashes are all that can be given of our forty-eight years, ten months, and one week together, of life that was an unknown future in July 1935, and is an unchangeable piece of history now. More details of the time before Fran's cancer was discovered can be found in the books L'Abri and The Tapestry.

The difference between live theater or a live symphony and a film is that whatever slips or mistakes are made in the live performance remain in the memory of the audience. These mistakes become part of history, unchangeable. The film, however, can be cut and refilmed with take after take. Each of us has an uncut history. We can't go back and do another take or play the music of our lives over again.

Walk around an old barn in the country near Grove City, Pennsylvania, and listen to Francis Schaeffer, young pastor now, talking to a farmer while he milks his cows and while Fran sands an old chair down to the walnut grain hidden by coats of paint. Later, chair under his arm and two-year-old Priscilla running hop, skip, and jump beside him, he tosses the chair into the back seat, Priscilla into the front (the days before baby seats!) and drives on to make his next pastoral visit. The congregation's problems are brought to him in barns, out in a field, by the kitchen stove, or in a back parlor as individuals are treated as human beings with individual worth. When a new church is built out of an old one moved from a flooded area, it is Fran who climbs the steeple to paint it.

By the time Fran is the new pastor in Chester, Pennsylvania, Priscilla is in kindergarten and it is a four-years-younger Susan who sometimes goes to make pastoral calls with her father. Many of the people in the Chester congregation are shipyard workers and so visiting at work is not possible. But there are old folks, handicapped people, and invalids to be cheered by a child and father. Communication is what it was all about, communication of the important truth of where life came from, the universe and its form, the basic questions of whether there is any meaning to life or any life after death. In later years Fran always said, "The questions are the same whether from farmers or shipyard workers or Oxford and Sorbonne students. The vocabulary may need to be different, but the answers are the same. Truth doesn't change."

The next home and pastorate was in St. Louis, Missouri. The "flash" in this case takes place ten years after the wedding! It is August 6, 1945, and the first atomic bomb has been dropped. Newspaper headlines and the strained voices of radio news announcers soon cover the country with the cry, "The War Is Over! The War Is Over!" It is a typically hot St. Louis night. Fran takes the two older girls to experience the victory parade and I stay home with three-month-old baby Debby.

The future husbands of our three girls were in tremendously different circumstances at that moment. Priscilla's husband, John Sandri, was a nine-year-old in Scarsdale, New York. John, a Swiss-American, was celebrating with his parents the good news that they could revisit relatives in Switzerland soon. The violin and piano communicated their feelings at that time, as in many other times of life. Four-year-old Susan's future husband was also a nine year old, but his excitement was over the return of his father, John Macaulay, from service in the South African army, fighting along the Suez Canal, and later in Italy. It had been a long and disruptive break in home life. As for baby Deborah's future husband, Udo Middelmann, when she was five days old and still in the hospital, he was five years old in Bruchsal, near Heidelberg, when Germany surrendered. That day meant a new life of great responsibility for the Middelmanns as

Udo's father was picked out by the military government as being one who had stood against the Nazi rule for twelve years. Now he was chosen to be mayor, head of the fire department, chief of police, as well as to work for the settling of refugees as they streamed out of destroyed cities and East Germany. Later, because of the outstanding job he had done, Mr. Middelmann was chosen to be comptroller of UNICEF, the world children's relief program.

Coming back from the chaos of the parade that August night, Susan received a cigarette burn on her arm ("He did it on purpose, Mommy.") put there by a rowdy soldier. Not one of us would have dreamed that each of the three little girls would be meeting her husband in Switzerland!

Perhaps the next flash should be the blurb written years later, on the flyleaf of one of Fran's books:

> Francis A. Schaeffer is one of the foremost Christian thinkers of today. Recognized and respected for his work in philosophy and theology, he is, however, most known for a special ability to communicate ideas to diverse groups of people. During the past twenty years, thousands have come to discuss and benefit from Dr. Schaeffer's study and counsel at his Europe-based L'Abri Fellowships and through his many books. *How Should We Then Live*, *The God Who Is There*, and *Escape From Reason* are among his works.[1]

L'Abri Fellowship began in the spring of 1955 in Chalet les Melezes, which amazingly was being built in 1935, at the same time as Steinway piano 281261. Neither that chalet nor the piano seemed to have any connection with Fran and Edith who were being married in Germantown, Philadelphia! The *timing* is fascinating.

The chalet was twenty years old that historic thirty-first day of March in 1955 when, after going through floods and avalanches and other traumatic experiences, the Schaeffers moved in. The Schaeffers had been married twenty years by July 6, 1955, so their marriage and the chalet's life had paralleled each other. And the piano was getting ready to move to Chatfield, Minnesota. It's interesting to watch the bits and pieces of history flash into sight, like threads on a loom, waiting to be threaded into a pattern.

1. Francis A. Schaeffer and C. Everett Koop, *Whatever Happened to the Human Race?* (Old Tappan, N.J.: Revell, 1979).

An Italian stonecutter squatted with ease as he chipped away at the grey stone for the fireplace being built at the end of the Chalet les Melezes living room. Three-year-old Franky squatted beside him, watching intently and chatting away with Italian words mixed in with his French. This fireplace was going to be the scene of many long discussions led by his dad, with people from all over the world who would be coming with their questions. Franky was there not only for each step of the making of the fireplace, but for many of the discussions throughout his childhood.

Another twenty years would go by before the three people bound up in the fireplace's existence would be working together on a film. Dr. C. Everett Koop (years later to become Surgeon General of the United States) gave that fireplace as a gift to L'Abri, so you could say that he was building it from the distance of Philadelphia Children's Hospital. Twenty years later Francis Schaeffer and C. Everett Koop were to narrate a film and write a book, both titled *Whatever Happened to the Human Race?* Franky Schaeffer would write the screenplay and direct the five-episode film. But on that day as the Italian stonecutter chipped away, he was only an inquisitive little boy playing with the chips of stone and asking questions. There was no preview of the future being announced.

Somehow it seems that the piano should be played by a great pianist within hearing as we see this flash fading against a backdrop of the marvelous range of mountains seen from that chalet—the "Dents du Midi," the glaciers and other peaks, and the Rhone Valley below. But piano 281261 was playing its music in Minnesota and an old upright piano was at the end of the Melezes living room.

Another blurb on another flyleaf says:

> Dr. Schaeffer has lectured frequently at leading universities in the United States, in England, Holland, Japan, Hong Kong, Kuala Lumpur, Bombay, Singapore, and other parts of the world. He is author of 23 books which have been translated into twenty-five languages, with more than three million copies in print. *How Should We Then Live?* is a ten-episode film series as well as a book, about which he said, "This book is a personal analysis of the key moments of history which have formed our present culture, and the thinking of the men who brought those moments to pass. This study is made in the hope that light may be shed upon the major characteristics of our age and that solutions may be found to the myriad problems which face us as we look toward the end of the twentieth century."

Do you know the little dirt road that leads to the left after you pass Chateau d'Oex not far from Gstaad? Fran and I were hiking along there one day. He had been verbally sighing, "The idea of doing a film series and book on the rise and decline of Western culture from the Roman age until now is too impossible to begin. I just can't...." Our hiking boots were making the clump, clump, clump that Swiss boots make while giving a wonderful security to your feet and making any path possible! Cows were playing their unconscious symphony of bells as they moved their heads to eat grass or to walk to a better spot. The harmony of those grassy slopes dotted with clumps of trees or chalets and old wooden barns made a silent music of their own. Suddenly Fran said, "Edith, do you have paper and pen with you?" I took off my light-weight, blue-plaid rucksack and produced a notebook and pencil. "Good, write this...." I perched on a rock and wrote:

> There is a flow to history and culture. This flow is rooted and has its well-spring in the thoughts of people. People are unique in the inner life of the mind. What they are in their thought world determines how they act. This is true of their value systems and it is true of their creativity. It is true of their corporate actions such as political decisions, and it is true of their personal lives. The results of their thought world flow through their fingers or from their tongues into the external world. This is true of Michelangelo's chisel, and it is true of the dictator's sword.

"There, that's the beginning," he said. It was a penciled scribble in a notebook stuffed back into the rucksack. We walked on at a good pace again, but a book and film had been begun.

What do writing and film making consist of? Hard, slogging work, keeping at it whether you feel up to it or not. It consisted of Fran, with sciatica so painful that he later had to be taken in an ambulance, going to the Cafe Deux Magots to sit at Jean-Paul Sartre's table and discuss existentialism while the cameras rolled. It consisted of Fran's saying his lines without wincing as a Roman chariot charged by him. They made take after take, with the horse coming closer each time, as the Italian chariot driver seemed to be trying to test him! Creative life is full of its high moments and low moments, of amusing things and tragic things, of human relationships helping or destroying a day's work or an hour's work. Unknown people built a railroad from Chur to St. Moritz up Alpine, rocky mountainsides. Schubert left a pile of music he never knew would be played. Human beings have affected history by slogging on in the face of discouragement.

The slogging work of writing *Whatever Happened to the Human Race?* took place for Fran all too soon after doing the twenty-one seminars with *How Should We Then Live?* But it was ready in time. In time for what? It was ready in time for the filming in August, September, and the beginning of October 1978. One might argue that it was in time to affect the whole abortion, infanticide, euthanasia question. One might even argue that history has since changed the possibilities of filming in the Sinai desert with Israeli help. Actually in the light of what happened right after doing the last filming and the last voice-over, the phrase "in time" is very appropriate.

Fran stood on the top of Mt. Sinai with the cameraman filming from a helicopter and the gorgeous peaks stretching out into the distance like wonderful waves on a sea of sand. He was able to say in this setting, one of the most important sites of the entire Bible, that the thing to notice about this epochal moment for Israel when God spoke with Moses and gave him the law is the emphasis on the reality of history which the Bible itself makes. Fran was given opportunity to speak on the road above Jordan, looking down over a bend in the river. He talked about the Israeli general Joshua while the modern troops marched through early morning dust to do their important job of guarding the land. Fran reminded people of the twelve stones Joshua had set up in the middle of Jordan at the spot where the priests who carried the ark of the covenant had stood. He pointed out that just as in the time of Moses God commanded various items to be kept as physical reminders of what He had done, so God did the same thing in the time of Joshua.

Fran went through the scene of Abraham and Isaac talking about the exciting reality of God's making clear to them what the substitution of the ram caught in the thicket meant in pointing to the Lamb. At the Garden Tomb, Fran read the passage in Luke of the story of the Resurrection. Finally, he spoke strong words in the sunset on the Sea of Galilee beside a fire and a boat full of fish, where Luke tells us that the resurrected Lamb of God cooked breakfast for the fishermen disciples. Fran then thanked Franky very fervently: "Thank you for giving me the very best opportunity I have ever had to make the message of the Bible clear."

The music written by Tim Simoneck for all this film fit gorgeously with the script and the scene. It was played by the London Philharmonic and directed by Tim.

Was *Whatever Happened to the Human Race?* filmed in time? Dr. Koop was later to become Surgeon General of the United States and would not have time to make such a film. Tim Simoneck was later to have a long hospitalization during which he couldn't have done his work. And on October 9, 1978, Francis Schaeffer was on the way to Mayo Clinic to discover that part of the heaviness of his legs in climbing up stairways and the hills around Jerusalem and part of the lethargy in getting up to wash his hair in the wee hours of those mornings was due to a raging case of lymphoma!

"In time" is not too strong a description for this piece of work which has made a difference in history.

The last 11.4 percent of our married life was to be one of the most productive periods. Because of making a home in Rochester, Minnesota, where we could return for checkups with Dr. Petitt, evening discussions opened up with doctors and other people coming to ask questions. L'Abri conferences also took place in Rochester and the California branch of L'Abri was moved to Rochester. Fran wrote the book *A Christian Manifesto*, which became a best seller with over 300,000 copies sold, and spoke in many parts of the United States, including Washington, D.C. What the doctors were doing for him with chemotherapy opened a period of time that was intensely important. That period after cancer was diagnosed was unique in both tribulation and in fruitfulness! One wouldn't plan 11.4 percent of a marriage to be woven with cancer as a part of the fabric, but often Fran would say, "I feel I can accomplish more with this condition than I could without it. When I walk down a hospital hall, for instance, I am one of the gang." For both of us, for our children and the ones they married, and for our fourteen grandchildren, that period was one of greater honesty and recognition of the preciousness of relationships than ever before.

The rush across the ocean in December, 1983, seemed as if it might be too late. Yet there was more of Fran's life work to be finished, and I was able to give him the gift of responding affirmatively to his request "to buy a house here near the hospital and bring over all our things from Switzerland." The response "Yes" seemed to me to be a part of what I had promised back in Germantown in 1935. "Are you sure, Edith? Are you sure it won't be too much?" "This is," I said, "what I was promising when I said, 'for better or for worse, for richer or for poorer, till death do us part.' Of course I'll look for a house and bring everything over so that *home* will be right *here*."

It was mid-February when I returned to Rochester from an eight-day time in Switzerland packing all the possessions of our married life into 269 boxes. Our familiar music was packed, along with all the familiar books, furniture and dishes, candlesticks, clocks, teapots, spoons and curtains, and so on. Sitting on the chalet floors, night after night, Prisca, Susan, Debby and I laughed and cried as we read old letters and pored over old pictures. It is amazing how unplanned moments in the midst of ordeals can turn out to be some of the most tender moments of life. The reality of love and loyalty, deep ties and shared memories cannot be portioned out into a time schedule of ten minutes a day! It is when an old letter comes tumbling out, or a snapshot of the first fish caught or a composition nine-year-old Franky wrote is discovered that laughter comes and memory blots out the immediate present. Memory of the wild winds and snows of that February is mingled with that of hot tea and toast tasting like ambrosia at two A.M. and of a new spurt of energy giving zest for the bittersweet task of breaking up a Swiss home of thirty-six years in order to take that home over to "Daddy" or "Fran" and to surround him with familiar sights and sounds once more. A huge container with everything I was taking to America disappeared down the mountain road in Switzerland to be seen about five weeks later passing St. Mary's hospital in Rochester.

Transplanted? Or uprooted? Transplanted.

The return to Rochester on a half-empty plane did not give the usual joy of having two seats on which to sleep. Too many times, I awakened weeping from dreams in which I looked for shoes under the bed and realized that it was an empty room—no bed, no shoes. At the airport, Mary Jane and Greg Grooms from the Rochester L'Abri staff met me with a question: "Do you want to go home first, or straight to the hospital?"

"Hospital? Why?"

"He had to be taken back in today. There is fever and staph infection. He's pretty discouraged."

That was February 14, 1984. In the next two weeks a surgical procedure had to be undergone to remove the Hickman catheter on the left side and to put another one in on the right side. Antibiotics had to be given constantly for the infection. And long phone calls were taking place as Fran talked with Lane Dennis, his editor, about various changes in the manuscript of his new book, *The Great Evangelical Disaster*, about to go to press. As doctors perched on the side of Fran's bed during that time, discussions were about ideas, not just the medical situation. "He's got so much he wants to say in the seminars he has planned to do with Franky, I think we'll give him a couple of transfusions and let him try at least one," said Dr. Habermann.

And so it was that on March 2, Fran left the hospital to go to the airport. A private plane had been thoughtfully sent for him to be flown to the first seminar. I did the needed sterile care of the site of the catheter, and gave the heparin shots, etc. Fran went on to appear for a couple of hours at each college—eleven of them—all over the United States, ending with a L'Abri Conference in Knoxville, Tennessee. The trip was broken by a couple of days back at Mayo Clinic for chemotherapy, and at the end we stopped with friends in Atlanta, returning April 11. At the stop in Atlanta, we were met with a wheelchair and it was an obvious time of weakening for Fran with water gathering in his lungs.

There are three ways of thinking of such a determination to finish a task in life. One could say, "It was too much. He should have been resting." Or one could realize that his sense of the urgency and importance of his message, based on his certainty that there is a truth which he called "true truth," gave him a longer time to finish a task. Some doctors have said it was his intense desire to work shoulder to shoulder with his son in speaking strongly in the area he felt was so profoundly needed that gave him a few weeks more than he would otherwise have had. But if one believes in the existence of God, and if this God responds to the calls of His people, there is a third interpretation: the extra time to finish a task was given by God.

During this month of travel and speaking, the container from Switzerland had arrived in Rochester. Mike Sugimoto, who had been in Switzerland while we were sorting and the moving men were packing, was now in Rochester! I don't think that was a chance happening. It also was not by chance that Greg Grooms and his wife Mary Jane, who had been a part of L'Abri in Switzerland, were installed in the work in Rochester before this final illness transplanted us. Greg had taken charge of organizing and directing a whole crew of volunteers and some professional workers who put in insulation, tore out rotting places, painted, papered, and generally restored the newly bought old house. Mike had a place that was ready when he opened the front door to receive the Minnesota moving men who unloaded what the Swiss men had packed.

The arrival back from Atlanta gave Fran two days in his new home—two worthwhile days of thankfulness that my promise in the wedding vows had been kept, and that those material things that made up the continuity of forty-eight years had been brought to surround him "until death do us part!" After that deep, though brief, satisfaction, he was back in the hospital. The cancer had changed from a small-cell lymphoma to a large-cell lymphoma which does not respond readily even to a more drastic chemotherapy.

It was Easter Sunday, April 22, 1984, that I was to hear the familiar request for the last time. "Edith, get paper and pen ready, I want to dictate something." He had been asleep and all the lights were out. Doctors and nurses didn't think he could really communicate. Suddenly the lights were snapped on, and the request was made in a clear voice. I grabbed a notebook and a pen and began to write Francis Schaeffer's last dictation.

The Critical Collapse of a Basically Flawed Universal

For a long time now, it has been held, and universally accepted, that the final reality is energy which has existed forever in some form and energy which has its form by pure chance. In other words, intelligence has no basic place in the structure of the universe from the Enlightenment onward. Therefore, we are to accept totally the basic structure of the universe as impersonal.

This means, therefore, that neither religion nor intelligence are in the universe. The personality issue does not enter into *what* the universe is, nor to *who* people are in this theory. Under this theory, there is no place for morals, nor for there being any meaning to the universe. And the problem here is that it [this explanation] is simply *not* what we observe about the universe—nor especially about man himself. In spite of this, modern man continues to press on, saying that this is what the universe is, and especially what the individual is. In other words, we have been told that in faith we must insist blindly on what the universe is and what man is. In other words, man is simply a mathematical thing—or formula—even though it brings him sorrow.

His voice was weak, but the words were clear and concise. I needed to bend closer to get every bit of it.

This is simply mysticism in its worst form, and the final denial of rationality. With understanding, one sees the proud egotism of holding this basic philosophic concept against what comes to man from every side.

What would we do with any other theory that postulated such a theorem? Certainly it would be put aside. Why do we continue to hold this theorem as to what reality is, when in any other area we would simply throw it out?

The answer is clear that it is simply a mystical acceptance. In other words, man is so proud that he goes on blindly accepting that which is not only intellectually inviable, but that which no one can live with in governmental or personal life, and in which civil life cannot live.

To go back and accept that which is the completely opposite—that the final reality is an Infinite Personal God who created the world—is rational, and returns us to intelligent answers, and suddenly opens the door. It not only gives answers, but puts us once more in a cosmos in which people can live, breathe, and rejoice.

If modern man would only be honest, he would say that it is *his* theory which is in collapse.

No other word was said. Fran turned over, pushed out the light buttons, and went back to sleep. Later I found this letter in the notebook, and realized that it was what he wanted to say to the family, to the doctors, and to others when he could no longer speak himself. His last written page, ending the books he had written, set forth once again the basic foundation he felt to be so important as a base for life, a world view.

Within that same period of hours I was faced with a decision. "He is dying of the advancing cancer. Do you want him to be placed in intensive care on machines? Now is the time to make the choice." With six doctors bending over me with expressions that were not unkind, waiting for me to speak, my mind played back snatches of the many conversations Fran and I had had concerning the difference between prolonging life at any cost or prolonging death. "You men have already done great things during these last years and these last few weeks. You fought for life and gave Fran time to complete an amazing amount of work, including writing this last book and making this last seminar tour. Thank you. Now, however, if I understand correctly, you are talking about making a choice between having his last period of time being one separated from me and from all he would love to hear and see, or being with me and in the home nearby with all his familiar things and his familiar music. I don't want him to be separated from us until he is separated from his body! You see, I believe God exists, though you may not. I believe with no shadow of doubt that when he is absent from his body, he will be present with the Lord. I don't want him to be absent from me, from his daughters, to be shut away in an intensive care unit for these last days. I want to take him home."

The response was almost entirely one of deep relief on the doctors' part. They seemed to say, "We wish more people would care for their loved ones this way."

There were phone calls to make, home-nursing care to be arranged, a hospital bed and oxygen to be rented. The bed was placed on the ground floor to face windows opening to the view of a tree trunk where squirrels ran up and down, and a bird feeder hung. Tiny leaves were appearing on the trees, and the grass was getting green, but no flowers had appeared yet. Debby, Mary Jane, Mike, Greg, and others pitched in to make a sudden "garden" in plain view, with pots of red geraniums, boxes of petunias, and a log with an old fountain fastened to it. (A bronze head of a boy that had been brought with the things from Switzerland. Ivy hid the hose that brought water to flow from the boy's mouth.) The things Fran could view from that bed, inside and outside, brought glimpses of different periods of life. It was a homecoming from four stark white walls into firelight, candlelight, birds of all kinds coming to feed...and *music*.

Music flooded the room. One after another we played his favorite records. Beethoven's symphonies and sonatas, Bach, Schubert, Liszt, Chopin, Telemann, Mendelssohn, and Handel. Handel's *Messiah* was played from beginning to end several times in the next days. He loved the full volume with the words and music thundering through him: "King of Kings, Lord of Lords, Hallelujah, Hallelujah." With Haydn, Fran responded, "*My* Lord, *My* Master." So often he had told our children of Queen Victoria standing in her box at the Royal Albert Hall to give homage to her King.

What a contrast—Handel's music wonderfully played and beautifully sung—with the noises of a hospital. I was so deeply thankful that I had made the decision to cross the sea and to bring him "home" over here for his last days. How do you measure time? How do you measure importance? I've toyed with percentages—what percent of a married life was made up of cancer. But I needed no percentage to tell me deep within my being that it didn't matter what percent of forty-nine years together these ten days came to. It was impossible to tie a price tag to the value of these ten days of being surrounded by loving care, by beauty and life, by flavors, sights and smells that brought back special memories, by music, music, and more music, as well as by words speaking of certain hope.

Was I placing a false value on these days? Was it an aspirin pill to take away some pain? Was it an illusion that music matters at this point in life, that beauty is important at this crisis point in a relationship, that there was something to communicate that had meaning to both the person leaving his body as well as to the persons remaining in the room and in their bodies?

For the family, the three of us there (keeping the others in close touch by phone), it was a satisfying thing to be able to share cups of tea, to put another log on the fire, to pray aloud when he said "pray," to read to him the words which bridged the gap with a promise of what is reality ahead. For us it was fantastic to recognize that music was not blotting out a future silence, but that music was really what is ahead. Music is a part of the future, so it was not unsuitable to have music to share as long as possible, until we too can share the future.

Nearly 3,000 years ago the prophet Isaiah wrote words that were quoted in 1 Corinthians: "Eye has not seen, nor ear heard,/Nor have entered into the heart of man/The things which God has prepared for those who love Him" (1 Cor. 2:9). That is a promise for a forever music that will be beyond the beauty of anything we have ever heard.

No, we were not having a false kind of time, we were not bolstering each other up with unreality. When Fran softly said, "Keep on...from strength to strength," it had meaning all right. It had meaning for us because he referred to Psalm 84 which he was too weak to quote in full, but which we could look up and read. He was pointing us to the continuity of the pilgrimage to be finished by each of us. How gorgeous it would have been to hear the sons of Korah singing that psalm with an instrument of Gath accompanying them. Verse 7 of that psalm says, "They go from strength to strength;/Every one of them appears before God in Zion."

Communication in music and words!

It was exactly four o'clock, two clocks were striking, when Fran's last soft puff of breath was followed by silence. He was absent. Absent from his body. But God says to us in the Bible that there is both a departure and an arrival. There is a reality of arriving and being present with the Lord.

Silence? I believe there is a burst of music unheard in the room of departure, but brilliant in perfection in "the house of the Lord."

Psalm 23 ends with David singing, "And I will dwell in the house of the LORD/Forever." David, I believe, goes on playing his musical instrument in the house of the Lord forever.

Family began coming. Plants, flowers, trees, telegrams, letters,

Edith and Francis at the 1982 Schaeffer family reunion in Switzerland.

phone calls, and people began pouring in. There were a letter from President Reagan to be exclaimed over and framed, and a cable from Sir Bernard Brain of the English Parliament and a deluge of comforting messages from all over the world.

The fifth episode of the film *Whatever Happened to the Human Race?* was a part of the funeral service held in John Marshall High School. It seemed fitting to let Fran speak that which he himself had said was the most satisfying message he had ever been able to give. So it was that Fran's standing on Mt. Sinai, his standing above the Jordan River as the Israeli troops marched by, his standing by the mountain watching Abraham and Isaac return after the glorious substitution of the ram, his sitting by the open tomb reading, and his walking into the sunset as the Sea of Galilee's waves splashed on the windblown shore were our view of him as he spoke that which had been so important throughout his adult life. His desire was that others might know the truth and come through the substitution of the Lamb of God and be with him in the house of the Lord forever. "Till death do us part" is a parting as real as any boat departure with a space of water widening and the shore disappearing.

Together has been replaced by *alone.* Does *alone* need to be associated with silence, cold, darkness, a desert, the wilderness, no purpose, no meaning? Does the word *death* cancel out the word *life?*

Forever music. Is there a "forever life" to enjoy a "forever music"?

CHAPTER 4

A Tribute to the Rescue

M y granddaughter Kirsty Macaulay was coming to live with me and to attend the Community College. "I can't have Kirsty in the house without a piano," I said to myself. "She simply has to compose and sing. A piano is a must." So the first of July found me looking at secondhand, upright pianos. That night I had a phone call at midnight from an old friend, Mary Crowley from Texas.

"What have you been doing today?" came her question. "Looking for a secondhand upright piano to put out of sight behind the wall in that alcove at the end of the living room." This was received with silence at the other end of the phone.

Then came, "You are not going to do that. You are not going to get an upright to put there. You are going to get a baby grand to put in the central spot of the living room." "But Mary, that is too much money and would take up too much space. Really, that's impossible."

After more conversation and a day of looking at pianos, another call came from Mary. "Edith, I want you to look and see if you can get a secondhand Steinway baby grand for the same price as I got one for a Baptist college conservatory of music. Try to find one, and I'd like to give it to L'Abri in memory of Fran."

I said, "Oh, thank you" a bit weakly. Now I was not speaking a bit weakly simply because it was an enormous gift and a wonderful one, but because I felt the search was going to end in failure! Where would I find a secondhand Steinway at that price? How could I start looking?

The other three houses in this branch of L'Abri are about two blocks away. I called Mary Jane Grooms, one of our workers, and told her of Mary C's request. "Where do I start?" I asked, feeling a bit hopeless.

My next call was to another Mary—Mary Lou Sather, a Mayo surgeon's wife. "Do you have any idea where I could begin looking for a secondhand Steinway baby grand?"

I made no more calls, but I did pray. Pray? Does God care about such a request with the world full of disaster, pain, famine, suffering and sorrow? Is music important to God, if there is a God? That day in July, I thought about Moses as he sang with the children of Israel, "The LORD is my strength and song, And He has become my salvation" (Exod. 15:2). That gave me astounding liberty to pray for a piano! The Lord who became Moses' song speaks in music, gives music. I prayed to the One Who *is* the song of Moses in the words of Exodus 15, and asked to be shown a baby grand Steinway—*if* that would be right for me to have in that living room. It seemed that with Fran's voice silenced here, a piano would be another voice appropriately communicating an aspect of what the universe is!

The next day two phone calls followed one after the other. The first was from Mary Jane Grooms. "Oh Mrs. S, guess what! Our piano tuner, Al Fisher, came this morning, and while he was tuning our piano, Greg asked him if he knew where to look for a secondhand Steinway piano. And he said, 'I have one to sell.' "

"That's amazing, Mary Jane, because—"

"But listen, it's even more amazing because he should have been tuning our piano a few weeks ago. But that day we didn't hear the doorbell because we were in the backyard with the children. Don't you see, we wouldn't have thought of asking him had he not been here on the spot today."

I had not walked away from the phone when it rang again. This time it was Mary Lou, Dr. Sather's wife. "Edith, listen to this ad in the Mayo Clinic paper." She proceeded to read me an ad for a secondhand baby grand Steinway! They turned out to be the same piano. Mary Lou went on to say she had called their church organist, the wife of another Mayo surgeon, Dr. John Woods. "Janet says she'll be glad to drive out to give her opinion of the piano after playing it."

I then called David Kemmer, a fine technician who tunes, regulates, and voices grand pianos for concerts and installs organs as far away as Florida. That sounds like a rather flat statement for describing an unusual event. Ordinarily, David simply can't be reached by telephone. To have him not only answer, but to be told he could have tea and go out to give his expert, impartial opinion of the piano within a short time of the call was a sensation, an event! This was to be followed by a series of events which I do not believe were coincidence.

We asked questions of David on the way out to the country, talked of organs, of antique pianos, of wood, and of music. Soon we had arrived at Allen Fisher's house, knocked, and were ushered in. There it stood! I had not read the first three chapters of this book then! I had no story of the history of that piano at all, except to be told that it had been kept in good condition. Then Janet Woods sat down and played. And the clarity and sweetness of the piano's voice filled our ears. David looked carefully inside and out, played some himself, and then remarked that he could not believe the age. "It must be 1956," he said, "because of the condition." However, he peered inside to see the number. There it stood, in that triangular place at the left —281261. "Yes, that is the beginning of 1936, made in 1935." As he said it then, nothing happened inside me. I simply nodded, and felt impressed that one look inside could tell him so much.

The decision was made after hearing everyone talk about the unusual condition of the piano, and the beautiful bass and treble. "This is a really excellent piano and I would advise you to go ahead with it." The price was exactly what Mary Crowley had said would be good! Mary Lou remarked that it had been quite unusual that she had looked through the Mayo Clinic paper so thoroughly. Also, out of curiosity she has looked since, and has never seen another Steinway grand advertised in it!

If this story were being accompanied by music, a very special Mozart would be in the background right now! That evening, July 5, I called Allen Fisher. "Yes, we will take it. Could you possibly have it delivered tomorrow? You see, my husband died just seven weeks ago and tomorrow is our forty-ninth wedding anniversary. It is the first wedding anniversary I have been alone. It would help a lot if that piano could arrive tomorrow."

"I'll do my best. I think that some fellows from Schmitt's could move it about noon."

July 6, 1984, the doorbell rang. A ramp was being laid across the front steps as I opened the door and greeted Allen. I looked at the Neuchatel clock and saw the hour. The preciseness of the timing made me feel prickles run up into my scalp. Forty-nine years to the hour since her wedding, the five-foot-two-inch bride of July 6, 1935, and the five-foot-one-inch Steinway model S baby grand 281261 of 1935 had come together for a celebration!!

To me this was not a chance happening, but a planned gift, a gift to gently introduce me to a new chapter of creativity. I was swept with a thrill of recognizing the pulling back of a curtain, just a tiny crack for a brief moment. Have you ever seen a curtain on the stage of a great concert hall move a bit so that you have a hint of preparation—a harp being set up, or a piano being rolled in, and a master technician standing near by? This was a different setting, but I had a glimpse of a beginning, a production about to take place, a preparation for a surprise! I felt a wave of both excitement and deep thankfulness at a time when I was expecting nothing but tears and sorrow and emptiness from dwelling on only memories.

Carefully the men brought the Steinway in, unwrapped it, and placed it in the corner where it looked its beautiful best. Sunshine poured in, lighting up the grain of the mahogany. My excitement and thanksgiving were because of the gorgeous tenderness of God, who does care about His children, and to Whom both music and creativity do matter. Within seconds I thrilled with the "turning of a page" as I was introduced to a new chapter of life.

"I *know* what I am going to do," I said to myself and to God. "Thank You for this. I will write a book about this piano, about Steinway, and about the history of pianos. I am going to immerse myself in research. But there is a second certainty—I want to have a thank-you dinner and concert for the doctors who took care of Fran. I want it to be in honor of Dr. Petitt, Fran's principal doctor these six years, and to have all the men and their wives for a very special evening. After that I'll keep having special high teas or dinners and have concerts, some discussion, and some reading. The piano will be another voice in this house, communicating through music not only about life and beauty, but also of struggles and death."

My spirits soared with awe and wonder. The *timing* was stunning! A telegram arrived from one of my children in Switzerland and a rose from another. They were put on the piano. Friends and L'Abri workers came with plants to bring anniversary greetings, and stayed to marvel at my exuberance. Greg played the piano. Then Anne Brown played it. We had tea, and I told them of my certainty of what I wanted to write and the concerts I was sure this room was made for. "It will be a little like the sixteenth century," I said romantically!

Then I asked Mary Lou to take me to the cemetery after a stop at a flower shop. There I found white and soft yellow chrysanthemums such as Fran and I often had for special occasions. I fixed them in a basket myself with some ivy trailing out of it. I felt I had to put something down on paper right then to make my thought of him that day more definite and concrete.

Happy Anniversary to you—up there, and to me—down here.

Love, Ede

I slipped it into the basket of flowers and placed it on his grave. There is an old tree there, and a young apple tree and spirea bush we had planted after the funeral. I left the flowers, and went back to my piano to think about the reality of chapters, or blocks of time, in our lives. This was to be a new chapter. To turn a page and start a new chapter does not erase former chapters, or diminish them in any way.

Creativity is quite possible in the midst of affliction and sorrow, sadness and difficulty. Creative flow is like running water on a bruised foot or putting an ice pack on a bruised knee. It is not being disloyal to begin a fresh new creative direction in the midst of bereavement. It is important for oneself, for other people, and for God, to take the gift of an idea, using the gift of whatever talent you have, to plunge into learning something in a field you had no time to study before. The universe is so full of fascinating diversities, it is important not to get into a rut—but to surprise people, and especially to surprise yourself, with a change of topic for conversations and for creativity. The beauty and the excitement of fresh discovery are a part of what human beings were given a capacity for and a necessity for!

There is a horizontal effect of human being upon human being. Sometimes that horizontal effect is devastating, and one person discourages another, or puts another person down. However, at other times a person can be the spark that lights a flame and gives a breath of air that fans that flame into a bonfire of creativity for others.

Mary Crowley, in her tribute to Francis Schaeffer, gave a gift of a piano to L'Abri. But so much more than that, it was a gift of a spark that lit many fireworks! Have you ever been at a Swiss First of August fireworks display or an American Fourth of July display? Mysterious objects are arranged on boards in various patterns, hidden by the dark. Have you watched the spark at the end of a piece of firelighting punk touched to the fuse which sets off a chain reaction until an amazing array of color and light makes clear that which had been only in the imagination of the designers of the fireworks? That piano became not only a precious comfort in itself, but was the punk that lit a chain reaction of sparks.

As I stood there with a flood of ideas coursing through my brain, the appropriate music to communicate my feelings and thoughts would have been Handel's fireworks music which he wrote for the King of England to accompany a gorgeous display of fireworks over the Thames. That was surging through me as I thought of having a thank-you concert and dinner. The menu, the instruments and performers, the flowers and candles all became vivid in my mind. Then the possibilities of going to New York to interview John Steinway, to see, hear, feel, smell the factory in Queens, the browsing in London bookshops and talking to violin makers—a veritable "display" took over my thoughts and feelings. Creativity bubbling up like water? Creativity spraying sparks down through darkness?

Where does creativity come from?

CHAPTER 5

Creativity Created

Y ou are sitting in your favorite concert hall. Perhaps it is the new Ordway Hall in Minneapolis-St. Paul, or Carnegie Hall in New York, the Royal Festival Hall in London, or Kennedy Center in Washington. You may be in Vienna, Stockholm, Tokyo, Amsterdam, Lausanne, or a tiny twelfth century church in Saanen, in the Swiss Alps. But wherever you are, you are caught up in the anticipation and excitement of the moment when the conductor stands with baton poised—the hush before the first burst of notes. Perhaps it is Beethoven's Piano Concerto no. 5 (*Emperor*). No matter where you are, or which orchestra is your special one, pause and consider for a few moments as the orchestra gives the first three chords and the soloist bursts in with the astounding cascade of thrilling notes, as brilliantly as a waterfall catching sunshine on the individual drops of its spray. Listen. Listen. What are you hearing?

Is it random sound? Is it a chance happening? What was combined in your own anticipation and expectation? Why were you willing to pay for the seat, to come in time? What gave you the measure of confidence that this evening would be worth all the rush it took to get here? Upon what was your confidence based? Whatever amount of knowledge you have concerning instruments, you have some measure of confidence that these instruments are good and will perform. You may know that the cello was made in 1705 and is therefore 250 years older than the slim, blond woman who is to play it. You may know that the first violinist has a Stradivarius violin, and you are ready to listen for the sweetness of its tones. You may be full of what you read in an article about the gold flute of James Galway or about

73

Waiting for music at Carnegie Hall.

the oboe. You may know that the Steinway 303 is especially beloved to the pianist who is playing the solo. Perhaps you know nothing at all about any of the instruments, but you have come to the concert with an assurance that the instruments will be of high quality—even if you could not define what "high quality" consists of in an instrument.

Another thing true of your eagerness for the music to flow over you is that you have some idea of the composer's genius. You may be a music student or a conservatory graduate; you may be one of us who will always be a part of the audience and not a performer, but you have your favorite composers and you are expecting that the program will bring pleasure to you. You are waiting to listen not just with your ears, but with a depth of understanding and appreciation. As you look at the program, you are reassured in seeing the names of the composers.

Programs make a bit of a rustle as people turn through them, looking for bits and pieces that have been written about the performers. Pictures of the soloists are there, and some paragraphs are usually written about their backgrounds, their studies, their achievements. Perhaps you know much more than is given in the program about every person who is performing tonight. Or perhaps they are just being introduced to you for the first time. The best friend of the soloist may be sitting right in front of you. People are mixed in the concert hall. To someone who is the wife, husband, best friend, or closest fan of a soloist there is always the "butterfly wavering" in the abdomen, which goes along with the brain's verbalizing a "hope he does his best tonight" or a "hope she is really 'on' tonight." The performers are the other ingredient you believed to be good when you chose to come to this concert. They are the ones who must bring music from the instruments. They must interpret the notes composed by other human beings in another geographical place, in another time of history.

You sit there with a measure of confidence that this evening will fill you with music which will blot out some of the tiredness from work, take away some of the cobwebs in your brain, relax some of the tensions caused by income tax forms, remove the echo of the unpleasant retort an associate made in the last conversation of the day. You are counting on those instruments, the composer's work, the performers, and the skill of the conductor to do this. You are ready for sheer enjoyment to some degree, without having to doubt the existence of these creative people whose creativity is being combined tonight.

Now add to the array of violin makers and the makers of each of the other instruments, the four hundred people who had a part in making the Steinway concert grand and the master technician who gave a careful toning and voicing to it just before the concert. This technician is faithfully standing in the wings, ready for any emergency (such as the breaking of a string). Add also the architect who designed the hall and all the people who built into it not only beauty but also acoustical excellence. Add to these people the stage manager who watches over so many details, keeping the house in order for the events which follow one another, day by day.

It is the combined creativity and skill of all these people that makes it possible for you to settle in your seat, adjust your glasses, be sure your handkerchief is handy and a throat lozenge available without a rustle when you reach for it, in case a tickle or dry spot becomes intolerable. In other words, you can relax because each one is prepared to do what he or she has a genius for. It is who each one is that counts, and the kind of mind and imagination and creativity that each one has for his or her portion of the whole.

Creativity is behind the cascade of trills and deep bass notes. Creativity is behind the movement of the conductor's hands and head. Creativity is behind the crescendo and behind the hushed soft contrast. Creativity is essential to all music. Whatever we hear in the concert has been in the mind of the composer. Beethoven was deaf when he wrote this *Emperor* Concerto. He could hear it in his mind even though he sadly never heard it with his ears. The beauty of what was in his mind comes into our ears. But—to have it played for us, the creativity had to take place in *that* man's mind.

Whoever the composer, whatever the music, creativity is the essential ingredient of jazz or classical, of gospel or country, of rock or Gregorian chants. Creativity is also the essential ingredient of instrument making. Talent, skill, hard work, faithful slogging, all go into being a performer. But there is an ingredient among performers that cannot be explained by the training or the practicing. It is "touch," "interpretation," "genius," "creativity"...call it what you will. There is an ingredient that has to do with what is heard in the mind, what is understood with an inner sensitivity which is *not* mechanical, and which needs to be classified (if one word is to be used) as *creativity*.

Creativity—whether in music, sculpture, painting, writing, film making, designing fabrics or gardens, ceramics, architecture, interior decorating, farming, cooking, boat making, and all the areas of science and discovery—needs *choice!* Ideas flood human minds, and a choice has to be made about which idea to pursue.

Do my theories about how the universe began fit in with creativity? Do they provide a base for the beginning of art and music? Do my theories about the universe allow me to have standards or ethics? Is there any meaning or purpose to life, on the basis of my theories, or the theories I have accepted?

Now, as I listen to this full orchestra, reveling in the music, does this glorious music fit in with my thankfulness for hearing, seeing, feeling, responding? Does my enjoyment make sense?

What *are* the choices of theory upon which to base your life? Will you choose a theory about some sort of "forever existing particles," plus chance, plus time equaling everything that exists, including you and me?

Let me mention a few theories very briefly.

The Anthropic Principle

The earth is an exceptionally hospitable place for mankind, with abundant water and an average temperature that happens to lie in the narrow range where water is a liquid.... The fact that the real universe does harbor intelligent observers therefore places certain constraints on the diversity of ways the universe could have begun and on the physical laws that could have governed its development. In other words, the universe has the properties we observe today because if its earlier properties had been much different, we would not be here as observers now. The principle underlying this method of cosmological analysis has been named the anthropic principle, from the Greek *anthropos*, man.

The anthropic principle has been invoked in cosmology precisely because the deductive method cannot readily be employed there. The initial conditions of the universe are not known, and the physical laws that operated early in its history are also uncertain, the laws may even depend on the initial conditions. Indeed, perhaps the only constraint that can be imposed on a theory reconstructing the initial conditions of the universe and the corresponding laws of nature is the requirement that those conditions and laws give rise to an inhabited universe.

At the least the anthropic principle suggests connections between the existence of man and aspects of physics that one might have thought would have little bearing on biology. In its strongest form the principle might reveal that the universe we live in is the only conceivable universe in which intelligent life could exist. It is fair to say, however, that not all cosmologists and philosophers of science assent to the utility of the anthropic principle, or even to its legitimacy.[1]

You, as an intelligent observer of the universe, need to think carefully and carefully observe! You are listening to music that was created with specific instruments in mind. There is discussion as to what should be played on the modern piano and what should be kept for the clavichord because music written for the clavichord sounds different from the composer's idea if played on a modern piano. You and I are delicate instruments if we may think of it that way for a moment. The anthropic principle suggests that the very fact that we exist as observers of the universe unlocks something concerning the *kind* of a universe it is—one that is hospitable to human beings. My mind tells me that there is a logical connection here that comes forth into my thoughts with a crescendo of excitement!

Out of Nothing?

An article by Dennis Overbye, "The Universe According to Guth," puts forth some of Alan Guth's theories concerning origins and relates his discussions with other men. Alan Guth is a brilliant young cosmologist at M.I.T. who discusses the speculation that the universe might have been created out of nothing.

> Not with a bang so much as with a pfft, it ballooned accidentally out of the endless void of eternity, from a stillness so deep that there was no "there" or "then," only possibility. For one golden instant all creation was a harmony of energy and matter ruled by a single godlike force. As the cosmos expanded, like a ripple on a pond, and coiled, that force fragmented, and then fragmented again. As each new force split away, the constituents of the early cosmos—quarks, gluons, neutrinos, gravitons, and other exotic particles—once able to change identities freely, were trapped in separate classes, permanently alienated from each other. Universes sprouted from tiny seeds of the evolving chaos, grew, and went their lonely ways, separated by fortress walls of energy.
>
> These events happened billions of years ago, when the universe was only a fraction of a second old. Today, physicists wander mentally through a fragmented cosmos, haunted by

1. "The Anthropic Principle," *Scientific American*, December, 1981, 114.

mathematical dreams, searching for a few relic clues to the lost order of the past.[2]

Do we *know* where the universe started? Overbye's article also mentions J. Richard Gott, a Princeton cosmologist and an inveterate universe creator, whose big bubble theory is similar to Guth's.

[Gott] avoids the dread singularity, the tiny, incredibly dense point that started it all, by putting it forever in the past. But more radical theorists are ready to create the universe out of nothing...

[Sidney] Coleman, among others, suspects that cosmologists trying to probe all the way back to the instant of creation may find some more surprises. "We still don't know why snowflakes are hexagonal," he says. "If you had never seen snowflakes, you would have a hard time predicting them. The same might apply to 'snowflakes' that might have formed in the early universe."

Coleman and Guth were in a Harvard lecture hall one April afternoon as a young Tufts professor, Russian emigre Alex Vilenkin, presented his version of genesis. According to him, the universe as a young bubble had tunneled like a metaphysical mole from somewhere else to arrive in space and time. That someplace else was "nothing." Afterwards the three physicists sat in the hall and had a conversation that Lewis Carroll might have enjoyed, about nothing. "What is nothing?" asked Coleman, pressing his fingers together in front of his face. "Nothing," said Vilenkin, "is no space, no time." Coleman pondered that for a while. "There is an epoch without time; it is eternity," he said finally. "So we make a quantum leap from eternity into time."[3]

Has everything we know as matter in the universe, plus everything we know inside ourselves as personality—ideas, creativity, appreciation of other people's music and art, cooking and knitting—sprung spontaneously out of *nothing* with no outside factor involved? Do particles plus time plus chance equal the universe and its form and human beings and their creativity? Or does no time, no space, nothing plus nothing equal the universe as it is with its orderliness and its form?

Can you have *faith* enough to believe this, and then simply go on comfortably listening to the next selection, thrilling in the familiar

2. Dennis Overbye, "The Universe According to Guth," *Discover,* June, 1983, 93.
3. *Ibid.,* 99.

order of Beethoven's Seventh Symphony or the Bach Concerto? Is your mind quiet and relaxed with this explanation? Do you feel satisfied to consider yourself to be "the measure of all things"? Do you feel satisfied to have "nothing" be the final reality?

The Ultimate Theory of Everything

Is there something more recent that helps? After all, three years have gone by! (*Discover* magazine, April, 1985, has an article entitled "The Ultimate Theory of Everything.") "Everything" ought to include creativity, genius, a base for ethics, morals, and choice, as well as an explanation of "you" and "me." The article needs to be read in full, but in essence we are being told that in an auditorium in Stockholm, Carlo Rubbia, who had just won the Nobel Prize in physics—along with his colleague, Simon van de Meer—described hitherto undetected particles that had come into sight: "Monojets and dijets, baffling phenomena detected at the huge particle accelerator at CERN, are tantalizing physicists seeking one grand plan that would finally explicate the universe."

> Only a year ago, physicists thought they had achieved an admirable understanding of the various fundamental particles and forces of the universe and had concocted, at the very least, the basic structure of the mathematical laws that govern them. Now Rubbia, who's a staff scientist with the European Laboratory for Particle Physics (called CERN, an acronym for its former name), outside Geneva, and a professor of physics at Harvard, has reported observations that don't fit into the standard notion of how the universe works. These observations may herald the existence of new particles, perhaps unknown forces and unknown forms of matter....It may eventually lead to what they irreverently refer to as the T.O.E.—the ultimate Theory of Everything.
>
> The pursuit of the T.O.E. is one of the overwhelming obsessions of high energy physicists. They hope to create a grand mathematical construction that traces back all the myriad of particles, as well as the forces that act upon them, to a common ancestor that existed in the very first moments of the universe. However, John Ellis, another theorist insisted that they would ignore all the new results except the monojets. "As a theorist," he said confidently, "if you want to interpret what's going on, you have to exercise a lot of judgment, and you have to be prepared calmly to throw away pieces of data that don't agree with your theory. If you try to fit absolutely everything you're going to go crazy...."

By early January, Rubbia was saying that all the ideas put forth to explain the results could be discounted for the time being—with the exception of supersymmetry...."Look," he said modestly, "whether supersymmetry is there or not isn't my choice. We're only going up Mount Sinai to get the tablets, not to write the commandments."

The other physicists of the UAI group were a little more cautious. "We've presented the data very honestly," says Rohlf. "We've come out and said these things aren't junk. It's easy to prove what they're not. Proving what they are is considerably more difficult...."

Despite all the optimism, both theorists and experimentalists are being realistic. They're too much aware that the history of physics is littered with the ghosts of apparently ironclad discoveries that later experiments proved incorrect, and with the rubble of years of theoretical work that attempted to explain the wrong results.[4]

Perhaps you are saying, "I don't care about physics and I don't care about particles." But it *is* important for you to find an explanation for your own existence and for your own creativity. Perhaps you feel that there is no need to consider the theories, thinking you can just vaguely accept whatever is the opposite of believing God exists. You may think all this has no connection with you if you are in some area of the arts, or are sitting waiting for a concert to continue. You may feel that the pouring rain outside affects you personally far more than any theory as to where the universe came from or how life began.

If you say, "I don't believe in God," "I don't think the Bible is different from any other book," "I don't think there is any meaning to life," or "I don't believe in life after death," you may think that ends it and try to shut out the ticking of the clock. But it is very important to *know* what it is you *don't* believe to be true. It also is important to know how the theories which you are perhaps putting in the place of God are shifting and changing.

As the violins gleam in wonderful tones of brown and red-brown, as the flutes catch the light and reflect it in their silver or gold, as the oboe's shape delights you, and as the trumpets shift up to the performers' lips, let's ask the question again, *"Where does creativity come from?"*

4. Gary Taubes, "The Ultimate Theory of Everything," *Discover*, April, 1985, 52–59.

For most of us, our brains won't let us have the dubious luxury of not asking the question, even if silently. "Where DOES creativity come from?"

There is no magic in the word used as the name of the first book of the Bible. *Genesis* is a Greek word meaning "origin," "source," or "beginning." The original Hebrew title is *Bereshith*, meaning "In the beginning." The Jerusalem Talmud supports Moses as the author of Genesis, as does the first-century Jewish historian Josephus. The early church openly held to the Mosaic authorship of Genesis. In all the range of Israel's life it would be difficult to find a man better prepared or qualified to write this book of history. Trained in "the wisdom of the Egyptians," Moses had been providentially prepared to understand and integrate, *under the inspiration of God*, all the available records, manuscripts, and the relay of true history by spoken words. (How could he know things that happened *before* he lived? And how can anyone write prophecy of things coming after his life is over? Only by special revelation from God.)

Indeed, God exists and He has not been silent. He has revealed Himself and has given the basic explanation of the order of the universe and the beginning of life, and the personality and creativity found in human beings—in a book! God has made clear *where* creativity came from in a book!

How does this book begin?

What is the alternative to the theories of the physicists?

"In the beginning God...."

What an overwhelmingly awesome four words.

What a stunning answer to all the questions.

What a final discovery.

What a final reality!

In the beginning was personality because God is personal. God is infinite and eternal in His wisdom, power, and love, but He is also personal because He is a Person. That means, in the beginning was thinking, acting, feeling! That means, in the beginning was an infinite mind with a myriad of ideas, an ability to choose, and all the ingredients for creativity.

Creativity is the background for the Creation.

The Creation needs a Creator.

The music we are waiting to hear had composers, creators who heard in their minds what we are going to hear on the piano, violins, cellos, bass, violas, flutes, oboes, trumpets! All creation needs a creator. And creativity existed in *The Creator.*

Listen to Isaiah:

"To whom then will you liken Me,
Or to whom shall I be equal?" says the Holy One.
Lift up your eyes on high,
And see who has created these things,
Who brings out their host by number;
He calls them all by name,
By the greatness of His might
And the strength of His power;
Not one is missing. (Isa. 40:25–26)

The signature of the Judeo-Christian God is CREATOR.
It is to this Creator that David sang in the Psalms. He sang with the gorgeous accompaniment of his harp.

I will sing a new song to You, O God;
On a harp of ten strings I will sing praises to You. (Ps. 144:9)

The psalmist sang of God's Creation.

To Him who by wisdom made the heavens,
For His mercy endures forever...
To Him who made great lights,
For His mercy endures forever—
The sun to rule by day,
For His mercy endures forever;
The moon and stars to rule by night,
For His mercy endures forever. (Ps. 136:5, 7–9)

It was the Creator who said through Isaiah,

Thus says the LORD, your Redeemer,
And He who formed you from the womb:
"I am the LORD, who makes all things,
Who stretches out the heavens all alone,
Who spreads abroad the earth by Myself." (Isa. 44:24)

It was the Creator who spoke to Job,

Where were you when I laid the foundations of the earth?
Tell Me, if you have understanding.
Who determined its measurements?

Surely you know!
Or who stretched the line upon it?
To what were its foundations fastened?
Or who laid its cornerstone,
When the morning stars sang together,
And all the sons of God shouted for joy? (Job 38:4–7)

God is gently but firmly sarcastic to Job as He asks these questions. In a later verse in this same chapter God asks Job if he knows all these things because he is so old! It is as if God said to me, and to you, "Do you know what you know because you were there these billions of years ago which you project in your theories?" "Do you know what you know because you have lived so many centuries and eons of time?" The actual question God asks Job is,

Where is the way to the dwelling of light?...
Do you know it, because you were born then,
Or because the number of your days is great? (Job 38:19, 21)

Oh Job, oh human being, how many light years have *you* lived? Do you know anything about "forever" by experience?

How then does this God expect us to know anything? Certainly He respects our minds by revealing to us in a book that which our minds can comprehend—to a degree. Also He gives us His Creation to study and to enjoy. But this Creator tells us there are things to be taken by faith. That is, there are very real things we cannot see and, being finite, we cannot always completely understand them.

In the book of Hebrews, which is in the Bible, we are told in words which we *can* understand, something about that which we *cannot* understand!

By faith we understand that the worlds were framed by the word of God, so that the things which are seen were not made of things which are visible. (Heb. 11:3)

Physicist Carlo Rubbia may tell us that "whether supersymmetry is there or not isn't my choice." I would say with him, in the same sort of way, "Whether truth is there or not isn't my choice. The universe is what it is. Creation is what it is. If God exists, His existence does not depend on my believing it. He exists. His Creation exists."

The thing we are talking about is _understanding_. It isn't just that we live in an atmosphere that is hospitable to human beings who need air to breathe, water to drink, ground in which to grow food. We need an explanation of how it is we are personal. Is it a personal universe? Or is it an impersonal universe? Do we fit in? Or are we an improbable accident of chance?

> For thus says the LORD,
> Who created the heavens,
> Who is God,
> Who formed the earth and made it,
> Who has established it,
> Who did not create it in vain,
> Who formed it to be inhabited:
> "I am the LORD, and there is no other.
> I have not spoken in secret,
> In a dark place of the earth;
> I did not say to the seed of Jacob,
> 'Seek Me in vain';
> I, the LORD, speak righteousness,
> I declare things that are right." (Isa. 45:18–19)

We do fit in because He made it to be inhabited. The book which God gave through Moses and other people gives a fantastically logical explanation that fits the reality of what we find within ourselves. "In the beginning God..."

The universe had a personal beginning, not an impersonal beginning. God had in His *mind* the singing of the stars together, as He told Job about the music of the stars, even as Mozart had the sound of music in his *mind* before he wrote it down. The difference is that God is infinite and eternal, and made everything from nothing. We are told, "He spoke, and it was." We are told that it was not an impersonal "force" who created everything, but a personal God. This is the alternative answer to where love, compassion, and communication—and creativity—come from. Because, you see, God the Creator created human beings in His image.

Perhaps you have heard these words sung. Perhaps you hear deep minor music as a background for the words. Perhaps you listen with ears only for entertainment. But please consider the astounding answer to where creativity came from that is bound up in the following familiar passage from Genesis:

> Then God said, "Let Us make man in Our image, according to Our likeness; let them have dominion over the fish of the sea,

over the birds of the air, and over the cattle, over all the earth and over every creeping thing that creeps on the earth."

So God created man in His own image; in the image of God He created him; male and female He created them. Then God blessed them, and God said to them, "Be fruitful and multiply; fill the earth and subdue it;..." Then God saw everything that He had made, and indeed it was very good. (Gen. 1:26–28, 31)

Isn't this spectacular? An infinite personal Creator made human beings in His own image! That means human beings were created; we are not a chance collection of cells! Human beings were carefully made in the image of their Creator. Don't you see—you were made to be creative. To be made in the image of God, the Creator, means that creativity is part of what human beings are in the very warp and woof of their beings. Human beings can't help being creative any more than they can help breathing, or communicating with other human beings. People differ from the rest of Creation in being able to create on a finite level. God alone could make something out of nothing. He gave people the earth full of trees, silver, and the raw material out of which to make brick houses, marble statues, landscaped gardens, cotton, linen, wool, and silk fabrics, stone roads, and a great diversity of musical instruments! Men and women, people, were given the earth to take care of, and to use in interesting, original, creative ways—ideas always coming first.

Everything that has been made—from space ships to handmade quilts—has first been an idea. It was Jabal who was the father of those who dwell in tents and have livestock. Someone first had an idea for making a tent in his mind, and took great pains to make it a reality. "His brother's name was Jubal. He was the father of all those who play the harp and flute" (Gen. 4:21). The tentmaker's brother made musical instruments! A creative family!

God not only created some fantastic music which we may hear some day, but He created birds with a stunning symphony of songs, notes copied by instruments, coming from the instruments of their throats. Now very *early* in the history which we are given in God's book, we find this mention of flutes and harps—instrumental music along with voices!

Consider this for a moment. God said He created people, human beings, men and women, in His "likeness." What on earth does it mean to have been made in the image of God? It means many things, but among others it means being made in the likeness of the One who first created music. No wonder human beings have the capacity for making instruments, composing music, and performing music—perhaps quite naturally in the hills playing a flute to the sheep, or a stringed instrument to accompany a song sung to another person, a king or a peasant!

J. R. R. Tolkien in *The Silmarillion* writes a first chapter called "Ainulindale"—the music of the Ainur. Now of course this is a mythological story, but as with C. S. Lewis, Tolkien often follows some parts of reality with his vivid imagination, putting it all into a mythological world. In this chapter he has music being created. He pictures instruments like trumpets, viols, organs, lutes and countless choirs making harmony together. He tells of this music going out "into the Void, and it was not void."[5]

I think when Tolkien read of God speaking to Job and asking whether he had already been born, whether he had been there when the "morning stars sang together," he must have thought of how that music would go out into a void which would cease to be a void!

Recently I heard the National Symphony Orchestra in the Kennedy Center for the Performing Arts in Washington, D.C. Mstislav Rostropovich marvelously led this wonderful orchestra in *La Mer*, in which Debussy portrayed the sea in three symphonic sketches. Now I can feel and see the sea by listening to this, if I carefully imagine "From Dawn to Noon on the Sea," and "The Play of the Waves," and "The Dialogue of the Wind and the Sea." But that night I had been thinking of what the morning stars might have sounded like singing together all those eons ago in what was perhaps the first great concert! As I listened to Rostropovich's fabulous crescendos and diminuendos and watched him bend from the waist, swaying intently from side to side, bring out of the orchestra the loud crashing sound which goes through one's ribs, then hold up his hands to gently bring soft tones from his instruments—I excitedly responded. I visualized stars making this music, led by God their Creator, at a distant moment of history. I almost said it out loud, but refrained of course. The words were very loud in my head and I had to clasp my hands to keep them from moving too much as my toes made movements inside my shoes. *This is it! This is it! The stars sounded something like this, I'm sure of it*—kept surging through my brain. I looked around, but no one was looking at me and obviously those loud words had been only inside my head!

5. J. R. R. Tolkien, *The Silmarillion* (Boston: Houghton Mifflin Co., 1977).

"Patrons are requested to turn off signal watches during concerts" the program tells me in small letters, but my excited thoughts were louder to my own ears than any signal watch. Yet no one else had heard it! What an amazing thing the human brain is. The brain responds to other people's creativity and enables the audience to be an audience. And yet it races on with ideas that come in the midst of response and give a springboard for new creative possibilities or to plans for actual projects.

What a strange way for chance particles to act. How much faith it takes to believe that particles plus billions of years of time, plus chance, will equal creativity, or will equal the brain, the mind, in which ideas form and from which creativity comes forth. It seems to me that what we have been given by Moses in Genesis is consistent with the way we ourselves observe things to take place. We observe in ourselves, and in others, something of the flow of ideas, something of the process of choice among these ideas, and something of the result of choosing to make a violin, a piano, a chocolate cake, a lawnmower, a bicycle, a pot of soup, a boat, a telescope. We find it understandable to be told that the things we see displayed in a museum were at one time in someone's mind. They were sculpted or painted, and now years later we can still know what was in that person's mind. It is not an irrational concept. It fits what you and I experience hour by hour in living, as well as fitting what we observe as we live among creative people. As I look about this room, I have no problem imagining the creator of the fabric of my green and white curtains, imagining the designer of the candles or the mug in which my coffee has been served. It is interesting to read the names of the authors of the books on the bookshelves—their lives can be read about also. And the paintings on the wall were painted by my son Franky whom I know well! I have no problem with needing theories about whether the brass candlestick came into existence by chance or not. Design of so many sorts fills me with admiration of the designer!

Where do artists and designers get their models?

Four hundred fifty years ago, Giorgio Vasari, an Italian artist, wrote books about the artists of the Renaissance, which were best sellers during that time. Just think of this man who at nine years of age was so well taught that he could recite in Latin a part of Virgil's Aeneid, as well as draw beautifully as he was taught by a French painter. This little boy of nine was taken to Florence by a cardinal to study with Michelangelo, and then later with Andrea del Sarto. It was this "little boy" who was to write about the lives of these men and others, as well as to be a painter and sculptor himself. To read this paragraph is like walking into a room in Florence and sitting with this man Vasari while he explains the true origins of creativity.

> Design is the foundation of both these arts [sculpture and painting], or rather the animating principle of all creative processes: and surely design existed in absolute perfection before the Creation when Almighty God, having made the vast expanse of the universe and adorned the heavens with His shining lights, directed His creative intellect further, to the clear air and the solid earth. And then, in the act of creating man, He fashioned the first forms of painting and sculpture in the sublime grace of created things. It is undeniable that from man, as from a perfect model, statues and pieces of sculpture and the challenge of pose and contour were first derived; and for the first paintings, whatever they may have been, the ideas of softness and of unity and the clashing harmony made by light and shadow were derived from the same source.[6]

How satisfying, understanding, convincing is Vasari's explanation of the origin of both creativity and the models for art. How thrilling to contemplate the wonders of the Creator God's Creation. Walk in the woods past moss-covered rocks and clumps of ferns, look at the variety of leaves and barks, watch the almost visible growth of snowdrops and violets in the spring. Think of the diversity of color, textures, shapes seen in one short walk in one small part of the earth's vast geography! Forgetting all else about "origins," think about the fact that human creativity in art draws from myriad models in that which was created by the Creator.

Now shift to music and the consideration of models for sound. Walk along a seashore and listen to the thundering of the waves. The sky may grow dark and as lightning streaks the sky, a clap of thunder adds a rolling of drums! Come again on a clear calm day and hear the soft lap, lap, lap, the regular rhythm of small waves, not only drawing you to sit close enough to let them wash over your bare feet, but bringing a gentle part of a favorite Bach to mind. Walk in a thicket of trees at sunset and hear the tremendous diversity of birds' songs in the English countryside, or concentrate on the crickets' chorus as the stars come out. Models of sound have also been created to stimulate

---

6. Giorgio Vasari, *Artists of the Renaissance*, trans. George Bull (London: Allen Lane, 1978), 19.

creativity. There is a staggering diversity in Creation from the silence of snow to the delicate sound of rain on leaves. Silence is a part of the sound of music as well. What amazing "models" have been made—not to be copied as if by Xerox or with a camera, but to give inspiration to creativity and birth to ideas in endless combinations and variations.

The captivating ingredient in the whole fantastic stream of reality is that the Creator God created beings in His likeness so that each one could be a creator on a finite level. But added to this overwhelming fact, God then gave both the models to inspire fresh ideas and the material necessities for making things. The right wood for violins and the right wood for soundboards in grand pianos depends on the right trees being created!

The blending and harmony of all this potential is like the best performers blending the best violins and violas—cellos and bass—in Bach's Concerto for Two Violins in D Minor. I have a disc on now, played by Igor and David Oistrach as the two soloists. This blending of strings and recorder or flute tones, like a tumbling crystal-clear stream washing over pebbles, ferns, and rocks as it comes down the mountainside, is going somewhere! The music speaks of something ahead. It speaks of life, not death. Respond to it. Move your body even if ever so lightly. As you move your head, your hands, you are responding to that which speaks, sings, throbs, trembles, soars, with life. The conclusion brings a sigh—which should be a sigh of expectation. Forever music? Is that a nonsense phrase? Is there a possibility it may be possible, probable, certain? Is there any hope for forever music?

Now listen with me to Clara Haskil whom we often heard in Switzerland before her tragic death. Listen to her amazing fingers as she so sensitively plays Beethoven's Sonata no. 17 in D Minor. The one thing to listen for is the life—the quality of continuing into a future. Human beings were made for creativity. They were also made for life! It comes out in certain music with definiteness because of the composer's understanding, or creeps in simply because of what a human being really is. These are not computers nor an accidental result of chance happenings in history. These are creators with a base upon which to create, even if they don't know the base is there.

But what happened?

The world is so full of ugliness. And there is also destructive music and harsh discord and violence in music. Where did it come from?

How can it be that God saw everything that He had made, and said that He beheld it and "indeed it was very good"?

Where in the world did death come from?

What is death all about?

Where did war, cruelty, evil, sickness, accident, malfunction of brains and bodies come from?

What happened to make human beings so horrible? Were human beings created to be cruel? If people were created in the image of God—and God is personal and infinite—does that mean God is cruel? Are people as we know them, are we as we know ourselves, the same as the people God created in the beginning and declared to be "good"? Or did something take place to change that?

Let's go on to Amadeus Mozart to do some thinking together in the midst of these questions and the answers. The movie *Amadeus* gives us some astonishingly vivid contrasts wherein we can come to some exhilarating and exciting conclusions. Seeing glimpses of some of the basic answers to life's meaning is not dull!

CHAPTER 6

Amadeus and the Fall

I f you have not seen the film *Amadeus*, you should at least *hear* it.
The soundtrack gives you part of an evening at a concert with
Neville Marriner conducting the Academy of St. Martin-
in-the-Fields. At other moments you hear excerpts from *The Marriage
of Figaro*, *Don Giovanni*, and *The Magic Flute*—operas staged by
Twyla Tharp with Ivan Moravec at the piano. It is a marvelous treat
that lifts you out of whatever you were doing that day into the gloriously satisfying music of Mozart.

The music in this film draws you back for a second time. You
will listen with increased amazement if you remember that Mozart
wrote his music without needing to correct and change bits. It flowed
out of his mind and onto the paper with a rare demonstration of the
kind of creativity that can take place in a human mind. Unless you
are a musician, you can't translate those black notes and lines into a
full orchestra that sounds complete inside your head! Mozart, however, not only heard it as he looked at the written notes, but saw and
heard the notes in his mind before putting them on the paper.

As you add what you are seeing in the film to what you are hearing, you are suddenly transported into another moment of history
and another part of the world. The lighting and photography take
you through ancient narrow streets with the charm that only old
stone and many years of living can give. You wish you could look
longer at the wrought iron lamps with their old glass and the door
knocker seen all too briefly as a door swings open to show an interior
hall full of wonderful shadows and shapes. If you were painting these
cobblestone city walks at night, you would need a lot of black in

93

your greys and yellows and soft greens as everything is foggy and at times snowy or rainy. The film was shot in Czechoslovakia, but the narrow twisting streets could be in the old part of Lausanne, or other old European cities. There is a flavor that makes anyone who has lived in such places and walked late at night in a quiet time of thinking or discussing with a kindred spirit feel that any other part of the world is too young to give a background for contemplation!

In this film you also see the lavish clothing of that period of history. You see the same Tyl Theatre in Prague where *Don Giovanni* was actually performed in 1787. It is exciting to see the people in the clothing of that time, performing the music, and being audience too, making one feel it possible to slip in among them in space and time, listening to the music at the very time it was born. The quality of photography and music makes such an illusion convincing, until the film ends and one turns away from Mozart's dismal burial in that pouring rain sickhearted that no happy solution had come to save him in his illness and to give time for more compositions to pour forth.

I am not attempting to be a film critic, but it is extremely important to consider this story as presented in the film. I am not attempting to assess whether the film is accurate to Mozart's life or not, but it does present a totally inaccurate picture of God because of Salieri's misunderstanding of God. You will see what I mean as we go on. First, let me give a bare outline of the story of this film which has been so well done and deserved all the awards it was given.

Antonio Salieri, the eighteenth-century court composer to Emperor Joseph II of Austria, is living out the last years of his life in an insane asylum. We see him there telling a young priest something of Mozart's life and his own—to make clear why he came to hate God and to accuse Him of unfairness.

As a young lad, Salieri vowed to God that he would live a celibate life if God would give him great musical talent. (Let me digress to say that one does not make a bargain with the living God. Too many people try to treat God as a vending machine by declaring "I will do this if you will give me this." They put so much in a slot and expect to get out a candy bar! And if the demand is not granted, the resulting attitude shows what was there in the mind and heart in the first place.) Salieri does have talent as a composer and a position of honor and power as court composer. However, as he hears of Mozart's ability, in both composing and playing, displayed by the age of

Portrait of Wolfgang Amadeus Mozart, 1789.

four, and as he begins to hear Mozart's compositions, he says, "It seemed to me I had heard the voice of God." Salieri wanted to meet this young man.

Salieri discovers two things when Mozart is introduced to the court. He sees that Mozart's talent is even greater than he had realized before. Mozart's gorgeous music seems to pour forth effortlessly from his fingers. The compositions seem to pour from his mind as if a tap were turned on letting a fast-flowing stream of crystal-clear water pour forth endlessly. Yet Salieri soon discovers that Mozart has an uncouth and unmusical laughter that bursts forth, shattering the magic! Also, Mozart is vulgar, coarse, ribald in his taste and actions. How could this unrefined man bring forth such elegant, polished, exquisite music? Salieri's exclamation is, "It seemed to me that I had heard the voice of God, and it was the voice of an obscene child."

The film shows an encounter of mediocrity with genius. Yet, Salieri is the successful man who has the power to squash Mozart and spoil any success during his lifetime. So often the music or art of a genius is not properly heard, seen, or appreciated until long after the lifetime of the artist. There is a quality of greatness in literature, music, art, architecture, roadbuilding, and city planning that lives on in spite of, rather than because of, the people who produced it!

Salieri continues to confess to the priest and the film shows what he is recounting of the operas Mozart writes, of their performances, of his marriage, of his lack of money and of his drinking and carousing. Salieri is convinced that it is his own fault that Mozart died in the midst of an illness during which Salieri was pushing him to write a requiem. The film pictures Salieri writing the notes as the dying Mozart dictates music Salieri intends to pass off as his own! Mozart dies before the requiem is finished.

Salieri is portrayed as having a strong jealousy of Mozart, but that jealousy is not as strong as his own frustration at being mediocre in comparison to the genius of Mozart's fantastic music. The hate Salieri shows for God when he tears down an enormous crucifix and throws it on a bonfire is a hate that arises from thinking that God has bestowed this glorious talent upon an unworthy cretin, while pious Salieri was bypassed! Salieri seems almost to worship Mozart's music as he covets it for himself.

The reality of twisted history is often as this film shows it. Salieri is the only person who truly understands and appreciates the greatness of Mozart's musical ability. Mozart's wife is shown to love him and be proud of him, but without any true understanding of the unusual quality of his music. The emperor is pictured as a man with no ear for music, nor any way to hear greatness even while listening to the notes. People are all shown to have only varying amounts of understanding as to the amazing quality of what is coming forth from the orchestra, voices, and clavichords as Mozart's music is played. It is only Salieri who understands with deep recognition and delight the excellence of this music. He alone could have responded in a way that would have helped Mozart, and the two could have had a friendship on the basis of a shared recognition of the music and discussion about it.

Mozart was without anyone to give a satisfying response to his creativity. And it was a devastating twist to have the response that could have helped him be hidden within his enemy's mind and being! Neither man really had what the other one would have credited him with having or envied him for having. Salieri certainly had no compassion for the frustrations of Mozart who was finding his operas pushed aside, as he, Salieri had the power to do. Mozart had no idea that Salieri coveted his brilliant talent and would give anything to change places!

How different history might have been if they had been able to be friends sharing their hopes and fears and sheer wonder about music—no matter *which* mind it had come from!

But there is another far stronger statement to be made about history: How different history would have been had there been no Fall.

No what? No Fall. You see, if you take the alternate possibility of the beginning of all things, rather than the humanistic theory, you have a full-rounded explanation and a measure of understanding of the origin of evil in the midst of all that had been created as good.

Salieri's hatred of God for "giving that obscene Mozart such an overwhelmingly marvelous gift of music" is the same kind of hatred that Baudelaire expressed as he, and Albert Camus too, concluded that if there is a God, He created the world as it is, with the bad created alongside the good. This point of view ends up with God being the creator of evil.

My husband's book, *He Is There and He Is Not Silent*, says, "Charles Baudelaire, who was a famous French art historian and a great thinker, has a famous sentence: 'If there is a God, he is the Devil.' "[1] My husband goes on to say that if one begins with the premise that there is an unbroken line between what man is now and

1. Francis A. Schaeffer, *He Is There and He Is Not Silent* (Wheaton, Ill.: Tyndale, 1972), 38.

what he has intrinsically always been, then if there is a God, he is the Devil. In other words, if the evil and wickedness we find in people is that way because of how people were created, then Salieri's actions make sense.

But Camus and Baudelaire and Salieri did *not* understand. Perhaps no one ever told them about the Fall!

"What?" you may ask. "Do you mean that myth about Adam and Eve? What a simplistic idea!"

No, please read on. It is not simplistic. It is profound and it is also the truth of how it all came about. The other theories of origins and of life springing from a series of unlikely accidents have *no* explanation for either the marvelousness of human beings, *nor* for the horribleness of human beings. Neither good nor evil makes any sense. If human life is simply a product of chance, there is no base for making a judgment about what good consists of and where the line is crossed into that which is "wrong." Words like *right* and *wrong* are so arbitrary within such theories as to become meaningless.

Reading the Bible's explanation gives answers that are superbly satisfying and are in harmony with history's happenings. Truth not only fits like a perfect key in a complicated lock, but truth is satisfying like air to someone who has come up from too long under water. The glorious air of truth gives fresh life to the intellect as well as to the spirit.

If indeed there is a Creator God, He has created the whole universe, the seen and the unseen. He has created the portion called natural and that which we call supernatural. Not only has God created that which we see with our naked eye, the telescopes, and the microscopes, but He has created the immense, unknown areas of the universe which the scientists say are undiscovered galaxies that make up perhaps 99 percent of everything there is. People have limited God in their idea of Who He is and what He is able to do, just as they have a very limited idea of what the universe is made up of and its extent.

Incidentally, it is fascinating in the midst of the present discussion by astronomers who are finding more galaxies and who are full of awe at realizing that "what can be seen of the universe is like foam on the surface of the ocean, snow on mountaintops. Beyond lies the shadow universe—invisible, unknown, unimaginably immense,"[2] to go back to David's nineteenth psalm and read,

2. Front cover, *Discover*, May, 1985.

The heavens declare the glory of God;
And the skies proclaim the work of his hands.
Day after day they pour forth speech;
And night after night they display knowledge. (Ps. 19:1-2 NIV)

The New International Version translates it "the skies proclaim the work of his hands."

You see, God has made known a portion of knowledge in His written word, and has also made known that He expects people to gain knowledge of Him from His titanically vast Creation. However it would take longer than any human being has to live to discover more than a small fraction of what there is to discover about the universe.

It is not surprising that God, the Creator of the vast universe, Who has existed forever, gave a book to make known the essential things about truth and a base for a world view, as well as things essential for understanding past, present, and future history. If a personal God created personal human beings in His image, then communication, one of the marks of personality, would be essential to both God and His created beings. Verbalized communication is essential to imparting information and knowledge. If verbalized explanations of factual as well as ethical bases for living were to be passed from generation to generation, it is perfectly logical to expect that all that people needed would be in a written form.

The Bible is not a mystical religious book full of hidden puzzles only the initiated can understand. It is written in grammatical language, using normal syntax and understandable sentences. It is meant to be read and understood with the mind. In the book of the Proverbs of Solomon, son of David, king of Israel, there is this at the beginning of chapter two:

My son, if you receive my words,
And treasure my commands within you,
So that you incline your ear to wisdom,
And apply your heart to understanding;
Yes, if you cry out for discernment,
And lift up your voice for understanding,
If you seek her as silver,
And search for her as for hidden treasures;
Then you will understand the fear of the LORD,
And find the knowledge of God.
For the LORD gives wisdom;
From His mouth come knowledge and understanding. (Prov. 2:1-6)

If from the Lord's mouth we are to expect to be given knowledge, then we are meant to get that knowledge from the Bible. Of course there is a vast amount of knowledge and understanding we cannot expect to have in our short time on this earth—but what we *do* expect is to have that measure we *have* been given be true. Truth may be searched for and found. Exhaustive truth and exhaustive knowledge are not needed to make the measure we are given be true, and be that which *fits* the form of the universe, and the nature of human beings!

In God's condensation of all truth (the Bible, a comparatively short book), He has given us all we need to know in order to have an eternity to find out what we have yet to discover! There is an endless time ahead to study the wonders of the immense universe. This book also is fabulously efficient at giving us what we need to know in order to live within the framework of who we are and in order to *fulfill* our purpose in history, and to *bring forth* what we each have creative talent to do.

Creativity and discovery will not end with this all-too-short life. The frustration of limited time and energy is not matched by limited ideas! Neither Mozart, Leonardo da Vinci, nor Einstein, nor any other person with a flow of creative ideas has sufficient time to study, or write about, or do, a fraction of what is still flowing through the brain at death. This is all because God did not create people to live such a short span of time.

Before human beings were created God had already created angels. When? The condensed book which God gives us does not tell us that span of time. We are told enough to know that angels are rational beings with the ability to make choices and decisions. Angels had a period of time during which they evidently had an opportunity to fulfill all they had a capacity to do as amazingly special creatures, made by the Creator and in good relationship with Him. However, the highest of all the angels, once the most beautiful, Lucifer, rebelled against God.

How you are fallen from heaven,
O Lucifer, son of the morning!
How you are cut down to the ground,
You who weakened the nations!
For you have said in your heart:
"I will ascend into heaven,
I will exalt my throne above the stars of God;
I will also sit on the mount of the congregation

On the farthest sides of the north;
I will ascend above the heights of the clouds,
I will be like the Most High."
Yet you shall be brought down to Sheol,
To the lowest depths of the Pit.
Those who see you will gaze at you,
And consider you, saying:
"Is this the man who made the earth tremble,
Who shook kingdoms,
Who made the world as a wilderness
And destroyed its cities,
Who did not open the house of his prisoners?" (Isa. 14:12–17)

You see, there was a revolt in heaven, an attempted coup, as Lucifer set out to exalt himself and to be like God, having other angels worship him and bow to his leadership. The conflict which began at that point in history has affected history ever since. Lucifer used his period of choice to choose to begin a war against God and to spoil His Creation in every way he could. He gathered a force of other angels. It would seem that the recruiting of protesters against the God of Creation and His moral base for life and work was similar to the recruiting which has taken place through centuries ever since that time. The angels who flocked to follow Lucifer, who made the kind of promises always made in the midst of mutiny—that the benefits of mutiny would far outweigh what they had at that moment—were many! How many angels followed Lucifer? We are not told. We do know that Lucifer, who is known as the Devil, or Satan, gathered an army who became the demons. All demonic activity, all the occult practices which are not pure fake, stem from Lucifer and the fallen angels.

The loyal angels who loved God and adored Him continued to be faithful in serving Him. How many were there who remained with God?

We are not given a total number, but there is a hint in a verse about a future time, when the angels will be singing to the Messiah. John, a Jew who wrote the book of Revelation, said:

Then I looked, and I heard the voice of many angels around the throne, the living creatures, and the elders; and the number of them was ten thousand times ten thousand, and thousands of thousands, saying with a loud voice:

"Worthy is the Lamb who was slain
To receive power and riches and wisdom,
And strength and honor and glory and blessing!"
(Rev. 5:11–12)

That gives a hint that there are an overwhelming number of angels. However many God made in the first place, they do not marry and have children and so it would seem that there is an unchanging number. However many rebelled make up the number of demons.

How long was it after Lucifer warred against God and was thrown out of heaven with the other rebels that God created the first man and woman to have dominion over the earth and to have the marvelous possibility of being one physically, intellectually, and spiritually? We are not told. We do not know either how long Adam and Eve walked in the garden in the cool of the evening, day after day, talking to the Creator with no barrier between them before they were assailed by Lucifer with his insidious suggestion. God had given His created earth to Adam and Eve, along with plant life, animal life, insects, birds, and fish, not only to live among, but to cultivate and enjoy. God had said clearly that every tree was good for them to eat, but that there was one tree to stay away from: "But of the tree of the knowledge of good and evil you shall not eat, for in the day that you eat of it you shall surely die"(Gen. 2:17).

Now that was a statement of fact that was distinct, understandable, and comprehensible to these two intelligent people. They did not need a book of rules, there were no rules. There had been a good open relationship in daily walks and talks with the Creator. The freedom to live in that garden with its perfection and to have a free reign for creativity and an unspoiled relationship with each other was a freedom like nothing anyone has known since. It was a freedom in the midst of a flawless situation. There was only one law to heed: don't eat the fruit of that one tree. The result was clearly stated. Utter fairness on God's part was striking as He made it clear that turning aside from the truth of His spoken word and deliberately doing what He had *said* not to do would bring death, would indeed *bring* death!

What Lucifer, Satan, the Devil, in the form of a snake did in attempting to tempt Eve was to flatly accuse God of telling them a lie. First as he spoke to Eve he questioned her, to sow seeds of doubt that God had spoken. "Has God indeed said 'You shall not eat of every tree of the garden'?"(Gen. 3:1). And when Eve replied, "We may eat the fruit of the trees of the garden; but of the fruit of the tree which is in the midst of the garden, God has said, 'You shall not eat it, nor shall you touch it, lest you die' " (Gen. 3:2–3), Lucifer went a step further.

He denied emphatically the truth of God's statement. And ever since then all the false promises of Satan dressed up in a variety of false religions and philosophies have denied the truth of God's Word. There is a mark, a signature that Satan leaves: that which he declares is true, which he sets forth as the way of life or the base for a world view, specifically, explicitly, and definitely denies the truth of God's Word, the Bible. His first attempt was successful, and he has continued it ever since with an amazing success. It is amazing because it is incredible how many people prefer to believe Satan's lies than God's truth.

What Satan said to Eve was, "You will not surely die. For God knows that in the day you eat of it your eyes will be opened, and you will be like God, knowing good and evil" (Gen.3:4–5).

Eve's reaction—and Adam's also—was to believe that Satan was speaking the truth. They desired the results that Satan promised— that is, desiring to have the knowledge and wisdom promised, and not believing that the result would be death, Eve ate, and Adam ate also. In so doing, they showed by action what had already taken place in their minds. They were putting their trust in Satan's lie rather than God's truth. It was a step of faith all right, but faith in Lucifer's lie.

You may know this story as a myth, or as a musical production, or as a fantasy, or as a religious account that some peculiar group of people believe. Read it again as an account of how the history of the world changed to a history of an abnormal, devastated, vandalized creation after Satan, the saboteur, succeeded in tempting the beautiful first man and first woman to choose to act on his lie rather than continue to act on the basis of the truth they had been given by the trustworthy God of Creation.

Actions are made on the basis people accept in their minds as a valid base for choice. So wrong actions come from an erroneous understanding of what truth consists of by listening to the wrong source!

These two first people heard God walking in the cool of the day—a lovely picture of sunset light coming through leaves and making flowers look a bit brighter as the evening songs of birds filled the air. Adam and Eve hid themselves from the Lord in the trees. The

Lord's voice comes forth clearly, "Where are you?" And the answer is that they are hiding in fear because of being naked. "Who told you that you were naked? Have you eaten from the tree of which I commanded you that you should not eat?"

Then the man hedges and says the woman gave him the fruit to eat. "The woman whom You gave to be with me, she gave me of the tree, and I ate." And when God turns to the woman and asks what she has done, her reply is, "The serpent deceived me, and I ate"(Gen. 3:9,11–13).

The blame was clearly on having made a free choice—first within the mind, and then in outward action. In the light of what God had made known, the choice was for death, in place of life.

God puts a curse upon the serpent first. He goes on to say that there will be a future man, or "seed," born of a woman who will bruise Lucifer's head, and that person's heel will be bruised by Lucifer. This is the first promise of a coming Messiah who will do something. The book of Romans, much later in the Bible, says, "And the God of peace will crush Satan under your feet shortly" (Rom. 16:20).

As God outlined the results of the choice that had been made, He first gave hope by speaking of the *solution* to death and separation. He then gave the specific verdict of how all of life would be spoiled and nothing would be what it had been. The flow of history will be spoiled by what had happened. A curse was placed upon nature as well as upon human beings. Nothing will be as it was in the beginning.

People who would be born would be affected by their heritage. From that point on, although each human being will always bear the image of God, it will also be true that each human being will be a descendant of Adam and Eve. The "genes" come from two who chose to dishonor God by believing the slander and vilification which Satan spoke. The "line" of human beings now springs from two who have sinned. It is a heritage handed down from generation to generation. No one escapes being conceived and born in this line of sinners. Also each individual makes choices to do things that are completely against his or her own code of behavior, no matter how primitive that code is. Whether a person has a base for saying anything is right or wrong or not, every human being makes some sort of value judgment, and breaks his or her own ethic.

People are bothered by wanting to be better than they find they are being. They want to be like whatever their ideal person would be like—but they fail. Whether a person knows about or believes in the

Fall or not, there is a struggle within human beings that longs for resolution. Of course this differs according to the sensitivity of the person and the thoughtfulness and honesty of the search for solutions, but there is some recognition of being imperfect which bothers everyone to some degree.

The historic fall from an ideal and perfect situation brought immediate and far-reaching results in the spoiling of the artwork of God in His creation of all things. The evil that bothered Camus and Baudelaire and Salieri *has* a source. There *was* an interruption, a sharp line, an outstandingly different "before and after," that changed what God had made as good. God being a just God fulfilled His justice by bringing about exactly what He said would be the result of not believing His word, and turning away from doing what He had said was important for continued life. Death was *not* what God meant human beings to have. People were made for an uninterrupted length of time. Death came into history as a result of the Fall.

Adam and Eve did not immediately drop dead physically. The first death was the death of their perfect relationship with God. Then came the death of their perfect relationship with each other. "She gave me of the tree" was the first accusation made in anger and there has followed a history of human beings struggling to have relationships with other human beings. Relationships need working on. Relationships do not fall into place without blood, sweat, and tears.

The Fall also resulted in a psychological imbalance rather than perfection within each person. No one has ever been perfect since that time. Adam and Eve experienced separation from God, separation from each other, and separation from their own emotional and psychological balance at that historic moment. Physically their bodies began a disintegration which causes people to say, "The moment you are born, you begin to die." This was not the way God meant it to be. It is a result of the Fall and God's warning, "You shall surely die." Death comes by disease, accident, and murder. Anger results in strained relationships and war between two people in a family, in a neighborhood, in a city, between states, and between nations. Cruelty has resulted as human beings are cruel to other human beings—whether in torture, or in exploiting them with the pushing of drugs or the making of slaves in one way or another. History has been ugly, ugly, ugly because of the Fall.

The first thing to be said quickly is, there is a solution. If the beginning of all things consisted of impersonal particles, then there is no absolute by which to judge what is happening in and through human beings today. There is no solution for present problems nor any hope of a final solution in a chance universe without a Creator Who has a mind in which Creation existed first and then a power to create by choice. But, if God the Creator does exist, and if the Bible is His revelation of truth to us, then it is crystal clear that there *is* a solution that affects our present lives and a solution that will one day give a new beginning to life and that will make "forever" have a practical meaning. That solution was gradually unfolded throughout the Bible and is *not* just "pie in the sky." Rather it helps people both understand and live hour by hour in the light of what the truth consists of.

Francis Bacon, who lived from 1561 to 1626, was a lawyer, essayist, and Lord Chancellor of England. He could be called the major figure of the scientific revolution, and he took the Bible seriously, including the historic Fall and the revolt of woman and man in history in a geographic location. He said in *Novum Organum* (1620):

> For man, by the Fall, fell at once from his state of innocence and from his kingship over creation. Both of these misfortunes however, can, even in this life, be in some part repaired; the former by religion and faith, the latter by the arts and sciences.
>
> For the curse did not make creation entirely and forever rebellious; but in virtue of that edict, "In the sweat of thy brow shalt thou eat bread," it is now by various labors (assuredly not by disputations or idle magical ceremonies) at length in some measure, subdued into supplying bread for man: that is, to the uses of human life.
>
> Natural philosophy is given to religion as a most faithful handmaiden, the latter manifesting His will, the former His power.

I was sitting on the floor with my back against some cabinets in a science lab in St. John's College, Cambridge University, beside Linney Dey in 1976. It was at a coffee break and we had just served cups of coffee carried from The Copper Kettle, thirteen steaming blue cups on a tray carried through curious crowds of students flocking the sidewalks at this mid-morning hour. The film crew had been served, and Linney was poring over an old, faded, beige leather-covered volume of *Novum Organum* in Latin. She was translating the quote Dr. Schaeffer had asked for, in order to use it in his script in the documentary as he stood in front of a window, all the scientific apparatus on one side of him, and church spires outside. "What a quote to be giving in a science lab, with the film showing the juxtaposition of church spires and apparatus for experiments!" I said. Then I said, "Please let me copy your translation of that next bit too. I am so thrilled with what Francis Bacon thought in his mind, and expressed in his writing, more than 360 years ago now."

What an understanding, I thought, *of the abnormal world following the Fall which introduced death and destruction! Yet, what an understanding of "the leftover beauty" of God's creation.* When Francis Bacon said, "For the curse did not make creation entirely and forever rebellious," he referred to what I call "leftover beauty." Some day during eternity I want to talk to him about it!

"Leftover beauty?" you may ask. "What are you talking about?" This is what helps me to understand the questions Salieri raised about Mozart. It also helps me explain to my children and grandchildren why it is that so often superb creativity comes from people living twisted lives or with hidden evil in their lives. It helps me understand why many times mediocre work is done by people who are following the teaching of the one true God of the Bible. What sense does it make?

The Fall devastated and vandalized God's perfect Creation so that there is no possible way for any of us to know what perfection is like. However, just as no one died until Cain murdered Abel, so other parts of God's Creation were not entirely wiped out. Avalanches have not spoiled all the mountainsides, nor earthquakes changed all the portions of the earth. We have glimpses of breathtaking beauty as we watch the sunset coloring the frothy white waves into delicate apricots and pinks as they crash against rocky shores, or giving that wonderful "Alpine rouge," a flame pink, to the snow-covered tops of the Swiss or Italian, French or Austrian Alps. We look into a water lily or into the heart of the first violet; we watch insects with gauzy wings or snorkel around coral and watch the various schools of fish gliding together in and out of purple and yellow-green sea plants, and we know we are having glimpses of what seems almost like "perfection." We shell a pod of peas or husk an ear of corn and compare "perfect precision" of form and color with one spoiled by a bug. We hear what sounds like perfect sound in compositions that are being played by master artists and we sigh as we hear Handel's *Messiah* and wonder whether any music could be more "perfect."

Glimpses...glimpses...glimpses of such beauty give a hint of what God's perfect Creation was like. We enjoy deeply bits of "leftover beauty" in nature, in things we see and hear—touch and feel as our bodies glide through water of just the right temperature, feel a breeze of just the right delicacy as we walk through a cool forest on a hot day, delight in the warmth of sunshine after a cold winter, taste our favorite flavor under what seems like perfect circumstances, smell our favorite smell—lilacs in full bloom, or freshly cut hay, or a broiling piece of fish or meat over coals of burning wood or charcoal. We say over and over again, "MMmmmmm—this is perfect."

Human beings not only were not immediately wiped out, but there have been generation after generation of children, and children's children, born in the "line" of Adam. Later when God chose Abraham for his faithfulness in believing and following Him, there has continued to be generation after generation of people—some coming from Abraham and therefore in the special line of "God's people" and others of the line which turned to false philosophies and false gods. Do we then have a clearly defined picture of human beings through history? Is there a distinctly separate action from a "line" that could always be counted on and a contrasting line that could not be trusted?

Let's jump to the Olympics for a moment. Watch and bite your lower lip in amazement, catch your breath in unbelief of what you are seeing! How can human beings dive like that, swim like that, do gymnastics like that, run like that, skate like that, ski like that? I can't. What's the difference? Then look at people from another point of view—health, beauty of face or form, brilliance in mathematics or languages, in science or in agriculture or in architecture. Such wide contrasts exist.

Now think of creativity in the arts—writing, painting, sculpture, music, making of instruments, composing, performing, drama, voice, architecture, landscaping, or planning of a city like Paris or Washington. Think of the art of interior decorating, of cooking and serving, of designing fabrics or clothing, of cutting granite or diamonds, of a myriad of diverse and original creative ideas coming forth in the form that can be enriching to other people.

Then think of personality—of the seemingly natural talents that come so effortlessly from some people: of gentleness, sensitivity, kindness, compassion, communication, thoughtfulness, concern for others across the sea, love for children and patience with neighbors, a zest for life and for the lives of others who need protection. Can all the positive qualities or all the superior talents or all the good taste, or all the finest health and so forth down the list be attributed to people who are innocent of sin in any form? No! We are clearly told by

God that everyone has sinned, that everyone falls short of the glory of God. Not one person is perfect in thoughts or in words or in actions or deeds.

No matter how much "leftover beauty" a person has, he or she still falls short of what God expects. And there must be atonement for sin. Achievements, cleverness, beauty of face and form and physical condition, a sympathetic personality cannot pay or atone for sin.

The way to atone for sin is not by trying to balance sin with good deeds as if on a scale. The way to atone for sin was understood by Abraham when he carefully brought a lamb, looking forward to the coming Messiah who would *be* the solution. That vivid, moving happening on top of a hill "three days journey from Beersheba," when Abraham obeyed God and took his only son Isaac to sacrifice, was to be an unforgettable demonstration of what the coming Lamb would do. When God spoke directly to Abraham and pointed out a ram caught in the thicket which God said was to be substituted for Isaac, the whole idea of a substitutionary atonement was being made more emphatic and clear. The lamb had been understood to be a substitution from the time of Abel's lamb, but now it was more clear. Isaac was untied and taken from the rough stones and the ram took his place. When the first passover occurred at the time of Moses, the understanding was made tremendously specific.

The solution of atonement in the form of a substitute has been provided by God in His great love in a way that satisfies His perfect justice. Love and justice meet at a point in history and have an effect on each of our lives. We are presented with another choice and the door is open to us to experience perfection forever. "Whosoever will" may choose life...or death. But am I talking about "leftover beauty"? Yes, because I am agreeing with Francis Bacon that "the Curse did not make creation entirely and forever rebellious."

First of all, take the word *forever.* God did not lock human beings or nature into a forever-cursed situation. A solution was provided and a choice offered. Hope has been offered all through the ages and is still offered. That hope includes complete restoration of all creation. Nature and the vast reaches of the universe will be brought back to what perfection was at the beginning. A new creation is promised and we shall see and hear things too astoundingly beautiful even to imagine in our present amount of knowledge. We will have new bodies, which will never know pain or tears, death or destruction. All this is ahead and is available to anyone. God could not have been more fair. Creation will not be forever rebellious, it will be restored. The prophet Isaiah said, "Your dead shall live;/Together with my body they shall arise" (Isa. 26:19).

Second, the word *entirely* deals with the *now* of history or the continuing *now* from the Fall until the restoration. I feel certain that we have glimpses of "leftover beauty" of God's Creation so that we may know something of what it would have been and so that we can recognize in the Creation something of the greatness of the Creator! God's signature is *Creator,* and although that signature may be blurred by the vandal, still there is enough left over in the beauty of the creation to recognize something of *who* God is, of the wonder of His artwork, His ideas, His diversity, His power, His infinite ability, His love of beauty and attention to detail. Yes, there is enough left over to give some idea of God. And we are told in His Word that He meant this to be so.

We are not only told in the Psalms that "the heavens declare the glory of God," but in Isaiah we read:

> "To whom then will you liken Me,
> Or to whom shall I be equal?" says the Holy One.
> Lift up your eyes on high,
> And see who has created these things,
> Who brings out their host by number;
> He calls them all by name,
> By the greatness of His might
> And the strength of His power;
> Not one is missing. (Isa. 40:25)

> Thus says God the LORD,
> Who created the heavens and stretched them out,
> Who spread forth the earth and that which comes from it,
> Who gives breath to the people on it,
> And spirit to those who walk on it:
> "I, the LORD, have called You in righteousness,
> And will hold Your hand;
> I will keep You and give You as a covenant to the people,
> As a light to the Gentiles,
> To open blind eyes,
> To bring out prisoners from the prison,
> Those who sit in darkness from the prison house.
> I am the LORD, that is My name;
> And My glory I will not give to another,

Nor My praise to graven images.
Behold, the former things have come to pass,
And new things I declare;
Before they spring forth I tell you of them."
Sing to the LORD a new song,
And His praise from the ends of the earth. (Isa. 42:5-10)

Not only does God continually point to the fact that He is the Creator, but He points to the fact that you and I can "lift up our eyes" and look at the starry hosts as a part of His Creation *right now.* I believe there is enough of the "leftover beauty" of the original creation that we can see with our naked eyes, our microscopes, or our telescopes, that we are meant to have not only a reaction of awe and reverence but also a reaction of appreciation and wonder of the Creator. "Who is honoring the Creator with just honor?" People rightfully gave Amadeus honors, giving credit where credit was due (at least partially), but who is honoring the Creator now? Who is singing a new song? Who is singing His praises from the ends of the earth?

There is enough "leftover beauty" in creation to notice and to recognize what might have been and what is coming in the restoration, in spite of its all being spoiled by thorns, thirst, sickness, famine, earthquakes, tidal waves, avalanches, and hurricanes.

I also believe there is "leftover beauty" in human beings. It is true that no two human beings are alike. That is so observable as to be unnecessary to point out. The diversity, however, includes enormous differences intellectually, emotionally, physically, and as far as a flow of creativity goes. It is not just that Leonardo da Vinci differs from a child with no artistic or scientific interests or talent, but Mozart differs tremendously in his composing ability from Salieri.

"Unfair," cries Salieri. "I want that talent and I'll pay for it with my celibacy." His mistake is that one cannot bargain with God. God does not just pour out talents and troubles, athletic bodies and physically weak bodies in a random way. There is a continuity in history of cause and effect.

Consider that God created the first human beings perfect. They used their free choice to choose to rebel and make a statement about their believing Satan in preference to God. This not only constituted the Fall, but it meant that as children were born, and the earth became peopled, there was a diversity of "leftover beauty" in these human beings, giving glimpses of what possibilities were there in the first place. Also, there was a diversity of results because of the rebellion. For instance, although Abel tried to follow God's command (through his parents' explanation) to bring a lamb in sacrifice, Cain thrust his own works and ideas of worship into his sacrifice of fruit and vegetables... in utter rebellion. The attitude of Cain came out strongly and visibly in his murder of Abel. The first death was a murder! And the first murder was one committed in rebellion against God's word concerning the one way to come to Him. (It never differed. The lamb throughout the whole Old Testament pointed to the Lamb, the Messiah.)

But it was from Cain's line that we have the first mention of musical instruments. Creativity in a person as a result of being made in the image of the Creator does not depend upon that person's being full of love and trust for the Creator-God.

The infidel who has great musical talent is able to compose, or to make instruments, or to perform music because he or she is created in the image of the Creator of music whether he or she ever acknowledges it or not. The unbelieving person who has a beautiful garden and is a kind neighbor to your children when they knock a ball into his flower beds has good taste, works hard, is kindly toward children because he or she has been made in the image of God. These are some bits of leftover beauty showing what people were meant to be like in the first place. People—like sunsets and the moon on snow-covered trees; people—like fields of ripe wheat and Dutch tulip fields; people are evidences at times of the wonder of God's Creation. How amazing that He was able to make such complicated things as eyes, and hands, and minds! How marvelously spectacular that God was able to make finite beings who could think and act and feel and communicate and love, who could have ideas and make choices and decisions and create on a finite level.

One can look at the great artwork of an unbelieving person and worship the God who made people in His image to be able to create such magnificent works of art. One can look at an outstanding bridge being built and bow before the Creator God who made that engineer, even if the engineer himself knows nothing about God. One can listen to music with a satisfaction and a thrill, full of thanksgiving for it—being appreciative of the composer and at the same time whispering an acknowledgement to the fantastic God of Creation who created not only the universe, but beings with creative brains and abilities!

Yes, of course Bach wrote his music to the glory of God. Yes, of course there have been artists like Rembrandt who really believed. Yes, undoubtedly these have combined their genius with a love of God, an appreciation of His direct help, a prayer for His strength to be given in the midst of projects. Yes, of course God has promised His strength in our weakness and His hand holding ours in times of fear. Of course there is a difference when a person has genius *plus* talent, a will to work hard *and* a steady trust in the God of Creation to Whom he or she calls out and talks to. I am not even faintly hinting that it makes no difference what a creative person's base for life and art is. I am not saying at all that whatever one starts with in the way of natural talent or genius is not affected by his philosophy or world view. It does make a difference.

But, the fact remains that two things have been true since the Fall. First, human beings are horrible, capable of treating other human beings with cruelty. We do this not only to our enemies, but to family members, and even to our own children. The Bible speaks of the ways of peace not being known to those who have turned away from God and have exchanged the truth of God for a lie, and who are full of all kinds of immorality, deceit, self-seeking, and shedding of blood. We are distressed when we hear reports of increased crime, of new ways of self-destruction, and of the destruction of others with a stream of diverse ways of evil treatment of human beings. How long has it been since these people who do these things were in their mother's arms or being fed in a high chair? Where do such awful people come from in such a short space of time since birth? Where does the low view of life come from during so few years of living?

Second, human beings are wonderful in their acts of compassion for starving people half the world away, in their bravery that is so often amazing, in their creativity—composing and performing exquisite music, making diverse and beautiful instruments, designing space shuttles, making computers, building hospitals and an array of fascinating art objects and diverse things, in their study and practice of medicine and their work to save lives and give relief to suffering people. Human beings are really astonishing in what they can do spontaneously or learn to do in such short lifetimes, whether in exploring unknown parts of the world or in swinging by their teeth from a high circus rope! Human beings are astounding in that they require so few years from birth to being an astronaut, or from the high chair to conducting a great orchestra. How could Leonardo da

Vinci have had so many ideas in his one mind, and have produced so many paintings, drawings, and models of his many inventions all in his one lifetime? One person—one lifetime.

The reality behind the second fact is that human beings were made in the image of God and are finite and limited but are personalities with purpose and meaning in history and with capabilities to be unfolded. "Leftover beauty"—beauty and capabilities and potential that have not been wiped out—gives glimpses of some of the sheer wonder that has been lost.

The reality behind the first fact is the historic Fall. "Man fell from his first estate." (Sorry, folks, but Francis Bacon thought the word *man* referred to men and women and wasn't afraid of offending someone who didn't know that.) That Fall is what has brought about death in every sphere of life. The Fall stamped the image of Adam and Eve over the original image. But the original reality is still there, though spoiled.

Restoration and perfect solution are ahead.

Mozart, like other geniuses, had a drive to write the music he heard in his head. As his compositions came tumbling out of his brain, that which he heard with the ears of his mind could be played on the clavichord and reach the ears of others. The inconsistency of Mozart's life is similar to a young mathematician who as a child still prefers playing children's games to discussing his understanding of mathematics with reporters! The capabilities of human beings do not mean that each one has been "selected" to have something no one else has. There is cause and effect history. There is the blend of ancestors, there is the "leftover thread of beauty" in one area or another, handed down in some way. Perhaps Mozart could have discussed his own genius with a friend, as one talking about a "third person" as he examined the phenomenon and the marvel of his own genius. He certainly showed the Fall in various areas of his life, but at the same time he showed a generous portion of that "leftover beauty."

As for Salieri, his abilities were sufficient to display "leftover beauty" also. He had capabilities in composing and conducting and in leading the musical life of the court. However, his envy and covetousness, his hatred for Mozart, his deceitful schemes, his fury at God, his plot to steal the requiem, all blended together to show the titanic effects of the Fall in his life! Unhappily, "tears forever flowing" do not atone for sin. Atonement is provided by God for those who come to Him with all their hearts, seeking His way to Himself.

Amadeus and the "leftover beauty"? Yes, but Amadeus and the Fall. Salieri and the "leftover beauty"? Yes, but Salieri and the Fall.

Let's go back to Francis Bacon. "Man, by the Fall, fell at once from his state of innocence and from his kingship over creation. Both of these misfortunes however, can, even in this life, be in some part repaired; the former by religion and faith, the latter by the arts and sciences."

I wonder how different the lives of Mozart and Salieri—and of Baudelaire, and Camus, and Sartre, and many other people because of them—would have been if they had understood the effects of the Fall and the existence of "leftover beauty" in Creation.

People have a reason to treat other people differently if they understand that all human beings are made in the image of God and have different bits of "leftover beauty." People also have a possibility of understanding themselves better if they know about the Fall.

CHAPTER 7

Instruments

F irst of all music begins in the mind, where every other creative work begins. The human mind is incredibly versatile as it can taste, feel, touch, compose poetry and other communication, and hear a diversity of sound. We may want to ask Mozart what it was like to have music flowing in tremendous completeness through his brain, his mind, pressuring him to put it on paper, or to play it on the clavichord. But, you can ask the same question of someone living now, like Levine of the Met, or Daniel Barenboim. Perhaps *you* are a performer, a composer, an instrument maker, or just a lover of music and perhaps you know all about "listening" to music no one else can hear, because it is inside *your* brain.

The exciting thing about having a personal universe is that we can have a measure of understanding concerning the sequence of creativity. Ideas in the mind followed by a choice as to what to make or do, and then--presto—a work of art, music, chicken noodle soup, something other people can see, hear, or taste that was once hidden in our minds. We know all about that sort of thing because it is the order, the sequence, the manner in which our own creativity works. We ourselves plus our own creativity are test tubes. Therefore we respond with a true thrill to finding out that there is a Creator of the universe, who had in His mind all that He has made, including our own complicated bodies.

All this and music too in the mind of the Creator? He made human beings with minds to have an endless diversity of ideas and a whole section of these ideas has had to do with bringing forth music to change moments of life for every other person who hears that music in a drawing room, in a court, in a palace, in a park, in a concert hall, gliding in a boat, sitting on grass as music drifts out of a window. Music comes not by improbable accident, nor randomly, but from creative brains, through instruments and fingers, and into the ears and brains of an audience that understands, with varying amounts of understanding and varying degrees of response and appreciation. Music has an effect on listeners, whether they understand it or not, and is woven into history—past, present, and future!

If indeed there is a personal Creator, then He has created the ears we hear with. It is overwhelming to realize that if music were only heard inside one composer's head, it could never be heard or appreciated. If people had no taste buds, the myriad diversity of food flavors in the fruit and vegetables of the world would never be tasted. If no one had eyes to see colors, then all the trees and flowers, the starry skies and the white clouds would not be appreciated. The eyes, ears, nose, taste buds, sense of touch, and mind of understanding do *not* make the truth of what exists true. But when God tells us in Isaiah that He made the world to be inhabited, it is a way of letting us know that He did not make it to be empty of enjoyment!

We are told that God made all things "richly to enjoy." It was the deceiver causing the Fall who wanted to cut off the joy. Performers need an audience. Instrument makers need performers.

Musical instruments are mentioned very early in the Bible. In the fourth chapter of Genesis, the descendants of Cain are outlined. Jubal comes along in seven generations (if the generations are given without skipping, and that we cannot know) after Cain. Jubal is said to be the father of all who play the harp and the flute. Tubal-Cain, a half brother, is the one who forged tools of bronze and iron. The flute must have been made of wood, or gold, or silver. The harp would have been made from wood and tautly stretched strings. It is enthralling to me that both wind and stringed instruments are mentioned together this early in the history God has recorded for us.

Just as the first human beings were made by God and then they were spoiled, so we can think of skills and creativity being gradually lost, rather than beginning at a low point and going steadily up to a high point. Museums of ancient artifacts give glimpses of lost skills. We can't know how beautiful Jubal's flutes and harps were to look at, nor can we know the sweetness of their notes, nor the extent of their scales. One thing to remember, however, is that this is the line of Cain—the one who turned away from God's truth and from God's command as to how to approach Him with the sacrificial lamb. Yet creativity was not stamped out. It was important to mention musical instruments because they were made by creative people who were made to be creative...in the image of the Creator!

Perhaps you remember in Genesis 31 what Laban said to Jacob when he ran after him and caught up with him in the hill country of Gilead. "Why did you flee away secretly, and steal away from me, and not tell me; for I might have sent you away with joy and songs, with timbrel and harp?" (Gen. 31:27). A farewell party consisted of music, and here the line of Abraham was accustomed to a variety of instruments. Wood had been sought out, selected, seasoned, and skillfully carved. Satisfactory strings had been stretched so that the performer could pluck them with his fingers or with a "plectrum" made from a small stone, a piece of wood, or a carved bone. Maybe there were thinner strings to make the higher, lighter notes, and thicker strings to produce low notes. Concerts were a part of life.

After David had been anointed as the one to be the next king, while Saul was still king, in the book of 1 Samuel we find a story of a search for "a man who is a skillful player on the harp." The harp was taken for granted; that someone could play it as a master musician was also a reasonable expectation. What the Bible calls a "harp" was actually more like a lyre. David was found to be such a skillful player, and we find that his playing refreshed King Saul, as he played the harp with his hand. What a central place music had! There was an understanding and appreciation of the refreshing effect of music for relaxation and therapy!

David also played out on the hills as a shepherd with no audience but the sheep. Or was there? If the things not seen with the eyes include not only the "satellite galaxies that haunt the Milky Way," but also what people call "the supernatural world," who knows what audience the harpist, or flutist, or harpsichordist has when playing with a garden, the woods, or an Alpine field as the background! If God the Creator exists, He listens not only to prayer, but to music as a communication from the people He has made. Music *is* a communication. It can be played with a deep desire to say something that cannot be said in any other way. If you are a violinist, you may be able to say only with a violin how much you love and admire the person that means most to you. And your violin may be the best way you can present your awe and admiration of God to His ears.

The Psalms praise God with music. Music is a natural part of communication of human beings with human beings—and of human beings with God. That is a statement that has had meaning through centuries, has meaning now, and is a forever reality!

> It is good to give thanks to the LORD,
> And to sing praises to Your name, O Most High;
> To declare Your lovingkindness in the morning,
> And Your faithfulness every night,
> On an instrument of ten strings,
> On the lute,
> And on the harp,
> With harmonious sound.
> For You, LORD, have made me glad through Your work;
> I will triumph in the works of Your hands.
> O LORD, how great are Your works!
> Your thoughts are very deep. (Ps. 92:1–5)

> Praise God in His sanctuary;
> Praise Him in His mighty firmament!
> Praise Him for His mighty acts;
> Praise Him according to His excellent greatness!
> Praise Him with the sound of the trumpet;
> Praise Him with the lute and harp!
> Praise Him with timbrel and dance;
> Praise Him with stringed instruments and flutes!
> Praise Him with loud cymbals;
> Praise Him with high sounding cymbals!
> Let everything that has breath praise the LORD.
> Praise the LORD! (Ps. 150:1–6)

What a rich declaration Psalm 150 is of the centrality and importance of music in expressing joy and articulating thanksgiving! Dull dreary monotone is not called for in being "spiritual." The reality is that there is something to look forward to and recognize when God restores that which has been spoiled by the Fall. And we can be confident that He will restore it, for He is trustworthy.

> Let Israel rejoice in their Maker;
> Let the children of Zion be joyful in their King.
> Let them praise His name with the dance;
> Let them sing praises to Him with the timbrel and harp.
> For the LORD takes pleasure in His people;
> He will beautify the humble with salvation. (Ps. 149:2–4)

Can there be beauty from ashes? Is there salvation from the horrors of evil? Is the word *hope* just a cruel joke, or does it have a meaning that is gloriously real and obtainable? Can there really be "strength for today and bright hope for tomorrow"? Or is that just a romantic piece of poetry to be sung by trembling, frightened human beings? If death comes next, what is there to sing about?

The beauty of a sunset and then moonlight on Mediterranean waves as they send white spray high into the air at the foot of the lighthouse rocks on the end of the point at Porto Fino is a beauty that brings a depth of sadness almost unbearable after the death of the person with whom that beauty has always been shared. Beauty is not a help if there is *no* such thing as hope of an open door at the end of the tunnel. What a contrast the words *alone* and *together* are! *Oneness* cannot be had without at least two persons. One person totally alone spells "loneliness." *Oneness* is a word to be used about God because the unity of the three persons of the Godhead is real. *Oneness* is what human beings have been created to be capable of. A man and a woman are to become one physically, spiritually, and intellectually and the fruit of that oneness is the beginning of a family—a new generation, within a framework of oneness. There is a oneness in the family unit as well as in the larger family of four generations. And within what is meant by the term *Israel* or *the people of God* the oneness is supposed to be verbalized by the *word*, but also to *exist* without words! "And I will be their God, and they shall be My people" and "Do not fear, little flock" and "There will be one flock and one shepherd" are all tender words gathering believers into a oneness that does not depend on denominations made by arbitrary rulings of people. Oneness that is a reality fits into a framework that is true and lasting.

The simplest musical instrument has a framework to contain the necessary elements for bringing forth a continuity of music. True notes, clear notes, notes that can be regulated to be "in tune" come forth from an instrument that is sensitively and skillfully made of the proper materials by an artist who was born with a talent or a genius, a flair or an aptitude for learning from a master how to make that particular instrument—or the originality to invent something for the first time.

Not one of us can really imagine what the first instrument maker walked through, as he had in mind something he wanted to make and determined to cut a tree that he thought would have the right wood. When, in Genesis, Jubal is singled out as the originator, the father, of

harps and flutes, notice that his brother made tools. Jubal could se-
lect a tool of bronze or iron that would be strong enough to chip
away at the tree. Perhaps logs had been cut for building or for furniture making, and some seasoned pieces gave birth to the idea of the
first harp. But the first step was selecting the right wood. And the
second step was the seasoning of that wood. And the third step was
the shaping of that wood, and the stringing of taut strings to be
plucked. Trial and error? A copying of the sound of wind in the trees,
or of birds singing? A desire to sing a song of love or a lullaby for a
baby? Who knows what occurred as the sound of music followed the
ring of the ax against wood.

There are exotic and uncommon archaic instruments like the
psaltery, zither, and dulcimer, along with so many others, that help
us to see the diversity of ideas people had about bringing forth music
from vibrating strings. As you look up the history of the harp you
may come across this, in *The Oxford Companion to Music*. "The harp
is ancient and universal; there is record of it, in some form, in every
age of human history and in every place inhabited by men or spirits—except Hell."[1] This fits well with the description of the twenty-
four elders worshiping the Lamb in the future—each with a harp.
Also this fits well with the account in Genesis referring to the early
use of the harp and the flute with the musicians named in a matter-of-
fact way: as the children of Jubal.

Actually, the flute that Jubal's family played might have been the
end-blown recorder made of rosewood or some other lovely wood.
But we can't know whether the precise word *flute* meant a side-blown
instrument was being used or not. There are end-blown instruments
ranging from a tin-whistle through a horn made of a sheep's horn, to
the enormous alpenhorn that is longer than the person playing it and
made of amazingly durable and wonderful wood! It fascinates me
that the two types of instruments—stringed and wind—are basic in
the Torah.

In the beginning, God. In the beginning, creativity. In the beginning, music.

To attempt to skim through the history of musical instruments
would be a horror to purists who have spent years in careful research
of one family of instruments and even then feel they have not satis-
factorily finished their subject. This is a tiny sip to taste the ambrosia,

---

1. Percy A. Scholes, *The Oxford Companion to Music*, 10th ed. (New York: Oxford University Press, 1970), 454.

so to speak, of the beauty in the history of human beings who have had the genius and incentive to make instruments—and to make music.

"A way to make a living?" "Only a tossup between making instruments and some other job like making fishnets?" Yes, perhaps for some. But there is the reality of the genius of artists in various fields—and making instruments is one of them, even as sculpture is another, and painting another, and building beautiful boats is another!

How many, many instrument makers there have been through the centuries of history without any genetic planning—no "frozen sperm bank" to point to and no "superior race" designed by Plato-like plans or dictator's schemes.

Think for a moment of the town of Cremona in northern Italy. Why should that little town, which had a thousand people at one time, reduced to less than five hundred at another because of famine and war and the plague, be the place of such tremendous inspiration for string music? Vineyards and a church tower, children playing on clean stone streets, women washing their clothes at village fountains, and the smell of pasta cooking with a spicy sauce being prepared in another pot. Rural, small town Italy . . . the birthplace of so much creativity. Listen to this quote from Scholes:

> In string music, Italy was inspired by the wonderful productions of the Cremona violin makers (especially the Amati family in the sixteenth and seventeenth centuries, and the Guarneri and Stradivari families in the seventeenth and eighteenth).[2]

There is no record of the birth of Antonio Stradivari because his father, Alessandro Stradivari, was probably among those who fled from the city with his family when the scourge of a plague raged all over Lombardy. Little is known of the early career of Antonio and no record of when he began to make violins under the master Amati has been found, although some Amati violins have a label indicating Stradivari as the obvious maker.

Antonio married Francesca Mazzini on July 4, 1667, and they lived in a small house until 1680 when, with five in the family (one small son had died), they were able to buy a house at No. 1 Piazza Roma for 7000 imperial lira, 2000 lira down and 4990 within four

2. Ibid.

years! The other ten lira were subtracted because Stradivari paid his yearly tithe to the canons of the Cathedral. What a simple few lines! Factual, dry words? No, see the faithful day-in-day-out work of a genius with a pair of hands that were his own hands, knowing how to hold his tools and work with them, as a skillful surgeon knows how to use his surgical knives.

What is the difference between good, mediocre, and great? The beauty of work well done, the attention to detail and meticulously careful workmanship, combined with a flair and taste that affects all the small choices—plus something that can't be taken apart and described or analyzed and copied—are what goes into making a work great or an artist outstanding throughout history. Greatness is the "leftover beauty" of what human beings were meant to be in the first place. I'm sure that as with the diversity of snowflakes, there would have been (without the Fall) diversity in talents but not the great differences and the abnormality which result from the Fall.

Whether we look at some aspect of modern genetic engineering or some other scheme to eliminate human beings by gas chambers or abortion—to try to keep only the "best specimens"—a study of the history of artists will show that it is impossible to design a human being. The "great" have cropped up from amazingly unlikely backgrounds and widely differing family lines.

If you are interested in studying the individual violins of Stradivari, their proportions, their wood, and their measurements (not all the same by any means), then read *Antonio Stradivari: His Life and Work (1644-1737)* by Henry Hill, Arthur Hill, and Alfred Hill. They tell of the differences between one or another model as Stradivari tried slight changes. Let me quote a bit to give an idea of the detailed differences. Please note especially that these violins are *not* mechanical, assembly line works with each piece being a carbon copy of the one before!

Also please remember that Stradivari was probably apprenticed to Amati when he was about fourteen, and he probably stayed in that relationship until he was about forty. This bit I'm quoting concerns his work in the early 1690s when he was about fifty years old.

> The varnish used by Stradivari after 1690 is with a notably few exceptions of a deeper and richer color than that of the previous years. We have hitherto been accustomed to see the traditional Amati yellow and its kindred tints....Now, the outline dimensions and general construction of the long pattern violin ad-

mirably demonstrate Stradivari's powers of originality; and that he should have been successful in adding 3/16ths of an inch to the total length, while retaining the relative harmony of top, bottom, and middle curves, is an additional proof of his keen sense of symmetry; and this is rendered the more noticeable when compared with the works of many of the other Italian makers, few of whom were wanting in originality, though some showed lack of symmetry in their designs.

The account continues with a description of the "*f*" holes and their length, and then it points out:

> Stradivari more frequently used backs in one piece for these violins, and we have seen several specimens of wood cut from the same tree—maple of native growth—marked with a small strong curl running nearly straight across. We now rarely meet with backs cut the slab way of the grain, though here and there he occasionally used one. His pine still continues, with but rare exceptions of fine grain....
>
> We wish to point out that the dawn of the century (now 1700) does not herald any eventful and brilliant transition or any sudden quickening in Stradivari's progress, but rather shows him silently plodding on with unflagging energy, producing yearly, nay monthly, fresh modifications in his works, which, though not always successful, attest on the whole the natural and fairly consistent development of the forms and models of the past years.[3]

"Plodding"..."unflagging"—what a picture these words conjure up of faithful work. He lived and worked in that house at 1 Piazza Roma for fifty years—daily making his violins.

His first wife died in 1698, and the next year he married again. With six children from his first marriage and five from his second, there were eleven children to laugh, cry, be told "basta" and not to touch the tools or pieces of violins, to run in and out of the house shouting and playing with the other "bambinos" and "bambinas" along the street. Italians love children and there is a sense of family togetherness in work as well as play. However, there must have been illness, crying, and death as not all of the children lived to grow up. There were dismal, depressing times as well as moments of excite-

3. Henry W. Hill, Arthur F. Hill and Alfred E. Hill, *Antonio Stradivari: His Life and Work (1644–1737)* (New York: Dover Publications, 1963), 47, 49.

ment when some royal family member of Spain or another country ordered a set of violins, violas, and cellos. There would be many "ooos" and "aahhs" when Stradivari made the rare and beautiful inlaid violins with flowers and other figures of inlay exquisitely done.

The house was three stories high, with one room on the ground floor as the shop. It was small—right on the street. Imagine clothing hanging out the windows or over the tiny balcony, and the attic and loft sticking up at the top like cupolas. Up there where the air could come through, Stradivari dried his priceless musical instruments. As he toiled up the stairs and fixed a varnished violin or cello in place, wouldn't he have been astounded to hear great performers playing his instruments in wonderful concert halls and palaces through the years to come? How he would have thrilled with satisfaction if a curtain could have been drawn back for him to hear the compositions inspired perhaps by the tone of one of his instruments, played with loving hands by an Isaac Stern, or an Itzhak Perlman, or Jaqueline du Pres. And if he could have heard someone making a "deal" to pay more for one instrument than he ever saw in a lifetime, I'm sure his mouth would have dropped open in disbelief.

Two of his sons became violinmakers, and one imagines them helping their father as he grew older. There is strong evidence that Stradivari went on constructing instruments until the last year of his life...with his own hands, hands then in their nineties! Those hands are remarkable to contemplate! Which hands are the more remarkable—the ones that made the instruments, or the hands that play these same instruments today? Watch Lynn Harrell as he plays the Stradivarius cello which he bought from Jaqueline du Pres who so marvelously played it until her terrible affliction (MS) changed the possibility of her hands using the skill that is still there, but silenced, locked inside her mind, for the time being. Look at that cello or listen to it on a record and imagine it drying up there, with a breeze blowing through the openings of the loft in Cremona, back about 250 years ago! What you are hearing comes from the minds—and then the hands—of human beings created in the image of the Creator to be creative!

Do you grow to worship music? Oh no, we should worship the Creator who created minds and hands and ears and eyes—and forests full of trees—that music might be a part of the continuity of human life, communicating from generation to generation.

Does such exquisite creativity have to be all in one time of history? Does it have to take place all in one part of the earth's

Guarneri String Quartet, "World's Master of Chamber Music." Arnold Steinhardt, violin; John Dalley, violin; David Soyer, cello; Michael Tree, viola.

geography? Does anyone make violins by hand today? Yes, there are many violinmakers today. As far as we know, no one has uncovered the secret of Stradivari or of the other old makers, but there are makers of good violins. You may have seen a production showing Wiebe making his violins, violas, and cellos in a beautiful wooded area of the western United States. He has come as close as anyone to duplicating the sound of a Stradivarius.

The young Englishman who gave me the book on Stradivari is a sensitive violinmaker, living frugally with his young wife in Hampshire, carefully working with integrity and attention to detail, along with a love for both the wood and the instruments. Will someone be playing his violins 250 years from now? Perhaps indeed.

Come with me to Minneapolis. I have been met at the airport by Anne Brown and Suzie Barber. Suzie is a cellist who played in the Caracas Symphony Orchestra for five years. Her cello had been injured on an airplane (in spite of her "indestructible case") and so we are taking it to a Minneapolis violin, viola, and cello maker who also repairs instruments—a kind of a hospital for stringed instruments!

Impressions? The smell of lovely wood—sanding sends that aroma into the air—and of a proper glue. An upward look takes in hanging violins, forms, and cello molds holding the shell of a precious old instrument. There are bridges and necks and other very important pieces of wood. I ask a few questions and make some discoveries. Sources of wood are the most difficult to keep finding. "We're lucky," says one of the two young men. "We bought a lot of wood from the supply of a violinmaker who died. He had a great supply of gorgeous wood he had collected through the years, and it was auctioned off."

"We use Englewood spruce for the fronts—and maple." "That's a 200-year-old bass viol we are repairing." "The worst trouble we run into is if the wrong glue has been used. If glue is stronger than the wood, you can't get the top off to repair it." They both shook their heads ruefully at that, thinking of the hours and hours of patient and painstaking work to get the top off without injuring the wood.

I listen as Suzie talks about her cello and tries it out after the repair. She sits and adjusts herself in the middle of the workshop—as if on a concert stage. The five-foot-seven-inch slim young man with his curly brown hair and mustache stands waiting a bit tensely as Suzie tries her cello. She shivers a bit, remarking, "I'm sister to any strings, as cold affects me as it does them!" She asks for the C string to be "darker," and so he moves the sound post just inside under the bridge.

"In a little further please," she says. He replies, "You realize this will dim the brightness of the A a bit too?"

Musicians, instrument makers, and composers have their own shop talk just as surgeons, doctors, engineers, and farmers do. In our finiteness, we as human beings cannot be involved in everything, but we need each other, and are made richer by each other's talents. What good would it have done to you or me to have Mozart write as he did—or Chopin or Beethoven compose what they did—if there were no instrument makers and no performers who were willing to take long hours to prepare, and to use their hands? Each one had his or her part in producing that which resounds through us as we hear it. The reality of a composer's work lasting through generations depends on other people making instruments, performing music, and mending cracks in instruments. Cracks in the framework of relationships need mending too, for people are too precious to throw away! There is supposed to be a continuity, and at times the cracks can be ruefully looked at, yet recognized as something important to cope with or mend.

There are also amateur instrument makers who carefully make instruments for their own joy in creativity and as a change from whatever their work is to the relaxation of working with wood and strings and metal and knives.

I was reading a book on the pianoforte on an airplane going from Minneapolis to Washington, D.C., when the man next to me asked if I were a musician. I said, "No, I'm the audience for musicians." He went on to ask various questions and ended up realizing that he had read my husband's books and also mine! Quite an amazing introduction. My questions as to *his* interest in music led this electronic engineer to tell of his making a simple violin and viola—"Felix Savart's trapezoid violin." (Later he sent me a book which enables craftsmen to follow the details that Felix Savart [1781-1841] had set forth on how to make "un violon trapezoidal.")

Mr. Charles Bush then went on to tell of his rebuilding the organ in his church, and also to describe the Sitka spruce forests in his area of the country, Washington state. So my flight turned out to be a really timely lecture which fit into my research perfectly. Education does not all come wrapped up in classroom walls, nor with a certificate at the end of a few weeks! Education sometimes comes in reading articles and books and letters and sometimes in listening to public lectures. But sometimes the most valuable lectures we can hear come from not wasting our time by talking about trivialities with people who have knowledge we need to have. So much time is wasted in small talk at dinners, receptions, parties. There is a lack of communication during moments that won't come again. Education comes in diverse wrappings, even a 747 at times!

If you go to one of the old instrument portions of the various museums, such as the Metropolitan Museum of Art in New York, or the Smithsonian in Washington, D.C., or one of the museums in Geneva, or London, or whatever area of the world you are in, you can have an impression of old instruments collected in that place. Fleeting impressions and the reading of captions do not give you the education of a thorough music history course, but the impression that will be left in your memory will be one of painstaking work done by the hands of people who loved and hated, made mistakes and cried, laughed and were stern, people who worked in the privacy of their little niche in cold and heat with springtime drawing them to walk at sunset or dawn. These people had no idea that their work would be gazed at by people walking on the other side of a rope in the museums of the world!

In the Metropolitan Museum of Art's music section, my friend Avis and I stopped to look at a harpsichord: "Zenti Rome— 1666— Italian thin cypress—separate case." The next one was also seventeenth century Italian and very ornate with carvings of a statue and three sets of strings to give a brighter tone. There was a painting inside the lid titled "The Duck Hunter." There were rich tones of brown: red brown, beige browns, warm woods. We stopped to look in the glass cases holding a 1694 and a 1727 Stradivarius, as well as an Amati violin marked 1693 that was thinner and longer. Silent instruments all of them! Instruments in a museum can only be seen, not heard. Their voices are locked up inside. It's a bit sad when you think of the abundant life that vibrated through these same instruments in the hands of performers.[4]

We need to turn to books to discover something of the background of the modern piano.

Many old manuscripts contain drawings of monochords on which the pitch letters of the Guidonian scale (Guido d'Arezzo introduced a group of six consecutive notes, regarded as a unit for purposes of singing at sight, in the eleventh century—c.990–

4. In the Metropolitan Museum one can rent a tape recorder with earphones and listen to the old harpsichords and pianos as played by John Van Buskirk.

c.1050) are shown on the side of the monochord. The string could be stopped, to give the notes of a scale, by the fingers or by a thin piece of wood or metal held in the fingers. From this it was an easy step to stop the strings by means of projection at the end of a pivoted piece of wood or a key on a keyboard and so make a clavi-chord (key chord)...

By the year 1400 the monochord had developed into a clavichord which had a chromatic scale and up to ten strings. It is said that the instrument was popular until the year 1800. The clavichord was remarkably complete with a small but sweet and satisfying tone...cheap to construct and portable. In order to produce fullness of tone, each note was sometimes strung with pairs of strings, and the bass was strengthened by combining each string with one which sounded an octave higher....The clavichord was a favorite instrument of most of the great composers from 1400 to 1800, including J. S. Bach. It was useful for teaching, and for accompanying the voice as well as for solo playing.[5]

The harpsichord flourished between 1500 and 1800. Now there is a great resurgence of interest. In Chateau d'Oex, a lovely small town in the Swiss Alps, an American harpsichord builder, Bruce Kennedy, lives with his wife and children. He has settled there to make wonderful instruments and employs thirteen Swiss people. Like most instrument makers, he can also play the instrument and give interesting lectures about the history.

As I quote from *The Oxford Companion to Music*, perhaps you will be inspired to search for more information about the harpsichord.

In its three forms of virginals, spinet, and harpsichord proper, the harpsichord was the favorite domestic keyboard instrument from the beginning of the sixteenth century to the end of the eighteenth. In its most developed form, that of the harpsichord proper, it also served as the supporting basis of almost every instrumental combination during the period of the development of chamber music and the orchestra...roughly 1600 to 1800. An understanding of its history and nature is therefore of the highest importance in the understanding of the history of music.[6]

5. William Leslie Sumner, *The Pianoforte*, 4th ed. (London: Macdonald and James, 1978), 21, 23.
6. Scholes, *The Oxford Companion to Music*, 457.

Very frequent tuning was necessary for the harpsichord—at least once a week—and each intelligent owner of an instrument is said to have tuned his or her own. Bach is reputed to have been able to tune his in a quarter of an hour! This frequent tuning is due, among other reasons, to the thinness of the strings and their comparatively long length.

I wonder what Florence was really like in 1700. The beauty of the buildings and the gates and outdoor steps and courtyards have made Florence an outdoor museum for so very long! The city itself is a museum. Michelangelo's David had been made two hundred years before, and at that same time (1501) Ottaviano Petrucci was working in nearby Venice printing music with movable type. The popular interest in music soon led to the popularity of opera in Florence. Art and music flourished.

Let's look at the unspoiled beauty of the buildings with their variegated marbles, the statues of breathtaking proportions, the *della Robbia* choir lofts carved with gorgeous singing children, the marvelous sculptured forms and faces in the gates of hell, the paintings, and Michelangelo's stairway which is like a song! Was cappucino and espresso sipped between workmen's concentration or only wine? Were children sent with a loaf of long Italian bread, hot and fresh from the oven, for papa along with some cheese and salami? Did they play "kick the can" with a stone or what was the game? Whatever, life was being lived, and ideas that were in people's minds were, through hard work, coming to be a part of history that would affect us.

If you have been in Florence in midsummer in recent years, the vandalism of twentieth-century graffiti on buildings and steps that are works of art is painful to look at. Bodies of destructive human beings, draped in such ugly profusion over the "outdoor museum" that is Florence, become living graffiti and obliterate the painstaking and genius-inspired artwork of the human beings who produced Florence in their time! War and destruction, a constant result of the Fall, consist of war and destruction against artworks and beauty, as well as *other* forms of war!

What about the continuity of creativity and life in the midst of the effects of evil and death? Can you imagine Amati, Guarneri, and Stradivari being born because of cleverly chosen frozen sperm? Genius has arisen from surprising places and sometimes it doesn't occur where we might expect it. Notice that the sons of Stradivari were not outstanding in their violin making. Would a bank of frozen "genius" sperm injected into women judged to be high in intelligence ever produce both genius and automatic moral behavior, sensitivity, and compassion? The restoration of the spoiled creation, the restoration of destroyed human beings, needs a solution beyond genetic engineering. And the explanation of why beauty so often pours forth in unexpected places and moments needs more than chance and a shrug!

Bartolomeo Cristofori, a harpsichord maker and then Keeper of the Musical Instruments for Prince Ferdinand de Medici, took a step forward that affects all the music you and I hear today! In the midst of all that was going on in the city of Florence in 1709, he put hammers in the place of harpsichord jacks (or quills) and made the *first* pianoforte which he called, *gravicembalo col piano e forte*. Quietly in his workshop, a new step in music took place.

> Cristofori's mechanism was ingenious. There was an escapement by which immediately any hammer struck a string it returned, so leaving the string free to vibrate; and there were dampers which, on finger keys being released, fell at once upon the string and suppressed its vibration, bringing the sound to an immediate end.[7]

Only two of Cristofori's instruments still remain. One dated 1720 is in Leipzig. The other is in New York in the Metropolitan Museum of Art. As Avis and I stood on the other side of the rope amid the silent whispers of tourists who were looking with awe at this plain black case with its simple beige colored keys (some skipping it altogether to go to the very ornate cases of an Erard piano inlaid with mother of pearl and metal from Liszt's era), I thought how terribly emphasized the silence was in that place of "music of the past." It was almost like being in a memorial cemetery and being reminded of the lives of the people who aren't really there at all.

Instruments, I thought, *like those of Stradivari give music for generations of performers. The work of the hands of the human being who makes the instruments lasts so much longer than the maker as well as so much longer than the performers.*

I stood there looking at first one, then another, instrument and then thought again of the title *Forever Music*—a meaningless phrase if instruments last so much longer than performers. The Creator of the universe created people, human beings, in His image. But since the

7. Ibid., 789.

Fall, they have died one by one, year after year. The work of God's hands in Creation lasts a shorter time than the work of the finite creators' hands; their art, statues, buildings, as well as musical instruments outlast them.

No wonder God speaks to us in the Bible of death as "the last enemy that will be destroyed" (1 Cor. 15:26). What an enemy of such a perfectly amazing Creation as a human being with his or her brain—and all the complicated possibilities of that mind and a pair of hands!

Forever Music speaks of the existence of "forever people." It speaks of a restoration of what has been vandalized of God's artwork. It speaks of a solution to "forever silence."

This book wouldn't have been written if there hadn't been a death—the death of my husband. It wouldn't have been written if it hadn't been for the gift of Steinway 281261 and the following of its story. But it is imperative to know what is in the following chapters if there is to be any solution verbalized to the contrast between "forever music" and "forever silence."

CHAPTER *8*

Steinway

I t was the day of the marathon race in New York, October 28, and as Don and Barbara Dey met Avis Dieseth and me, they looked a little anxiously at their watches. "We have the route all carefully mapped out to avoid traffic jams, but we'll have to get right along if you're going to be in time for the concert." Finding the way was of central importance since a wrong turn would be more complicated than on a normal day. The blocked-off streets changed the shape of the city, so to speak. Funny about freedoms in life, isn't it? Freedom to run through the streets of New York suddenly gives another large section of people new fences within which to move. Freedom always has two sides to it, and it needs a proper base, or framework, so that it doesn't become a prison to someone else. Mind you, I'm not objecting to marathon races or bicycle races either. I'm simply musing!

"We'll be on time," we said a bit breathlessly to each other as we hurried along 57th Street toward Carnegie Hall. "There's Steinway's where we'll be going tomorrow. Now, let's cross the street right here...oops." Trucks, cars, people were all hurrying to be somewhere else—certainly not wanting to remain where they were at the moment.

Avis, from Fergus Falls, Minnesota, and I had been invited by my New York friend Terry Feldman to attend the concert she had put together to help "bring back Mrs. H.H.A. Beach and her music to the attention of music lovers." Terry had worked for weeks to make the complicated arrangements, as well as to practice her own portion of the singing for the Masterwork Music and Art Foundation to present *Grand Mass in E flat* at Carnegie Hall. The event was taking place a day before my appointment at Steinway and so our coming from Minnesota fit in. How many central events of the day are there over-lapping in one city? There were marathon runners triumphantly fin-ishing off months of training, puffing in happily to the cheers of friends. There were singers and musicians hurrying to get into their proper clothing and their places on the stage. There was the audi-ence, each person the central point in some whirl of life...and thou-sands upon other thousands of New Yorkers were in the midst of trivial or tragic, beautiful or ugly, centrally important times. Impor-tant to whom?

"Who is Mrs. H.H.A. Beach?" you may ask. Has she any impor-tance at all?

> BEACH, AMY MARCY. Born in New Hampshire in 1867 and died in New York in 1944. Phenomenally gifted as a child, she soon acquired a reputation as a piano virtuoso, but this was later superseded by a recognition of her accomplishments as a com-poser. She was the first composer in America to write a symphony of importance ("Gaelic" Symphony—Boston Symphony Orches-tra, 1896).[1]

A tiny paragraph covers seventy-seven years of life! What speaks with greater clarity about what she had in her mind and "heard" inside her head is her music. We sat in the balcony, filling our eyes with the satisfying beauty of Carnegie Hall: its beautiful propor-tions, the colors of the red plush seats, the cream and gold walls, and the crystal chandeliers—background for such a performance. The or-chestra and singers in their black and white clothing with the touches of red...the gleaming brass, gold and silver of the horns, the bas-soons, the flutes...the varnished wood of the string instruments catching the lights and shining...the beige of the bows, and the drumsticks, and the hands of the conductor and the pianist.

There was a constant flow of motion as arms of players moved in response to the hands of the conductor. One felt caught up in that flow of movement which was as alive as a ballet. The music poured forth as a movement of sound, in and out of ears, vibrating one's bones, immersing one. Human throats, lips, tongues, breathing—the human instrument—brought out not only music, but words, verba-lizing in a way that other instruments cannot do, "gloria in excelsis"

---

1. Scholes, *The Oxford Companion to Music*, 91.

with a depth and passion and crescendo. "Gloria." "Gloria." But to whom? Is there an unfulfilled need for glorifying someone who is worthy of all glory? That need is unfulfilled for those who live in an empty universe.

In Kauai, Hawaii, there is a helicopter ride that takes you in and out of the mountains, close to waterfalls. A feeling of being immersed in the beauty of waterfalls and pools too wonderful to describe is the same feeling that comes when there is music full of glory that needs to have a person to glorify, or to say "Thank you" for and to. "Glory to the Highest!" "The Highest" indicates the one true God, the only Creator. But we were not in the exhilaration of a helicopter. The sweeping motion and beauty for ears as well as eyes was coming from the mind of a woman who was not there to see or hear it. We were caught up in the creativity of Amy Beach who died a mere forty years before, but whose music had been woven into the fabric of our experience that night.

It had been just about four months since Steinway 281261 had been carried into my living room in Minnesota. I had been in England and Switzerland and had been studying books in researching this book. But now I was again getting my exercise walking along 57th Street hurrying toward the Steinway Hall for my appointment with John Steinway. Avis and I remarked on how close this was to Carnegie Hall and talked about the *old* Steinway Hall which had been in this area and had been the center for artistic and cultural events since 1866. It was about 1890 when Carnegie took over. Closing, or squinting, one's eyes and imagining gas-lamp-lighted streets with horses and buggies trying to find parking as ladies in taffeta and velvet pulled up their skirts a bit as they stepped out of buggies and imagining top-hatted gentlemen who gave them their hands or arms to steady them was enjoyable, but didn't shut out modern traffic noises very successfully!

Looking up at the modern New York skyscrapers, the Steinway building sits among them in proud disregard of playing copycat. The flavor of history which European cities have is so often bulldozed in America, even though America's buildings are not really very ancient. It is a pleasure to look at the outside or to enter a building with some historic background. To enter an old building whose walls have seen more history than one could write about is like entering a forest with trees that have taken hundreds of years to grow into what they now are.

So often rootless people walk around in rootless areas of the earth, with torn-up history all around them (new buildings, new parking lots, small new plantings, and torn-up families). We feel deeply sad about all the refugees of the world, but so many other people are busy turning their own lives into the refugee pattern of torn-up roots, and then they wonder why they need psychiatrists to try to find some avenue to stability. Roots are meant to give a stability so that the "props" are not needed for the growing tree. The roots help what is above ground to resist the winds of life. In the Scriptures there is a reference to the possibility of being "rooted and built up in [the Lord] and established in the faith."

We were warmly greeted by the receptionist who had record of the appointment, and, calling to check the time, asked us to wait a few minutes. We looked around the museum-like, round room with its vaulted dome ceiling, and the feeling of elegance of another era caused a respect for the pianos displayed there. Oil paintings and tapestries were on the walls and mosaics were on the ceiling. Marble columns went straight up to the high ceiling while a crystal chandelier hung down, brightening the day whether it is rainy and grey or the sun is being shut out by the surrounding skyscrapers. Four of the five grand pianos were gleaming mahogany or walnut, and one was white. There were also a small spinet and a baby grand. All of them looked so elegant standing on a Persian rug that it seemed correct to whisper!

On the elevators we had barely enough time to enjoy the wonderful wood paneling and inlay pattern of wood with the Steinway insignia of gold on one panel. On the second floor, we walked past rooms with pianos and portraits in them, coming to an office at the end of the hall. As we entered the door the surrounding of history became a delight as old etchings of every stage of Steinway's past covered the walls. A thick workbench with its evidence of much creative work in the deep gashes and marks almost spoke aloud with the story of all it had seen while pianos were being made through many years! A deep, dark green, leather couch, well worn and exuding welcome and an invitation to sink down comfortably (rather than gingerly on the edge of a chair!) added its unspoken reception to John Steinway's verbalized, "Do come in. We've just come back from Germany. Excuse the disorder." The "disorder" consisted of stacks of unopened mail on both his big desk and an equally big, old desk of his brother Henry. It was, in fact, orderly chaos and a familiar sight to anyone who comes back from a trip when mail comes in to lie unopened day by day!

Avis and I sat on the inviting couch and John Steinway sat in his swivel chair and swiveled in our direction. We looked at the fireplace and the big coffee table in front of us, and then I replied to his, "Now, what would you like?"

What would I like?

I had already read a short history of Steinway and Sons. I had already been captivated by the traditional story that in 1797 in the Harz Mountains of Germany, Heinrich Steinweg was born to a modest forester as his sixteenth child. I had already felt overwhelmed at the survival story of Heinrich. His father and older brothers had gone off to fight in the Napoleonic Wars, so it is said, and his mother tried to supply food and care for the rest of the family in the mountains. When the father came back, only Heinrich and two other children were there to welcome him. The rest had died from hunger and cold. Not long after this, all the family that were left, except Heinrich, were killed by lightning while working at the roadside. How can you explain survival? This "thread" in history, Heinrich, the sixteenth child (not aborted!) and the only survivor of eighteen people (counting his mother and father), once more survived the Battle of Waterloo, with hundreds dying all around him. He won a medal for bugling in the presence of the enemy. Heinrich Steinweg had an inborn or natural dexterity for working with wood. This kind of skill, it seems to me, is a combination of a love for wood and a recognition of the right wood while making a choice of what to use for making something. After the war, in the garrison he made a mandolin, a dulcimer, and a zither, and then became a cabinetmaker in an organ factory. A diversity of creative works is produced in the lifetime of anyone who is an artist with wood and who has a natural sensitivity in making choices in using wood, even as Michelangelo knew how to choose marble for his works of art.

Heinrich Steinweg presented his bride, Juliane Theimer, with a piano he had made himself with two strings for every note. This was his wedding gift! Another piano he made took him thirteen years of long evenings to make—careful, methodical, faithful work. Anything that gets done takes hours of just plain work—work with no measure of the monetary value of each hour! Whether it is a cabinetmaker working to inlay wood or to make a leg for a piano, or an artist carving the entrance to heaven on enormous wooden doors (as in Florence), there is a portion of time that goes on and on in the same slogging that takes place in the life of an early settler clearing forests and planting fields in any part of history or geography. Where you find things happening, you find *someone* working hard—past the required hours. Talent, or even genius, has to be accompanied with work or it remains dormant. When Heinrich won a prize at the state fair, he decided to make his life work that of piano making.

It didn't take long for those paragraphs to run through my mind—faster than reading! I looked around that office and saw not only pictures, but the workbench as I considered my real reason for coming.

"What would I like? I'd like some first-hand flavor to the story of Steinway and Sons. Of course, it can be read in books, but..."

As John Steinway talked, it was satisfying to know that the continuity of that family had continued by being involved with producing beauty of sight and sound in a piano whose name is synonymous with "tops"—right on to the fourth and fifth generations. I know there are writers who like to debunk various parts of history as a career or a pastime. Although I know that there are no perfect people and no perfect situations, I would say that the more I observed and listened, the more interested I became to discover added facts and to have an increased understanding of the mystique of the Steinway name and piano itself.

John settled comfortably into his chair and spoke as informally as if we had come in as next door neighbors: "Henry Engelhard Steinway came to New York, landing on June 9, 1850, with his wife and seven children. He was at the time fifty-three years old. His son Charles had come to America in 1849 and insisted that the rest of the family follow. Charles had taken a job as a cabinetmaker. One son, C.F. Theodore Steinway, the eldest son, stayed behind in Germany to run his own piano factory. The others soon found jobs in piano building in America. It was 1853 when they started Steinway and Sons in New York City. Operations were begun in a rented loft at 85 Varick Street, not far from the present entrance to the Holland Tunnel. Doretta, the eldest daughter, was the star salesman and sometimes offered to give free piano lessons to the prospective buyers to close the sale!"

Within a year their rented loft space was not enough, and a move took them to more adequate space at 82–88 Walker Street. A photograph of this factory shows a building along the street with steps coming down to the sidewalk and with railings similar to so many of the old London streets. Horsedrawn buggies are in the foreground. The people standing in front with their rather stiff poses, dressed up in coats, scarves, and tophats, are the Steinways and the staff of that time.

America was an amazing land of free enterprise and opportunity for anyone willing to work hard and produce well-made, fine products. However, as in any period of history, the demand for a product influences the growth of the company. And the demand has at times been affected by a wide range of events, and by other people's lives and talents. No one lives unto himself or herself. Each individual who has ever lived has had an impact on other people, negatively or positively, and so each person is significant. A person's death affects other people's lives, as well as a person's life. Choices made by one person cannot affect only that person, whatever the choice is. This fact is exciting at times and tragic at others. People may feel they are making a wonderfully humble statement when they say, "I don't matter to anyone; my life is worth nothing." But in fact no one can live without affecting other people's lives and affecting history—even if they choose suicide.

A little Swedish girl was to affect the fortunes of the Steinway Company in a surprising way! Jenny Lind (1820–1887), born in Stockholm, had a gorgeous instrument with which she was born: her soprano voice! She became known as "The Swedish Nightingale." Her debut was made in opera in 1838 as Agathe in *Der Freischutz*, but in 1849 she gave up opera and came to the United States for a tour from 1850 to 1851. Talk about the threads of lives being woven in strange patterns at times—it was P. T. Barnum, the showman, who arranged the greater part of these tours. Her opening concert at Castle Garden was probably Steinway's first major musical experience in the new world. There is always a "first"!

Theodore Steinway says this in *People and Pianos:*

> It was during the middle years of the nineteenth century that the piano became established in its permanent position in the eyes of the American public, both as a musical instrument and a piece of furniture. Interest in music was growing fast, as evidenced by Jenny Lind's triumphant tour in 1850-1851, and more and more people could afford to indulge their tastes. More than ever in homes where music was loved, the piano was becoming a member of the family.[2]

2. Theodore E. Steinway, *People and Pianos*, 2d ed. (New York: Steinway and Sons, 1961).

Jenny Lind undoubtedly stirred up great interest in singing and having pianos.

John Steinway greeted his brother Henry as he came in for mail, introduced him to us, and then went on with his reminiscing: "Because of growing success we moved from the Walker Street place and built a factory on Park Avenue from 52nd to 53rd Streets. Imagine what that property holds now! That property was all sold in 1906 when the railroad was covered over, and we moved out to Astoria, Long Island City, now near La Guardia Airport. That factory location in 1906 is the same that is used today. You see, Park Avenue became fancy and nonindustrial, and so in 1906 there was a complete move to Long Island. Nineteen years later the building we are now in was built with its showroom. That was 1925, and we have remained here until now. The history of our family and the corporation has all taken place in New York."

He went on to tell of the ethnic groups in New York and how the early Steinways all married Germans. Not until John's father's marriage did a Steinway marry a non-German. "Our original great-grandfather was seeking a place to get away from the war in North Germany, but also he had a desire to go where economic freedom and private enterprise made it possible for ideas to be free to develop, and where hindrances to creativity were removed. He felt America was the country of golden opportunity for development."

John stressed the fact that the family had always felt a responsibility as citizens of their new country. All the early Steinway men were in the Union army in the Civil War—and they fought with fierce patriotism for their new country. At Bard College (a part of Columbia) where John attended, they had long, evening discussions concerning ideas in these areas.

After college John and Henry started at the bottom by pushing logs in the lumberyard! They each spent three years in the factory actually making the pianos with their twelve thousand parts. They know the business from every angle and have lived with it throughout their lives. Now retired, they come to their office daily, except when in Germany at the other factory or headquarters.

As I listened there, surrounded by the pictures of the past on the walls, and the old furniture, and the flow of history in the story being told, I was very conscious of what has been uniquely American. America has been unique from the beginning because everyone came from another loyalty, everyone had had an allegiance to another flag, everyone had some conviction that had brought them to the point of being ready to transfer their strong fidelity and love. There was a passionate desire to be patriotic. I know there has been no perfect set of singleminded people nor any golden period when everyone's motives were pure. But there was a spirit of adoption that permeated the growth of America as people merged together in "a melting pot" from such varied countries and backgrounds.

I felt in what John Steinway was stressing and in what I have researched about that period of growing industry, that there was a passionate desire to defend this young country of true adoption whose ideals and standards, freedoms and opportunities were worth working for and fighting for. I remembered the story of my husband's father, whose family also came from Germany, throwing his father's Iron Cross in the furnace. Why? Because he wanted to indicate to himself, to his wife, and to his small son (and to the cellar walls!) that he was truly American at the time of the First World War! John Steinway went on to say, "Four of our family were involved in the First World War and all of our family were involved in the Second World War." These are patriotic Americans who have actively worked to preserve what they appreciated of this country's real freedoms with actions as well as words.

Technically, the Steinways were quick to adopt the overstrung scale, in which the strings are arranged radically in two layers, the treble below the bass, yielding greatly improved tone quality and power. The first of many prizes awarded the firm was for overstrung square pianos with full iron frames, exhibited at the American Institute Fair in the New York Crystal Palace in 1855. A disastrous fire destroyed that building in 1858 and Steinway lost seventeen beautiful instruments. However, it was after that loss that Henry Steinway brought forth his epoch-making invention: the application of the overstrung scale to the grand pianos.

I discovered that the old Steinway Hall was the scene of many cultural events from 1866 to 1890 when Carnegie Hall was built. These included:

1867—a reading by Charles Dickens himself!
1871—a concert by the Vienna Lady Orchestra
1877—a political meeting from which communist demonstrators were ejected
1877—the first demonstration of music transmitted by wire— from Philadelphia to New York

Imagination can soar into flights of fancy in looking at old pictures of these events. One almost hears the voices and feels the emotional responses to Dickens reading one of his books, to the beauty of music and the thrill of the first steps toward radio transmission of music into homes. One realizes that discussions in the area of ideas that involve freedom and tyranny would have been hot and diverse! What an evidence of freedom of speech! It is enormously impressive to me to think that a manufacturer of pianos—one that desires to produce the best in artistic and functional quality—could have such an interest in providing the general public with evenings of stimulation— enjoyment, and discussion, and provocative thinking. What a combination that was! How far it was from being purely commercial with no thought of helping people with their life as a whole. The phrase "community spirit" has a deeper meaning in this context.

My interview was over. "Dutch television has sent a crew here, and I have to go to be with them now," said John Steinway as he warmly shook our hands and led us to the door. The proper thank-yous and good-byes were said, and as the door opened a man stepped up to me, "Mrs. Schaeffer, I have been asked to take you down to the basement where someone wants to meet you. Please follow me."

We followed him down the hall, stepped into the elevator, and enjoyed the wood inlay again as we went down to the basement. Now "the basement" of the Steinway building should really be written in capital letters, as it is a famous and very exciting place. You see, this is where artists of the keyboard, the top pianists of classical music, and also the top jazz artists (who are called Steinway artists) come to try various pianos which are there for the purpose of being chosen for a New York concert. Picture Avis, who herself is a pianist, and me eagerly looking around as we walked through the basement hall with rooms opening on either side, full of concert grand pianos. Sounds of both tuning and playing went on around us.

A rather plain door was opened to a large room that certainly had no glamour in its cement floor, fluorescent lights, drab walls, and very plain ceiling full of plumbing pipes. But the room had an air of excitement about it. Concert grand pianos at all angles filled the room, some opened for playing, some closed as if in storage, some taken apart with the keyboard and action portion out on a heavy oak workbench. The excitement was made up of an atmosphere of music, past, present, and future. It was as if the music played here by Rubinstein, Serkin, Horowitz, Watts, and others, was still floating in the air, affecting one without making any sound! As for the sound of tuning, it's not monotonous if you know what it is preparing the piano to do. It is a note or notes of anticipation made audible! A little hesitantly we picked our way among the pianos, not quite sure what was going to take place. "Who," I wondered, "wants to meet me?"

Suddenly, there was a rush of wind. A quickly moving man had left his careful work on a piano in his corner to welcome me with a European kiss on two cheeks, and the words in a charming accent, "Oh, Edith Schaeffer, I am so glad to meet you at last. Your husband's books and your books have meant so very much to my wife and me. Come, come, sit down over here and let us talk." I sat by his desk, just to the left of his workbench. The piano he was adjusting and tuning was on my right. Above his desk was a calendar with a woodsy view on it and a few pictures and notations of what he had to do. But my attention was riveted on the story that flowed forth, an amazing story that I realized was going to be part of my book. *How surprising, how unexpected,* I thought as he talked. *I came down that elevator looking at the craftsmanship of the woodwork. I entered here thinking about the wonder of pianos and artists, composers and performances. And suddenly I am confronted with the overwhelming wonder of the Creator God who has not only done so much to this man's life, but who has also arranged this meeting!*

"She is being romantic," are you saying? "How naive."

You see, at the time I did not know Franz Mohr by reputation. When I went back to Minnesota, I found that a book given to me by Dr. Monty Petitt and his wife, Karen, literally just before I left and so with no time to read it had an article about Franz Mohr. You can imagine my astonishment when I started to read this book, *The Lives of the Piano,* and found that article and many pictures of Franz in it taken in the basement where we had just been introduced.

At that moment, while listening to his story (very condensed right then), I was filled with awe at the realization that this meeting had not been a chance meeting any more than the gift of the piano 281261 had been a chance happening. I knew I had to come back to New York again, and take full notes, to hear in detail the story of Franz Mohr's life—the background of the master technician at Steinway.

We said our good-byes in order to hurry to the office, many blocks away, of the public relations person from whom, we were told, we needed help to get permission to take pictures in the Steinway factory in Queens. I had already engaged a photographer for the next day, Peter Schaaf, who was recommended by my nephew John Van Buskirk, who is a fine pianist himself. "Peter," he told me, "has

Edith and Franz Mohr, master technician at Steinway.

done some work for me. He is very good, and also is a Juilliard graduate in piano. He would be the right one for taking the pictures you want in the Steinway factory." As my time in New York was limited, I had gone ahead and made arrangements with Peter before being sure I could get permission and learning how much time we might have in the factory.

After a long wait we got in to see the public relations person. She was cordial enough, but thought we could use the pictures already taken. I very much had wanted not only to have our own taken, but to see, smell, and feel the atmosphere of the factory. But it was Halloween, she was going to a party very soon, and I was an end-of-the-afternoon-no-time-to-go-into-this-now kind of an appointment. "We'll see" was the most that could be said, along with, "Here are some pictures you could use." And she turned to hand me a few while she picked up her mask for the party and said a gracious "good-bye."

That evening I phoned Franz Mohr to find out whether we could take some pictures the next morning of his voicing a piano. He agreed very warmly, and so I arranged with Peter Schaaf to meet him at the Steinway building at ten the next morning, when Franz said he would be getting out of the elevator after a board meeting.

It was November first at precisely ten in the morning when Peter Schaaf entered the doors with his camera equipment and Franz Mohr stepped off the elevator, hurrying over to meet us with a radiant smile. As we walked over to another elevator, he began explaining how different each piano is. "No two are alike," he said. "Each piano has its own personality, its own voice. They are not mechanical, not at all."

As we walked along through the basement's various rooms to the doors of his room, Franz continued to talk, explaining how pianists, artists indeed, come to Steinway's to practice, and how some musicians who play other instruments also like to practice in the basement when they are in New York giving concerts. There is a list of those who are given entrance—Steinway artists for whom the basement is home for a short period from time to time. An artist who is in New York to give a concert at the Metropolitan Museum or at Carnegie Hall or at Lincoln Center is invited by Steinway to come to the basement and pick a piano, Franz told us.

That basement may have plumbing pipes on the ceiling and may remind you of a workshop in the cellar of an old house, but as with so much beautiful creative work throughout history, the most outstanding work has been done in very stark or humble surroundings.

It is what is in the mind that counts. The understanding, the ability, the sensitivity, the knowledge of what to do to get the right results in a creative work is in the mind of the creative person, not in the surroundings. The hands must be trained (as well as having a natural aptitude and skill) to do what needs to be done, for there is a thin line that separates a poorly done job from a good one. Excellent work takes place in this basement!

As Peter Schaaf set up his camera, Franz introduced me to the technicians who work with him—Ron Conners, his assistant, Ludwig Tomescu from Rumania, and Dan Jesse. Each one shook hands with enthusiasm, saying something about my husband's books and mine. I was astonished to find that these four men who work together so closely to keep these wonderful concert grands in tune and speaking with the right voices are very much in tune with the Creator of the universe, having all become believers. In an unusual way, therefore, they are in tune with each other too. While I was exclaiming over finding these jewels so to speak, another man dressed in a formal business suit came through the door. "This is Mr. Gene Inman, vice president of Steinway, Edith Schaeffer," Franz said. Again came the warm greeting of being glad to meet me because of having read Fran's books and mine. And then he said, "Is there anything I could do for you? I'd be glad to help in any way."

"Oh!" I exclaimed. "Yes there is, actually. I'd like to go with Peter Schaaf to see the factory, and to take some pictures for the book."

"I'll arrange it for you. When would you like to go?"

"Thank you so much. Would two o'clock this afternoon be all right?"

The afternoon before it had looked as if it would be impossible to make that arrangement during the short time I was going to be in New York. But I needed to be *in* the factory to understand more of what takes place there as well as to take pictures. Now we had time enough for a light lunch after taking the pictures in the basement, and then the taxi ride to Long Island City.

As we bumped, swayed, careened around corners, went uphill to a bridge it was all to the music of screeching brakes and a chorus of horns. The solos of bus horns, taxi horns, a police whistle, an ambulance siren, city music with the hum of moving traffic as the background accompaniment, swelled while the soloists took center stage at least long enough to turn our heads at times to look at the soloist. The song in my head was louder than the traffic. It was a bubbling excitement that went something like this: *I'm on my way right now to see the birthplace of that dear piano, that beautiful baby grand made almost fifty years ago. I'm on my way to see a place that has not changed all that much, and to feel, smell, touch, see, absorb that which I have imagined and read about. I've already tried to be careful and exact in my writing about 281261 so that the "pregnancy" and the order of the "prenatal growth" throughout the nine months before shipment would be properly described. Now I can have the freedom to look at the workers and watch things that capture my interest. It may not be like going to Cremona, Italy, to see Antonio Stradivari's house, but—well—yes, it is really. Steinway has been in existence for 130 years and this factory was completed seventy-five years ago. Just think... my inner voice trilled a thrilling trill at that point...Just think, our piano was made when the factory was only twenty-five years old! 281261 is not only one of the very first of the five-foot-one-inch model S baby grands to be made, but it is two-thirds as old as the factory itself.* History to be history does not have to have taken place two or three hundred years ago. I was indeed on my way to feeling and seeing a piece of past history—history that has so much to do with many, *many* people's lives.

We were not on our way to Buckingham Palace. There was no St. James's Park to drive through. We were not going to find an Alpine peak, and so we did not pass the lake at Montreux, Castle Chillon, nor did we drive through breathtaking scenery of valleys and villages with fields full of flowers, or snow-covered jagged peaks. This was Long Island City in Queens, New York. There were butcher shops, laundries, churches, houses, and grocery stores. No music accompanied us and no roll of drums announced us. We simply drove up in front of a red brick factory, paid the cab driver, and walked to a door. A plain, small lobby was on the other side of that door, and a pleasant young woman sat at a table. Yes, we were expected. Yes, if we would wait a few minutes, we would be taken to see the factory by Mr. Vince Orlando. He'd be here soon. We could sit right there. Mr. Orlando, the manager, welcomed us warmly and took us through the office section to sit at his desk and have some facts explained. A veteran of thirty years, Vince Orlando was not reciting a spiel—his words were too genuine. As I came to know other people at Steinway, I realized that despite any sarcastic articles written about the Steinway mystique, there is a love of the history of the Steinway, a feeling of belonging, a pride both in the finished piano as well as in the individual portion that a person is making. I don't mean that all the people who work at Steinway are joyously satisfied people. But I did find something unique and special among twentieth-century workers.

There is an atmosphere of camaraderie, personal responsibility, and involvement in producing an excellent piano in every part of the twelve thousand pieces, which is felt as well as expressed. There is also a feeling of being a family working together. It may sound idealistic, but it has existed, and for the time being still exists, it seems to me.

"Let's go out first to the lumberyard," said Vince Orlando. "That is the logical place to start." We walked out, and looked up, and up, and up! The lumber was methodically stacked in piles: "the Sitka Spruce here, all the sugar pine and maple there, and those are mahogany, walnut, poplar, and cherry." I patted the rough wood rather respectfully, thinking of what it would be doing, and looking like, and sounding like in a few years. Years? Yes, as the piles stand there in rain and shine, winter and summer, it takes about three years for it to age properly. A corrugated covering protects the lumber, and cross pieces of wood keep air going through the piles.

The neat piles of wood stacked carefully to let air circulate reminded me so much of Saanan, a village near Gstaad, Switzerland. When you cross the railroad tracks at Saanan, to take the wonderful walk along the rushing torrent, past chalets, past an army camp, past a riding school, through woodsy areas, you first pass a lumberyard with piles of lumber stacked just like this. Saanan slipped into my mind's eye not because of the similarity of the lumber piles alone, but because of the connection with music. You can see in Saanan the tower of a small thirteenth-century church with a clock in the white plaster. It is here that the summer music festival of Yehudi Menuhin takes place. I felt as if I had gone back and would soon be sitting with all my children and grandchildren to listen to the Zurich Chamber Orchestra and James Galway with his gold flute as soloist! What an experience it is to listen to such music in the midst of ancient wooden walls, as well as in the midst of the murals painted on those walls, and the carved wooden rails of the balcony. Wood. Wood that acts as a sounding board in various ways.

Here in Queens there may be no rushing mountain stream in summer, no cross-country skiers going past in winter, no Alpine rouge at sunset time, only piles of lumber surrounded by red brick factory buildings. But with a difference. This lumber has come from some fantastically different woods and is going to turn into that which will feel, hear, produce and be a part of music itself. This wood will be the center of attention in great opera houses, in concert halls—great and small—in churches of all sorts, in synagogues, in

Edith Schaeffer inspects the work of Steinway craftsmen.

homes that are mansions, palaces, the White House, or in homes that are humble and small. This that is now "lumber" will turn into so many different and essential parts of pianos to accompany great symphonies, operas, ballets, jazz singers, masses, church cantatas, singing of great choirs, and the singing around a family celebration. This wood will become pianos which will be a source of music in many countries of the world and in tremendously different places—colleges, conservatories, and some old folks' homes, in theaters, arenas, and at the Queen's garden party! What a future these piles of wood have, indeed! This lumber, first in the hands of those who will skillfully make the parts of the piano, and then in the hands of those who will perform with expertise, will produce music that will be scattered over space and time—traveling through the airwaves of the world by way of satellite, by television and radio, by recorded tapes and discs.

Yes, my pat of awe and wonder on the rough wood was in place! It was kind of overwhelming. Three years the wood is there being aged after many years of growing. Carefully cut boards, all the proper width and thickness, are blended together in piles for a time. But soon they will be cut further, some into proper parts for pianos, and some because of flaws must be burned for the heat that is so necessary for part of the work. It is amazing, really. Part of the wood will be inside the piano, not to be seen by many people, but to be heard, some will be highly polished, while some of it will be on another fortifying layer, necessary and so significant to the whole. And some of it will be burned to give heat that will dry the rims made of other parts of the wood. As we looked at the piles we couldn't know what portion would be used in what way. All are equally important.

Not long ago all this wood had roots in forests that were widely separated. I remembered my "lecture" on the airplane as Charles Bush from Washington state described the Sitka spruce forests so that I could visualize them.

The Sitka spruce is not planted as an economic thing, as faster growing trees are planted first. There are beautiful properties where the Sitkas are growing naturally in mountain terrain. They need damp but well drained ground. Slow growth is important. Sitkas are used when they are two to three feet across and the trees that are used are about 500 years old!

Not damaging the forest is so very important, and so the trees are carefully cut and taken out by helicopter. These old growth forests have not much undergrowth because the sun doesn't come through, and light is shut off. They are so cool and quiet! The new or second growth forests, after eighty years of growth, are again silent with a carpet of green.

He went on then to talk of the Sitka wood:

> This lighter, stronger wood is perfect for sounding boards and for making musical instruments. At present the Japanese are buying at highest bids. Violins and guitars are made of Sitka although the fronts and backs are usually maple. Did you know that Segovia plays a Torres guitar, which is the most famous classical guitar? Well, Torres built a papier-mâché body with a Sitka spruce top—two pieces split and glued, the two pieces matched, the same as a violin. The necks of most guitars are made of Honduras mahogany. Mahogany seems to be alive when you knock on it; it seems to sing—like people!

Yes, the wood grows in forests that are not only thousands of miles apart, but forests that differ in so many ways. Like people who come together in marriage and have widely different backgrounds, who have grown with their roots in very different forests so to speak, the wood needs to mature a while and then be blended in a workable pattern. The pattern must have purpose so that the piano brings forth music, but it can also bring forth discord and noise if banged upon instead of played!

We went on to get impressions, to stop to let Peter take his pictures, to listen to Vince Orlando give us his careful explanations. We watched two dark men intent on their work as they meticulously handled wood that was being shaped into a gorgeous curve. The saw they were cautiously feeding the wood to was making five thousand revolutions a minute, spewing out wood dust in a cloud of smoke and zzzzzing sounds that came in varied tones—zzzzing in high, medium and low key! The absorbed look on their faces seemed to indicate an intention to get that curve precisely as it should be.

As we walked through room after room, smells were as vivid as sights! The smell of wood is a favorite fragrance of mine, and there was a rich variety. We stepped into the drying room, where the frames were standing to dry, and felt the 106° heat as if we had stepped into a sauna. I was impressed by the row upon row of beautiful frames which would enclose the inner reality of pianos. What good is a beautiful frame, if it never encloses the reality of the voice that is meant to be there? An empty frame! What a sadness that would be. It might be an artwork in your living room, but it would be empty of its real purpose. It would be an unfulfilled possibility!

We stepped into another room and walked between pianos in various stages of being made. Twelve thousand parts is a lot of parts. Four hundred people working on each individual piano at one stage or another is a lot of people. Nine months to a year is a lot of time. I was having a small glimpse, a short visit, a tiny impression—but a lasting memory. Never will I forget looking at two cheerfully smiling Blacks as they called out to Vince Orlando, who in his thirty years of work at the factory has obviously had a good relationship with the workers. People know each other. "Hi!" and a smile is a real communication in the midst of polishing, rubbing down the metal piano strings, polishing a leg, or carving an ornate and intricate leg for some special order. "Hi!" came from two men preparing an enormous box. "This is where the pianos are packed for their trip out into the world." Their glance at two pianos waiting to be packed was full of an attachment that was more than pride in the part being done by them. It was pride in the results of the entire joint effort of producing that beauty which was now going out to be on its own, like sending a son or daughter off to college!

We stopped in another room to watch the women weighing the keys. A tiny weight was carefully put on a key. The expertise of the two women is in recognizing whether the key is too stiff or too loose and to make appropriate adjustments. Another weight was tried and another key was tested. It is a painstaking job to bring about an accurate result. Patience is needed, but also a deep understanding of the importance of that one step in making a great piano. In life so often people don't realize what an importance there is in living their own part of history well, in being what they can be, in making the next step of some portion of history possible. If the keys are not weighed properly, then the next step cannot go as it should and the tuner cannot regulate the voice as he must do.

Does it *feel* important to work with the making of that essential soundboard? Do the men over there painting a lacquer finish *feel* significant because of the shiny beauty they are adding that will reflect the light of candles, chandeliers, or blend in with the varnish on a nearby violin? Does that wiry looking little man with a tattoo on his arm so earnestly working with the keys, with a small frown of concentration, *feel* the importance of his necessary contribution? I was getting more of an impression of concern in doing work well and an understanding of the whole than the average factory worker would have. I'd have to say, "Yes, I do think so...to a very real degree."

One reason for this dedication is that many of the workers have musical talent themselves and find this is a satisfying place to be. For instance, the young woman in the office had studied in a conservatory. Part of the appreciation of the final product and part of the desire to do their work well is connected with a basic love of music and appreciation of the Steinway piano's history and part in music in the present day. That sort of a reality of having good workers does not come by simply picking people out of thin air. The list of qualifications for employees has grown through the years with the company. There is an involvement that is far more than "a day's work," or a job.

Peter Schaaf, who himself studied piano at Juilliard and could have been a pianist but has turned to photography as his first love now, was busy taking photographs for the inside of this book. He, too, was loving his time in the factory. Anyone who loves music would.

We turned away from the long rooms with their mixture of sounds—a C note and the zzzzzing saws—the smell of wood and glue, of lacquer and turpentine and oils, and the sight of the faces of each unique person working, and the pieces (out of the 12,000) that have caught our eyes. I looked again at the beauty of the action portion (an art work to me), the shape and gleam of the brass hitchpins, the one-eighth-inch thick Brazilian rosewood for the hammer shank knuckles. These component parts were more lovely than art works of some kinds—functional, necessary parts, yet with a beauty in themselves. It was time to go and we had just begun to see something, to feel something. My mind was a buzz of ideas. My memory was full of photographs, even more than were taken by Peter that day! But, as with so many things in life, the time was too short for fulfilling the interest that had been generated.

Now we turned into the suitable place for ending our browsing around. "This is Ralph Biscagle." "Ciao....Buon Giorno" ... "Ciao"..."Good to meet you." A concert grand filled the room, and we walked around it to get to the bench where Ralph was working. I sat on a chair beside him to watch his careful tuning of this new concert grand before it has its legs removed and is shipped in the big box being made for it. The balancing of the tone quality is literally the last thing to be done. Yes, it has been tuned and well adjusted before. Yes, it will be tuned, tone-regulated, voiced, carefully again and again, before it is played—before each concert. But Ralph was working with as much perfectionism as if his was the only tuning this

Each key is precisely weighted for proper action.

piano would ever have! I looked to see where the burst of symphonic music was coming from and found that Ralph works with a radio tuned to an FM station for a constant stream of classical music.

"I was born and brought up in Bari, Italy," he began, "and my father took me to opera before I was four years old." He nodded his head with a dreamy look of remembrance. "Si, si. I grew up loving music." He banged on the key he was working on and then said, "You hear how awful that is? Harsh! Metallic is garbage! We wanna make it soft." He started jabbing with his needle-like instrument at the hammer. "The harder the hammer, the shorter the tone. The softer the hammer, the longer the note carries." He went on to tell us that his own instrument is the guitar. He worked at Juilliard for seven years. He was forty-nine at the time we talked. "Now listen to that note. Hear the difference? That's a nice sound now...nice." He told me I should look up the records and see who the final tone regulator was on my piano. "See who was here in 1935."

We said our good-byes all through various rooms and the office and made our way to another taxi waiting for us. The taxi driver began a running commentary as we moved slowly out of the factory area. The day was finished and people were streaming out. The doors opened and shut, seeming to spew people out in spurts, like a kitchen spigot that doesn't work smoothly, one of those that bursts forth and splashes you, and then runs in a thin trickle. Their clothing was varied—raincoats of all colors and sorts, red, blue, plain, checked, jackets, blue jeans, cords, turtleneck jerseys, sports shirts—a mixture of work clothing and a mixture of ethnic backgrounds. There were blacks and whites and browns, Italians, Greeks, but all Americans, all with music as an interest to some degree, all on their way home to carry on other interests, home, family, hobbies, joys, sorrows, struggles, each one a craftsman or a craftswoman and each very significant in the production of pianos. How many know they have a significance in history? How many see the creativity and the Creator behind the universe in the way they see the bits and pieces of those twelve thousand parts of the piano? I wondered as we bumped along. The taxi driver was talking.

"Yeah, this is Astoria. That's the Egle Electric Company; that truck belongs to them. That's a Roman Catholic church. Yeah, a lot of Greeks here—more Greeks in Queens than in Athens. Yeah. Brooklyn's Polish now. Where did you say you wanted to go? Way up on the West Side? Up to 940 West End Avenue? Yeah, we gotta go through Harlem—that's 106th up to 125th...okay."

CHAPTER *9*

Franz Mohr

C hildren. What comes to your mind? A swing hanging from a
lovely tree and soaring up and down with apple orchards
stretching out in rows nearby. A seesaw with two tots fairly equally
balanced and an anxious pair of mothers, one protecting each end. A
merry-go-round in Tuileries garden in Paris with a slowly walking
person substituting for a motor—a continuity of a new generation
with past years! A little bridge over a stream with laughing children
throwing sticks and leaves in the water on one side and running to
peer over the other side to see whose stick is "winning." A lilac bush
with children setting up housekeeping underneath with hollyhock
flowers as cups and shoe boxes for doll beds.

In today's world, unhappily, the word *children* also conjures up
many sad pictures of kidnapping and disappearance, of war and ter-
rorism, of starvation and neglect, of bewildered little people being introduced to problems too heavy for their short experience in life to
deal with.

A farm in Germany might have given an ideal childhood to the
children of Grandfather Mohr as he tilled his land and his boys
helped him. But one son chose a nearby village in which to become a
mail carrier, and later to work in the post office. This Mohr had three
sons. Tony, the eldest, taught himself to play an accordion and practiced hours and hours, filling the village house with his kind of music. The next son, born in 1927, was named Franz. Music was part of
his earliest memory, and his natural talent was for the violin. That
gift showed up so early, he advanced so quickly, and his teachers felt
he was so gifted, that he was soon being urged to practice seriously,

159

and to take up violin as a profession. When Franz was four, the family moved to the town of Duren, seven miles away. That move was in 1931, and the youngest son, Peter, was a part of the family by then.

The regular German school soon became a part of the day-by-day family life. Tony's accordion, Franz's violin, and whatever music Peter made were all a part of the sound that filled the house—along with recitations of poetry which is always a part of a good German primary education. The town of Duren is between Aachen and Cologne, and so preparation for Cologne University was a natural next step for Franz. You can be sure that both studies and violin practice were being urged daily with an encouragement to put first things first. Mozart and Brahms filled the air, and the history of composers as well as a good grasp of literature and languages were basic. European education fills childhood with a base that can only be described as "a good classical education." It includes a good knowledge of art and literature, languages and history, as well as mathematics and music! In Switzerland, to be accepted in the normal school to prepare to be a primary teacher, one of the requirements, along with passing other stiff exams, is to be able to sing and to have sufficient knowledge and ear for music to lead four-part singing. Germany would have had the same kind of emphasis.

Yes, in September 1939, little Franz had many hours of study and violin practice in the midst of family life, village life, and school life. The distressing piece of news that Hitler had marched into Poland came without adequate understanding of the why, and without adequate answers to the question, "What is going on?" Fear comes in the dark of the night at all stages of life, but especially to children who mull over things and try to figure them out, with only blurred voices and foggy glimpses of information. How much is known about all the facets of what is going on in today's history, behind a diversity of walls shutting out the view of cruelty?

Franz's father had Jews as his closest friends. One day he said to the boy, "Look son, Hitler is sending Jews to some kind of work camps. It is an awful thing. I don't know where they are going, but I know that this is the end of Germany." Franz's father was a Roman Catholic and not given to reading the Bible, but he quoted from the Old Testament book of Zechariah:

> "Up, Zion! Escape, you who dwell
> With the daughter of Babylon."
> For thus says the LORD of hosts:

"He sent Me after glory, to the nations which plunder you;
For he who touches you touches the apple of His eye.
For surely I will shake My hand against them,
And they shall become spoil for their servants.
Then you will know that the LORD of hosts
Has sent Me." (Zech. 2:7-9)

"It's the end of Germany, boy. 'He who touches My people touches the apple of My eye.' That's God speaking, and the Jews are His people. Mother has prepared sandwiches and other food for my friend Ben the butcher who is in the station. They are taking Jews away to some work camp. Go. Take this food. Go and get it to him somehow."

Franz got a friend his own age, and boy-fashion they ran off, determined to get past the guards. They found the building, an abandoned factory by the river. The river side of the building was unguarded as there was a locked door on that side. There wasn't much foothold, but they were able to climb and make it to some broken windows.

There they saw the Jews waiting, packed together in the factory room. One had his yarmulke and a prayer shawl on, with a candle burning. In awe they listened to the quoting of Psalm 121: "I will lift up my eyes to the hills—/From whence comes my help?/My help comes from the LORD,/Who made heaven and earth."

Their package of food had a name written on it, and after the psalm was finished they handed it through an open place in the window, jumped down, and got away without being detected. Children. Fear. Tears with no comfort. Such unresolved problems.

Another time, Franz stood with other young boys to see what was going on at the railroad station. Jews were being pushed into trains; tears were flowing; good-byes were being called out; luggage was being heaved on; chaos seemed to be everywhere. Franz ran home to tell his father. "Daddy, Daddy, oh Daddy, I saw our friends. I saw Mr...." and with sobs he told what he had seen. The father replied, "God help us. Germany is gone now...it is gone." But the assumption was that the Jews would be made to work very hard in camps. That was a horror to the Mohrs, and a fearful thing that was resulting from totalitarian rule. Rule by terror on the part of a dictator or a totalitarian government brings fear of saying much in wrong places. The gas chambers and all that was going on was not known to them during that time.

Franz continued to progress well in school and to show real genius with the violin. He was barely fifteen years old when he was accepted at Cologne University to major in music. As a day student, Franz rode the train every day. It was a short ride, and the trains ran every forty minutes during the days. A fifteen-year-old was going to school during war. Childhood comes only once for each child. In war, famine, or other brokenness, that's it. That's childhood. What was it like to go to university during a war? On certain days the air raid of the night before meant bombed buildings would be passed on the train. Fear is like a knife twisting inside with no warning. Fear of bombs or fire is not as terrible as fear of all that goes with totalitarianism. Anyone could be a spy for the state. The word *trust* loses its meaning like a leaky pail losing water. A dryness comes to people who can no longer trust anyone.

One morning as Franz got off the train and came to the auditorium building, he found it in flames. The sight was horrifying, but the sound was an unforgettable music—a sickeningly awful music. Hot air from the heat and flames was playing the organ pipes like some monster out of hell. A ghastly, hideously discordant music was playing, like the groans of a dying person, not one however, but many. There stood the sensitive music students listening to the ruptured sounds, shrieks as of wandering souls in outer darkness, sounds that would never be wiped out of their memories. They stood unable to move while the dissonance faded into silence—the silence of the death of an organ, the death of an education, the death of people also dying. Was this the end of music?

Forever? Forever discord? Forever silence? Would there be no hope?

Where did Hitler come from? Or Lenin? Or Mao? Or Stalin? Or Amin? What about the Berlin wall? What about Afghanistan?

What is the cause that brings an effect into the place where it is seen, smelled, touched, heard, felt? How do actions come?

In the mind. Just as creativity is in the mind first, so devastating destruction is in the mind first. Violence is in the mind first—from *ideas*.

Ideas come first.

Ideas matter.

Ideas give birth to action—good or bad.

Ideas give people their world view.

Ideas push people into heroism.

Ideas drive people into vandalism.

Ideas are meant to be handed down from generation to generation. People are not born as finished products. Teaching and instruction, the passing on of ideas, takes place, whether it is true or false teaching. The God of Scripture speaks in Deuteronomy very clearly:

You shall love the LORD your God with all your heart, with all your soul, and with all your might.

And these words which I command you today shall be in your heart; you shall teach them diligently to your children, and shall talk of them when you sit in your house, when you walk by the way, when you lie down, and when you rise up. (Deut. 6:5-7)

Discussion of truth with the next generation is being pointed out here. It is to be not just a rote memorization, but discussion of ideas while hiking in the woods, walking along a city street, sitting by a fireside or at the kitchen table, at bedtime. This is an admonition to give the next generation a base for action developed on the existence of God, and a real putting first of a love for God. The commandments of God set forth action based on love of God and then action based on love for other human beings.

One generation is responsible for the next—whoever is doing the planting of ideas. The parents, or teachers, or professors in universities may live a life of actions based on what is left over from some other teaching. That is, it is quite possible for people to have an ethic that does not belong to what they are teaching the next generation. They are then surprised and even dismayed when the next generation, their own pupils, begins carrying out in action what they have been given in the realm of ideas.

You might contemplate the effect of Hegel's relativism on Hitler's ideas. Think of Hegel's effect on Hitler's ideas in the realm of his providing a base for Hitler's actions. People do open doors down for following generations—down into the depths of despair for thinking young people, down into drastic action for others. Suicide follows for some. Cruelty to other people follows for others. Hegel lived from 1770 to 1831. Nietzsche lived from 1844 to 1900. Hitler lived from 1889 to 1945. Ideas and philosophies don't just end up in people's minds or on the pages of books, but in actions of individual lives and nations.

What was it Hegel introduced not only to German universities, but to the teaching of philosophy in every country of the world, and hence into action in the twentieth century? It was Hegel who came up with a totally new idea, an idea which led to the prevalent teaching that truth does not exist. Before Hegel's philosophic teaching, philosophers agreed that antithesis exists, that something is right and something is wrong, that cause and effect go on in a straight line and have meaning. Hegel came along and stated that there was another way— a totally different way of approaching everything. It may sound like something that doesn't affect you at all, but indeed it does. What Hegel set forth is what is taught to you and your children in most of the schools and universities of the world.

Rather than there being true truth, and the opposite being not true, what Hegel set forth in his talking, or on a blackboard, or with a set of marks scratched in the sand, was that the opposite to a thesis is antithesis. And then, putting a higher mark above those two, you can bring the opposites together in a synthesis. This does not remain fixed, however, but becomes a new thesis—with a new antithesis— and on you go. There is no resolution, to speak of it in musical terms.

This can't be a chapter on philosophy, but I feel we cannot understand present-day history without understanding that what is being taught in high schools, colleges, universities in the area of ideas upon which to base one's thinking is at the same time affecting actions.

The people who bear responsibility for the actions taken in different periods of history are those who inject ideas into the minds of the young, one way or another.

The relativism which resulted from Hegel's teaching permeated everything. In fact many people today think that no educated person could possibly believe that there is any unchanging standard for ethics and morals. Rather, since everything is in a state of flux, and since everything is relative, it would be impossible to say that it is "wrong" to kill people because they have blue eyes, or red hair, or anything else that one might arbitrarily pick out. Hitler chose to rid his kingdom, as he was thinking of it, of Jewish people and of those who were weak or in mental institutions because he made up his own rules based on what was acceptable to himself. When people are taught to believe that there is no base for law, no base for morals, no base for ethics, then it is a short time until some actions will come forth which they think no one else can have a base for saying, "That is wrong; we are going to stop you from doing that."

If God exists; if Scripture, the Bible, is His Word; if the explanation of the Fall gives us the background of the Devil and also of the abnormality of the world, then it is easy to see that relativism is the kind of lie you would expect from Lucifer who declared to Adam and Eve, "You will not surely die."

The one who brought in death denied death's existence to those who would die because of his deception. What a spine-tingling truth—which so many people reject.

Death was on every side in Germany. What was not being seen by those teenaged students who were smelling the burned musical instruments as well as seeing the devastation, was being talked about. Dresden had been bombed—180,000 people had died in that one city—and the refugees were pressing into homes wherever they could find a place, while others were sleeping and cooking outdoors. It is not surprising that this beauty-loving, sensitive musician called Franz was by now feeling the fierce fire of hate burning within him. These flames of hate leapt high, kindled by the sights, sounds, and smells of war—total war not contained by some sort of military bounds. *Nothing will ever change this hate*, thought Franz. *I will never forget.*

Franz was not yet sixteen when he was drafted into the army. Classes had stopped, no more school existed. The Russians were on one side, and the Americans were coming. This young, emotional, bewildered boy was drafted into the army. How many there are of those young boys today under sixteen in so many of the world's present wars! Franz had an intensive six-week training—a one-year training in six weeks. They were given makeshift uniforms. It was a desperate act at the time of losing, as sixty-five-year-old men and young boys were pushed into a short training and given minimal equipment to fight the Russians marching in from the east, and the Americans from the west.

As Franz's unit was retreating more and more during November of 1944, it came to the town of Aachen, not far from his own town of Duren. Most of the people from both these towns were evacuating. Franz asked for a leave of absence to go the six miles to his home to see his parents. The sergeant let several of them go.

When he got home his mother and father both said, "We are not going away from here. We have no desire to go any closer to the Russians who are coming the other way. The Americans are coming from the west. The war is over, we will stay here." Many others were running to the middle.

Franz realized that home would never be the same. Shells were falling daily. Many changes had taken place in family life already.

They were living down in the cellar of the house, as neighbors were too. The walls of these houses were two and one-half feet thick and seemed to give good protection in the cellar. It felt like a castle wall! Then the hallway floor was concrete and that gave a concrete ceiling for protection. They felt safe under there, but they were going up to the kitchen to cook. Franz's younger brother Peter and his father had been working on safety measures. They had built an emergency exit through the hall out into the garden. They had also made a steel door with two handles like the doors between compartments on a ship. All of his mother's carefully "put up" home-canned goods had been painstakingly buried in the clay of the cellar floor, available for meals! Yes, life at home was a peculiar sort of shipwreck.

It was the fifteenth of November when Franz came home, and he had been given two days. At dawn on the sixteenth one of those typical, grey, thick mists covered everything with quietness. This morning was quiet with a peculiar eerieness. Everyone felt clutched, as if something terrible was about to happen. The family discussed their feelings but concluded it was really unexplainable. They had forty to fifty rabbits in the backyard for the luxury of eating one every two weeks, and after talking about their strange feelings Franz's mother said, "Go out and feed the rabbits, Franz." He came back to the breakfast table to report that the rabbits wouldn't eat anything. They talked together and decided that they'd better get away from the city. "Let's go out into the country as soon as possible. Everyone get busy. Something is coming; I think something is coming."

The men prepared the bicycles and the mother prepared the sandwiches. At two-thirty Franz went out to see what could be happening. Such silence. He had never heard such silence. There was not even the sound of a shell, nor a movement of a plane. He climbed out on the roof and before the silence was broken he saw to his astonishment B-17 planes approaching. Then came broken silence suddenly and a smoke signal so near. "Mom, Dad, it's for us, it's for us!"

There was no time to retrieve the lunch or the bikes. All hell broke loose and in twenty minutes 90 percent of all the population of Duren had died. In twenty minutes the town was rubble. Twenty-two thousand to twenty-four thousand people had died in twenty minutes, and all the streets of houses had turned to burning rubbish. A rubbish dump—flaming—smoking—there was no town left. They had run down to their cellar shelter along with some others. When there was a lull in the noise, Franz ran upstairs and found the whole side of the house was gone. He was looking out through the emptiness to a furnace of fire, with people walking in the burning flames like human torches, burning alive. Their bedroom was in flames and he looked long enough to have a memory of familiar things burning. Just then he heard another surge of planes coming, and he ran back down to the cellar.

Hearing the roar of the planes, his mother cried out, "God help us! Oh, God..." Franz yelled back, "Mom, shut up. Shut up! There is no God."

Something had snapped as he looked through the flames of the bedroom and saw the people walking to their deaths...the rubble...the roaring sound of planes coming. "Shut up, Mom! There is no God." The hate within him flamed up higher and higher to include God, as well as Hitler and his horrible war of conquest, and the Americans, British, and Russians with their fire bombs. *God*, Franz thought, *must either be behind it all or nonexistent. I hate God....Oh no...there is no God. If there is a God, how could he allow all this?*

His hand now went over his mom's mouth to stop her prayer, but that was the last touch of anything human before he was surrounded with noise, heat, flame, screams, falling bricks, plaster, smoke, choking fumes, thick dust—all in quick succession. Things were falling, falling, falling. Their house had been hit. It was all a frighteningly hellish mass of broken glass and broken furniture, walls, boards, bricks, flying, falling, shattering, burning, and in minutes there was no cellar as the walls had collapsed. Somehow, in the middle of everything burning that was burnable, and the falling bricks and plaster, Franz saw a hole open up and blindly scrambled for it with no consecutive thoughts about anything—no thoughts now, just an instinct to get away from the heat and the rubble that would soon bury him. How he crawled out, he can not really describe, simply that instead of scrambling from the inside, he was now running, running, running, and finding that all his hair was in his hands as he glanced down. He had pulled it all out in desperation, quite unconsciously. There were no streets—all was like some sort of a dump with mounds of burning refuse and hot pieces of cement and bricks, wildly piled rubbish with no relationship to anything familiar. Out, out, out.

The town was in a valley with hills rising on both sides, and so "out" meant up...and Franz ran up, up, up. People were running without stopping. Some were carrying their dead with them; one dead man was being pushed along on a bike. It was bizarre, grotesque, yet with no reaction coming except to go on and on, running up and up. Delayed-action bombs kept bursting with fire and noise, spraying fear. Up and up and up he ran until he paused a moment and looked back down on the town. Separate fires were merging into one column of fire and smoke. The memory of his sudden thought at that time has stayed indelibly in his brain. "Although I didn't believe God existed," he said to me, "as I stood looking, the story of Sodom and Gomorrah flashed into my mind. You know, where it says in Genesis, 'And Abraham went early in the morning to the place where he had stood before the LORD. Then he looked toward Sodom and Gomorrah, and toward all the land of the plain; and he saw, and behold, the smoke of the land which went up like the smoke of a furnace' " (Gen. 19:27–28).

Soon after that he stumbled into a farmer's doorway...and fell. They carried him to a couch where he slept utterly exhausted for ten days without stirring. Then suddenly he awakened with his first thought of his mom and dad. "Where's Mom? Where's Dad?" Then, "Where's Peter?"

It had been November 16, 1944, when his town was bombed, and almost everyone he had ever known in his life had died. He had nothing but the torn, burned rags of clothing left on his body. He had slept for ten days, and hunger had returned. It was now November 26, bleak, cold November and the weather was made more dismal by the smoke still rising. The town below looked no more stable than a child's sand town on a beach after a wave. ("All gone, Daddy. Let's start again.") But it was not a sand castle that had been demolished; it was not a day's earnest creative work on the part of a vacationing family designing castles, making proud turrets, with twigs for trees. It was a section of history and whole families of three generations that were wiped out. Start again? On what foundation? For what purpose? With what courage?

People put out signs along the paths on the hill:

HANS AND DOROTHY HERE—
LOOKING FOR FATHER BACHMAN.
WOLFGANG HERE—
LOOKING FOR LEOPOLD.

He decided to put out his signs in his daily search.

FRANZ HERE—LOOKING FOR FATHER
AND MOTHER MOHR AND FOR PETER.

A small village surrounded the farm, but it was a time of chaos and confusion as people were dazed, or injured and unable to walk around. Just before Christmas Franz found his parents—but not Peter. They were actually in another house in the same village.

In mid-January they went together to try to find the location of their house, and to attempt to dig Peter out. But they didn't get far— too much rubble...too heavy a work. They heard a moaning outside the town, a moaning like the frightening part of a dark and mournful opera. But this was no opera, this was not a stage setting. Someone was still alive—but where? They called and called at the top of their lungs, throats sore and scratchy, deep gulps of breath, "Is someone there? Is *someone* there? Are you alive? Where? Where?" Their calls sounded like echoes of hopelessness. The task was hopeless. As they called and stumbled over broken mounds of collapsed houses they felt there was no place to even begin, and so they left. Franz was close-lipped, but the words formed inside his mind, *Nobody, but nobody, will ever get me to go to church again. There is no God.* Dark thoughts of meaninglessness came to his mind. He thought no new thoughts, if he had known that, but followed along with Solomon in Ecclesiastes.

"Vanity of vanities," says the Preacher;
"Vanity of vanities, all is vanity."

There is no remembrance of former things,
Nor will there be any remembrance
Of things that are to come
By those who will come after.

Then I looked on all the works that my hands had done
And on the labor in which I had toiled;
And indeed all was vanity and grasping for the wind.
There was no profit under the sun.

And how does a wise man die?
As the fool! (Eccles. 1:2,11; 2:11,16b NIV)

Despair and cynicism are not new. These are a part of truth. They are what God tells us is the only answer—without God! Franz was arriving at a realistic understanding because despair makes sense. If there is no truth to be found, if no absolute exists, if everything is relative and what is right today is wrong tomorrow, or what was wrong yesterday will be quite acceptable tomorrow, nothing makes sense. Nothing has meaning.

Two unmarried aunts lived in a nearby village, and Franz and his parents went to live with them. "Life" continued. But what is life? Having something to eat? Sleeping a certain number of hours? Going to the bathroom? Washing some clothes at certain times? Washing face and hands and body at certain times in whatever water is available? Tribespeople in Nepal, or Africa, or the hills of China do these things in primitive conditions as all they have ever known. Refugees from so many countries, whether on boats or in jungles, attempt these things. "Life" goes on. But what is life for creative human beings who have been made with capacities for diverse creativity in many areas? What is life for human beings who have been made with the capacity for communication with and love for other human beings, and the capacity for love for and communication with God? Isn't the basic ingredient of life more than caring for the physical?

Despair in the face of war, famine, earthquake, volcano, floods, avalanches comes from facing with sharp and sudden reality the fact that the minimal necessities have been swept away. Is survival worth struggling for? Life needs to be more than food, elimination, water to drink and wash in, and sleep. What is the purpose of surviving?

Despair comes also to thinking people who have plenty of the minimal physical requirements of a human being, and a great deal more—to the point of sheer luxury. Thinking people come up with questions as to whether life has any meaning at all. Thinking people may not be able to find an answer to where creativity came from, nor where personality came from, nor whether love exists at all, nor how it is that death can cut off communication and any further continuity. Thinking people have the same conclusion as Solomon—life is utterly meaningless.

Everything Is Meaningless

Listen to Dustin Hoffman as he speaks to an interviewer, Gary Smith:

> "You know, I walked through the Whitney Museum the other day; they had the life and work of Milton Avery on the walls of five or six rooms. I look and I say, yes, I'd like to have that when I'm gone. But then I thought, who cares?"

> He is up now, gesturing, walking circles around a coffee table—no, stomping, pulsing with the knowledge that man is just worm food, and suddenly his arm shoots out and his voice explodes. "It means NOTHING! Who the hell really cares about

Charlie Chaplin? He left a legacy. So what? All it's going to be when I die is a paragraph in 'Milestones' in *Time* magazine.

"Okay, let's just *say* I could cash my body of work in, and for it I could get a thunderbolt with my name on it, and it would go off at five o'clock every night, and it would be a nice thunderbolt that could make you laugh and make you cry and leave you with insight. It *still* doesn't mean anything, because I'm not there to see your expression when it shoots across the sky."

He sags onto a sofa, suddenly exhausted, and talks from far away. "And so the work just disappears...the work doesn't mean anything....nothing means anything...."[1]

Despair comes to people when everything is wiped out, and they are left with literally nothing. And despair comes when people have an understanding as to how meaningless everything is if death can wipe out personality—"poof." Continuing life is a yearning that needs satisfaction. While cross-country skiing in the Engadine, my husband and I used to sit on a bench in the deep snow on a peninsula into the lake near Sils Marie, under a rock with a quote from Nietzsche inscribed on it. The view was breathtaking, too beautiful to stand if death was going to blot out beauty. Nietzsche spoke of beauty lusting for life. You see, ugliness brings despair, but beauty also brings despair. Beauty is often too much for a sensitive person to stand in the face of the existence of death.

Solomon, King David's son, contrasts his speaking of everything being meaningless without God, by speaking of the need in finding answers because there is God:

> Incline your ear to wisdom,
> And apply your heart to understanding;
> Yes, if you cry out for discernment,
> And lift up your voice for understanding,
> If you seek her as silver,
> And search for her as for hidden treasures;
> Then you will understand the fear of the LORD,
> And find the knowledge of God.
> For the LORD gives wisdom;
> From His mouth come knowledge and understanding. (Prov. 2:2–6)

---

1. Gary Smith, "The Lives and Deaths of Dustin Hoffman," *Rolling Stone*, February 3, 1983, 13. Copyright © Straight Arrow Pub., Inc. Used by permission.

For those who seek truth as a precious treasure, there is an understanding to be found, and a solution to be discovered that satisfies forever.

Franz Mohr, that overturned January, began the new year without noticing the change of years. There was no school, no job, and his full occupation was searching for food for his aunts and his family. There were a few potatoes and turnips to dig from some scraps of ground, and the forlorn gardens had some surviving beets and cabbages too. Under the aunts' cellar floor there were some canned goods to dig out.

The last day of February 1945, the Americans came into the town and began to dig out bodies which were under the rubble of houses. The charcoal collapsed when touched. These bodies were put with shovels into sacks and into crude coffins. The family stood near their razed house. The body of Peter was recognized by a few small signs; bodies of five others were gathered in the same sack and then in the coffin. They stood beside the box weeping and watching the Americans bulldozing a road through what had been the town main street past their house. Numbly with a deep fatigue they watched, while tears raced down their cheeks almost unnoticed. Peter. Neighbors. Everyone. Gone. A jeep stopped, and a huge American officer came up and stood beside them, holding their hands in his, weeping without words. They understood no English, he understood no German...they wept together without words.

As Franz told me, forty years later, he wept in remembrance and said, "It was heart meeting heart, in silence. The American formed words in English. The German formed words in German...and they understood without understanding! No language was needed to share a true sadness over Peter together. The American weeping over a dead son of an enemy! The German family weeping and holding hands with the enemy who killed him. How could it be? Only two months after it had happened! There was something beautiful!"

"Yes," I said. "My explanation is that it was a part of what I call the 'leftover beauty.' I am sure there is a terrific diversity of 'leftover beauty' in the midst of destruction. All God's creation has been vandalized. War is an expression of, or at times a necessity of, stopping the cruelty of a bully like Hitler to the Jews. But when the stopping had taken place, then that amazing thing you had just seen is possible...possible because of the 'leftover beauty' of compassion and kindness in the midst of the most impossible circumstances."

How gorgeous human beings would be if they were perfect! But they are not, and those glimpses of beauty in gentleness are not enough. The glimpses in the creativity of music are not enough to wipe out the other sins of a life.

My son-in-law, Udo, who was a five-year-old little German boy during this time, also knew American soldiers to be kind. As a young child he experienced the contrast between French Moroccan soldiers coming in as conquerors and the Americans. He said the Americans seemed to use the force they had in the line of duty to free the prisoners, or whatever, but that then they showed kindnesses and were friendly to children. Were Americans perfect? Far from it. But the difference of their coming from other ideas as a base, from a place where people mattered still, and human beings had value, and life had some worth, showed up in how they responded to people. This he told me when I related Franz Mohr's family experience on that memorable February 28!

May 7, 1945, was V-E Day. The war in Europe was officially over. Americans were celebrating in the streets of American cities, New York, St. Louis, Philadelphia, Boston, Washington, Los Angeles, Dallas. But in some places Americans were still dying. Embrace of human being for human being—killing of human being by human being. Love, gentleness, compassion—hate, violence, cruelty. WHY? Why the contrast? If Adam and Eve's choice was history, and not myth, the answer is clear. Adam and Eve already had been given love, beauty, gentleness, creativity, and life. They knew these things by experience. They could have passed them from generation to generation. But when they were tempted and chose that which introduced them to hate, ugliness, harshness, destructiveness, and death, they now by choice experienced these things, and passed them from generation to generation.

We have been affected by that choice and we have also made bad choices. We do know something of bits of "leftover beauty" in various areas, but we do not know by experience what perfection consists of. We may however have hope, and look forward to future perfection—forever! That too is a choice. Unhappily, many who are concerned about freedom for choice in today's world evade the consideration of the choice they have the freedom to make which will affect their own future history. Choices!

In the spring of 1945, Franz and his family moved back to the edge of their town, into a few rooms, without a roof. There were only a few people left. There was a garden behind this place which they cleared in order to grow some things.

With no school and no jobs, Franz and some new friends found some instruments and formed a band! It is incredible to watch human beings in history begin to have ideas in the midst of an agony of affliction. Affliction and suffering do not stamp out creativity, even when people have passed through despair! This band consisted of a violin, a guitar, a saxophone, a trumpet, clarinet, and drums. They named it "The Dixieland Jazz Band"—a teenaged German-American jazz band. And the war was not yet over! Talk about resiliency and adaptability. The imagination and resourcefulness of young creative minds even in the midst of stress beyond the comprehension of those who have never gone through severe disaster is amazing to contemplate. Competence shows up at such times! There is a determination as well as an ability to improvise and invent creative work, which shows up the most during depression—or during a devastating situation such as flood or war, drought or avalanche. Ingenuity that shows up then goes on in other parts of life to do a variety of things with expertise and skill.

As the Dixieland Jazz Band was practicing in the open, or in a roofless room, they of course could be heard! One day an American colonel and a black American driver overheard the jazz and stopped their car. They listened some more and engaged the band to come and play in the club for Americans. They were paid in cigarettes. The cigarettes sold for eight marks each at that time, so they had some money when it was impossible to have a job. The money meant that they could buy some food as there were some stores open.

All wells and all sources of drinking water had been destroyed, but as soon as the Americans came, they helped to bring drinking water. Living people were being given food and water—otherwise they would have starved to death. In spite of this provision by Americans, some of the young people began to form a communist party. The slogan "Workers of All Nations Unite and We Will Bring Peace" sounded good, so Franz drifted into that as the answer for which he was searching. All of his friends were atheists and communists. However, in spite of all his strong declarations disclaiming the existence of God, he felt uncomfortable with this solution.

I don't really have it all together—I don't have the answers, he kept thinking as he listened to what was being said.

One day, quite by accident, Franz came to a home where he had been invited by one of his jazz band friends. An Englishman named Dr. MacFarland, a dentist from Cardiff, was giving a Bible study. He spoke excellent German so Franz could understand the words, but he did not really understand anything. When it was over, the dentist tried to talk to Franz some more, one to one.

"I was very rude to him," Franz told me ruefully. "I said, what do *you* have to tell me? You are an Englishman, my enemy. What have *you* to say about God?"

"Franz, I tell you your heart is on fire with hate and only one person can change it—Jesus. I want to give you this Bible." (It was a German Martin Luther Bible.) "Read it, and write to me. I have put my address in it, and I will pray for you every day."

Franz went on remembering out loud, "His face was full of real love, and I couldn't handle it! I couldn't handle his quiet, loving manner, and so I couldn't say 'no' to his gift. I took it home expecting never to open it. I forgot everything he had said and taught that night and put the Bible on a shelf.

"However, through the next months one verse came back to me, and I didn't know where it came from. This kept going through my mind at odd times: 'Seek first the kingdom of God and His righteousness, and all these things shall be added to you.' I wonder...*seek*...I wonder, but no, there is no God. So...NO. Then I thought, but somebody has to react to war with love, to come with love to hate."

It was just at that time that Franz got word that his older brother, whom they had not seen or heard from, had been captured by the Soviets. He had been walking with the other prisoners through Hungary to a Russian prison camp, and had been shot, and left by the side of the road because he could not walk fast enough to suit them. The boy who brought the story to Franz said that the Russians simply shot anyone who fell down with fatigue or an injury or couldn't walk on at the pace they were going. Tony and others among those prisoners had been shot and kicked aside as a normal way of treating unimportant human beings.

Franz's heart fumed with hate, more hate, disturbing hate. But the basic questions kept coming. Where did human beings come from? Is there any meaning to life? Where did war begin? Why? Why are people cruel? He found no answers.

On Saturday nights the Dixieland Band had German engagements. In a small village near Duren, they had discovered a hall that had almost no roof left, with all the windows blown out and full of debris. By dint of hard work the band members cleaned this up, shoveling out debris, sweeping the floor, and made a makeshift platform. They made rough posters themselves, and put them up where the young people of the area could see them. The posters read something like this: "A Dance on Saturday Night—Dixieland Band playing." Franz says it couldn't have been a more pathetic attempt to provide a cheerful, sparkling, jubilant evening! But the young people came in droves. Of course it was not a big area, but it was full, Saturday night after Saturday night. The local priest made a remark in his sermon one Sunday, "A raw new young society is dancing on the bones of their comrades." Yes, the unburied dead were under rubble all around. Twenty-two thousand and many more had died in that area. They were not yet buried. Yet, has not history always gone on, dancing on the bones of the dead? How gruesome it is if that is all there is to life and if that is all there is to the future!

But the band was not deterred, nor were the young people. The debris was outside. They packed the hall so that the dancing did not consist of much movement. But music filled it. One of these Saturday nights Franz met Elizabeth, and a new kind of feeling filled his heart. He experienced a falling in love that was as real in that crowded, pitiful crush of people trying to have a good time as it would have been in a lovely apple orchard, or on a terrace of some beautiful home in the Bahamas! They became engaged. A new commitment for an expected future, for an expected beginning—not with thoughts of an ending!

It was soon after that (although about a year from the time he had received the gift) that Franz reached up to the shelf and began to read the Bible, starting in Genesis. "In the beginning God" is where it begins. That is the statement that gives the other alternative from "in the beginning, particles" or "in the beginning, nothing." Franz began to read, and to consider his basic questions. When he came to Cain and Abel he stopped in amazement and spoke out loud—to himself! "Murder—that's murder. Here is one family, and inside that one family you already have violence and murder. How can I blame God for war? Wow! It isn't God; it is man who is responsible. God made the earth for people, and people are killing people! Why, that family were the stewards of the earth. What an awful choice they made."

He read on until he came to Noah. He felt something of the reality of the sorrow of God seeing the whole earth filled with corruption and violence. He read of God's decision to put an end to it all with the flood, making a new start with the family of Noah. He read of how there was time for choice on the part of the jeering people who laughed at Noah for making a boat before the flood. The door was open for a period of time. But what struck Franz at the time was not the open door and the period of time for choice, but a sweeping realization that God was indeed a judge who knew people's lives. He stopped reading and began to think of what would happen if he were to be fairly judged for his own life and actions. He thought about standing before God and came to this conclusion. *I must better myself. I must live a better life.*

But he found that by making such a resolution, he did not have any way of keeping it. He simply could not keep his list of resolutions. *I have such hate inside me. I love Elizabeth, but that love does not stop my hate for other people. I cannot stop my hate with love. What shall I do? I am not able to change. And now I plan to begin a new family. I have no foundation to build on for a new beginning. I am miserable.*

Franz's nerves were on edge those days. He smoked heavily and had developed ulcers, and further nerves from the smoking. Often these physical problems kept him awake. It was during one of those sleepless nights that his unanswered questions kept pounding through his mind with an inward boring that seemed to be almost physically painful. He got out of bed, threw on some clothes, and went out into the woods to walk and think, run and think, on and on and on. When he came back into his room, it was after four-thirty, and day was breaking. Streaks of light on the horizon were turning the darkness into dawn.

Suddenly a new idea came into his mind, like the new day's dawn. "Why don't I pray? If God *is*, then He can hear me."

He swung out of bed onto his knees. But what should he say? He didn't want to recite the Roman Catholic prayers he had been taught in childhood. He just wanted to talk to God, if He existed. While he was trying to find words, the scene of the death of Jesus came into his mind, his memory. He had often wondered in childhood why it was Jesus had to cry, "My God, My God, why hast thou forsaken me?" while He was on the cross. He remembered those two thieves hanging on either side of Jesus, and that He had spoken to one of them saying, "Today, you will be with me in Paradise." *How amazing*, Franz thought. *Salvation must be free. The thief didn't have time to do any works.*

Now, he had never heard that. He had always been taught that good works would take him to heaven. It is hard for him to put this into words, but even forty years later the deep wonder is still there as he tells of the suddenness of the light of understanding. Like the sudden light of dawn, he saw. His "eyes of understanding were opened" like a curtain going up on the next act in a ballet. It was clear to him that salvation was a free gift, not to be paid for by good works, not to be paid for by purgatory. What happened was not an emotion. It brought emotion, but it was not an emotion. It was something that took place in his mind, with intelligence. His questions were being answered. There was a solution! The solution was available to him!

Yes, God will bring people before Him to judge, but there is an atonement for sin. From the beginning the solution was gradually unfolded. To Adam and Eve, to Abel, to Abraham, to Moses...the solution never changed. There was a lamb they presented as an atonement, looking forward to the coming Messiah, the Lamb of God, Who would one day be the atonement for all who believed and looked unto Him believing. This Messiah was to be of David's line, and to be born of a woman and to die for the sins of His people. He had to be alone because He was forsaken by God the Father as He took sin upon Himself. He was forsaken so that those who believe might never have to be forsaken. He was alone, so that we might never have to be alone. He died, so that life would be possible for those who would believe. He was raised from the dead, so that those who believe could one day have new bodies like His glorious body. He opened the door to eternal life and to the possibility of restoration and change of all that has been spoiled. His death was not a defeat, but a victory. Each despairing person who is bowed down with a sense of defeat may claim that victory.

No one had ever explained this to Franz. He did not have even one paragraph to read, like the one above, let alone a whole book giving a bird's eye view of the Bible, and a careful explanation of how to become a child of the living God, a believer, a Christian. No, Franz simply had this astonishing recognition of what the answer was—of how his own sin could be forgiven, and of how he could go on. He excitedly grew certain that Jesus had been alone on the cross for him. He believed that this death was for him and that therefore he was now a Christian.

He fell asleep for an hour, and then his mother came to waken him. "Franz, Franz...hurry, wake up." "Oh Mom," he said, eyes wide awake, all sleep gone. "I became a Christian last night!" "What on earth do you mean?" exclaimed his exasperated mother. "Why, you don't even go to church."

CHAPTER *10*

Tuning and Voicing—People and Pianos

Franz's mother's shrug of the shoulders and disbelieving scorn were followed by the worry of both parents as he continued to read his Bible. What he said to them conflicted with their doctrines. They soon invited priests to help them talk and argue with Franz as they kept telling him that he was crazy to believe he could go to heaven without going to purgatory or suffering more for his sins first. When he pointed out the wonder of what he had found in the free gift that Jesus had died to make available, his parents became more and more angry. He really was not ashamed of what he had come to believe as truth, and was thrilled to find the assurance given in Romans that salvation is for everyone who believes, for the Jew first, and also for the Greek (see Rom. 1:16).

It was a hard time for Franz. The amazing assurance that his questions were answered and that he now could have peace in a lasting way *inside* was combined with a turmoil stirred up *outside* by his parents. "You are crazy, Franz," they argued. "Even the Pope can't say he is going to heaven as soon as he dies."

His dad finally threw him out of their home. "Out, out, you go. I lost two sons in the war, now *you* are lost to us. Go now, go...go!"

He left with Elizabeth that day, and her parents took him in for a while. Then he went to Essen to visit Willy Blech, who he heard had become a Christian in prison camp in England. This was his first Christian friend. These two were a help to each other.

Music was now Franz's life. He felt he could not live without it. However, his wrist showed a weakness which made it impossible to go on with the violin. At this time he became an apprentice in the piano factory in Westphalia Schwelm—the Ibach Piano Manufacturing Company. This brought him close to his beloved music, as he learned to make an instrument other performers would play! Learning piano building in that factory combined his talents in music with the dexterity in his hands. As time went on he felt he had found what was perfect for him—learning to build a piano in school at night and working to tune pianos in the day. His studies in these two areas ended with final exams at the end of three and a half years. Passing with flying colors, he received a diploma for being a piano technician. He then had two more years of working there.

Coming to understand pianos as individual pianos is similar to coming to understand people as individuals! No two are alike and both time and sensitivity are needed, combined with an ingredient that does not come with teaching, but is something a person is born with. How can you define the differences between doctors all graduating from the same medical college and trained at the same clinic? How can you explain the difference between two talented artists, or sculptors, or cooks? There is a knack or a genius that emerges as a person lives and works, and suffers, develops and grows. A piano technician's expertise is one of those skills that differs from person to person and also develops with experience.

While his studies and work with pianos continued, Franz continued to visit Elizabeth at her parents' home. But he began to realize that he couldn't marry a non-Christian. That couldn't bring harmony, and also he grew to feel that it wouldn't be right. The evening came when, difficult though it was going to be, Franz decided he must talk to Elizabeth and break off their engagement. Mustering his courage that night Franz said, "Elizabeth, I *have* to talk to you." Her reply was a bit breathless. "But Franz I have to talk to *you*." He let her begin—happily! "You've been pestering me about reading the Bible, Franz. Now I want to tell you I've been reading John, the sixth chapter, over and over again, and I have come to believe that it is all *true*."

She had been reading about the time close to the Passover when Jesus had been talking to five thousand people on a mountain above the Sea of Tiberias. The day was growing late, and Jesus thought the people would have a long walk to get home—too long to go without food, so He asked for bread to feed them. Simon Peter's brother, Andrew, said there was a boy who had five barley loaves and two small fish, but he said it to indicate that what Jesus had asked was impossible.

Do you remember the story of the miracle of multiplying those small loaves to be sufficient to feed the whole crowd, with twelve baskets left over? If Jesus truly is the Messiah Moses had written about, it was no problem for Him to multiply bread in that fashion. Creation of bread in this way was similar to the providing of the manna in the wilderness, and whether it is manna, or bread, if the Creator of the universe is doing anything, there is nothing too hard for Him to do! The problem is not whether God the Father and His Son the Messiah *could* do such a thing—but a more basic one of the existence of God as first...and all else as having been created by Him.

Later on the other side of the Sea of Tiberias, people were looking for Jesus, and He told them that they were looking for more bread—a free handout. He made it clear that the important thing was not to find a free source of food which perishes, but to seek and find "the food which endures to everlasting life." Their reply was a question. "What shall we *do*, that we may work the works of God?" (This had been Franz's question too.)

Jesus' answer came firmly and concisely: "This is the work of God, that you believe in Him whom He sent." Later Jesus enlarged upon this and said, "I am the bread of life. He who comes to Me shall never hunger, and he who believes in Me shall never thirst."

Elizabeth had now come to believe *all* this, and had realized for herself what it was that Franz had been talking about so much—that it was necessary to *believe*. "Franz," she concluded, "I have become a Christian."

What Franz had to tell *her* changed radically after this, and a burst of music inside their heads accompanied their decision. They were going to get married, and very soon—the wedding date was set. I now know Elizabeth and I can see her eyes glowing, and her very special smile responding to Franz's own vivid joy. Franz's enthusiasm lights up his face, and his gestures are as eloquent as his words. The "inside music" would have spilled over to their friends.

The excitement they were sharing at that moment was not simply that of two people very much in love looking forward to physical and intellectual oneness for a lifetime of growing as personalities and of having new areas of interests and experiences; *but* it was an excitement over the fact that they *both* had come to realize that this fabulous gift of salvation was based on the death of Jesus, the Messiah Who had so long been promised. They realized that what Elizabeth had "seen and believed" in the book of John was the same thing Franz had come to see alone that dawn! It was what Jesus said in John 6,

"This is the work of God, that you believe in Him whom He sent." A gift of forever...free! A free gift of *life*.

Both sets of parents rejected them and would not come to the wedding on June 4, 1954. Only a few friends came. Willy Blech who had become a believer in prison camp was one of them. He had been taught by that special dentist in Cardiff, who had visited the prison camp. Some friends coming from Cardiff to visit Willy also came to Franz and Elizabeth's wedding. This gave it a beautiful continuity with the giving of that first Bible to young Franz, who now was twenty-six years old. The transformation of so much hate into loving forgiveness, the recognition of the Creator of beauty and the explanation of evil, the love of beauty in music and the desire to go on in that important circle of life made a very rare and beautiful beginning for these two standing to make their promises to begin their own family. However, the rejection by their parents cast a shadow on the joy, like a cloud drifting over the sun.

So many moments in life are happy but sad—or sad but happy. The fact that there is no perfection is not an academic discussion, but is constantly demonstrated in each of our hour-by-hour experiences with working in a career or living in the progressing history of personal relationships. Imperfection should not be allowed to erase joy, or response to beauty, or memory of a wonderful moment which cannot be repeated. A wedding day, or the moment of understanding the wonder of eternal life, or the birth of one's first child, or even the sharing of a flower or a sunset with another human being who responds with the same appreciation, is not something to be spoiled by imperfections. As if you were an artist making a sketch, erase the lines in your memory's sketch, and let the uniqueness, the unrepeatableness of the moment remain uncluttered.

In 1955, Franz quit Ibach and accepted a job with a Steinway dealer in Dusseldorf where the man for whom he would be working was also a concert manager, arranging concerts for musicians. So it was that after the first year of marriage, Franz began to have his first exposure to tuning and regulating pianos for concert pianists.

Franz and Elizabeth continued to attend the church in Essen where they were married since Dusseldorf is only a short distance from Essen. The Baptist churches in Germany had a publication with articles, news, and advertisements. Among other ads Franz repeatedly saw this: "ANYONE WANTING TO COME TO NEW YORK WRITE TO THE GERMAN EMANUEL BAPTIST CHURCH." He wrote a letter to the pastor, in his neat German handwriting, with the lines evenly spaced: "I am a piano tuner, a concert technician. Could I come to New York with my wife and children?"

The pastor called Steinway giving Franz's credentials, and got him a job right away. He wrote back with this news, and also with the news that there was an apartment ready and waiting for them. Franz and Elizabeth began to pray for assurance that this was the right thing to do. After their second boy, Michael, was born in 1962, they left for America with Peter, now two years old, and the new baby. It was five years later that the little family moved into the home in Lynbrook on Long Island where they still live, and where all three children grew up. Transplanting of trees and plants is an interesting thing to watch. "Root shock" differs from plant to plant, but if the soil is good and watering and proper care take place, plants often do better in the second location than they would if not given a new place. The transplanting of human beings is that way too if there is a conducive "soil" for roots to be put down, a spot in the sun with space enough to grow, and plenty of watering in the way of encouragement, incentive, scope for growth and productivity. When this happens, human beings often bring forth a greater harvest in a new location. It is well to remember that there is a God, the Master Gardener for His own plants, and when the Mohrs prayed for help in making that choice, they were putting themselves into His hands in this matter of transplanting.

Not too long after the marriage, there was a reconciliation between Franz and Elizabeth and their parents. A growing interest on the part of the parents led to their studying the Bible all together. So the communication across the ocean was a warm and very real continuity as a family.

When Franz prepared to come to America, the thing most important (so he thought) was to have translated into English (at great expense) all his credentials which proved that he was qualified! The papers included his certificates of piano building apprenticeships, diplomas from schools, everything he felt would prove his qualification. But when he presented himself and his papers to the vice president, he was told, "Just put those away, we'll see from your work what we need to see. You can start at the beginning." For two years Franz worked as a tuner and regulator in the rental division. He then was moved "up" into "the basement." The basement of the Steinway building on 57th Street is as far *up* as you can go in prestige as a concert piano technician.

Master concert technician at Steinway, William Hupfer, was a legend among top pianists. He was Paderewski's man. That is, he was the technician who was the choice of the famed Polish pianist, composer, and statesman. Paderewski made his debut as a pianist in Paris in 1888, in London in 1890, in New York in 1891. He became one of the most famous international pianists. (I'm giving you some facts to brush up your memory.) Paderewski began composing when he was six years old. At first he wrote mainly pianoforte solos based on songs and dances of the Polish Tara mountain dwellers. In the 1890s he wrote the violin sonata, the six Humoresques de Concert for pianoforte (no. 1 of which is the famous "Minuet in G," one of my earliest memories of childhood!). His opera *Manru* in 1900 had its first playing in Dresden, and then at the New York Metropolitan in 1902. In 1903 his sonata for pianoforte, twelve songs to French poems by Mendès and a set of Variations, was first performed in Boston. William Hupfer tuned, regulated, and voiced pianos in a way that Paderewski depended upon. Throughout those years William Hupfer was a very important factor in Paderewski's concerts.

The diversified life, the struggle to help his country and individual people, the burning zeal to right wrongs, and a variety of suffering are all part of the whole person—Paderewski. So often a name brings only one area of a person's life to mind. This man not only was an outstanding performer and composer, but he worked ceaselessly for the Polish cause, especially during the 1914–1918 war years. When Poland was created an independent nation in 1919 he became Prime Minister and Foreign Minister of the first government, but retired a year later after disagreement with other politicians. In 1922 he began to give recitals again to raise large amounts of money for war victims. He also established scholarships and sponsored several competitions, showing a concern for the next generation of musicians. It was in 1936, when Steinway 281261 was being purchased in Minneapolis and fifty years before this book would be published, that Paderewski appeared in a film, *The Moonlight Sonata*. He was in New York when he died in 1941—and Poland was again enslaved![1]

Delight and heartbreak, joy and sadness, victory and defeat—all have been mixed up in the music world, in compositions, and in performances, in the lives of all who are involved in the making of music. There is no more vivid arena in which to be conscious of the magnificence of human beings nor of the tragedy and horror of hu-

1. Michael Kennedy, *The Concise Oxford Dictionary of Music*, 3d ed. (New York: Oxford University Press, 1980), 754.

man beings, than in the creativity that has been given expression in music. In other words, the superb creation of creative human beings by the Creator can be recognized in the music human beings compose and perform. And yet the reality of the devastation of the Fall can also be heard in the music of those who have lived through the realities of the abnormality of history, not just in reading about it, but in their own lives.

The life and work of Paderewski portray something of what I'm attempting to deal with in this book. And the importance of his concert technician to his playing points up what this chapter is all about—the interdependence of our lives!

All this helps you to understand the enormity of this next factual sentence. In 1965 Franz Mohr took the place of the retiring William Hupfer in the Steinway basement. This meant not only that the historic, heavy, oak workbench of William Hupfer was given to him on which to carry on the work, but that the leadership, the honor, the responsibility, the sheer hard work passed to him also.

Although I spent five days with Elizabeth and Franz in their home in Lynbrook, talking over history and taking notes, as well as traveling each day to the Steinway basement, I'd like to quote from *The Lives of the Piano*, a book of essays by various people. Chapter four, by Dominique Browning, is "Finding the Sound" or "Portrait of a Master Technician."

> Since 1965 Franz Mohr has been the chief concert technician of Steinway and Sons. His job is to keep fine pianos alive. Mohr is one of a populous breed of craftsmen who build and maintain pianos in private homes, in music schools and in concert halls. His trade is widely malpracticed and misunderstood, but Mohr is universally regarded by his peers as a master. He presides over a legendary collection of artists' concert grands under the Steinway showroom on West Fifty-seventh Street in Manhattan, known among musicians all over the world simply as "the Basement." By the charter of William Steinway in 1865 any artist may borrow a piano to play in concert from the Basement (or one of the three hundred outlets across the United States) for the cost of the necessary tuning and round-trip carting.[2]

It was February 1985, when I visited Steinway Hall on West 57th Street for several days. Elizabeth and Franz had invited me to their

2. James R. Gaines, ed. *The Lives of the Piano* (New York: Harper and Row, 1981), 101.

home so that I could take notes as Franz told me the story of his life and be with their family and friends. However, except for Sunday which we spent at church and with friends, each day I was introduced to the life of a commuter. It was a fascinating opportunity to try out another lifestyle! We caught a 6:30 A.M. commuter train by running, but running slowly so as not to slip on ice, down the blocks to the commuter station. We then hurried to the ticket office. After being given the important bit of cardboard, we hurried up the outside stairway with an icy metal railing to grasp and found the best spot on the platform where long experience dictated that one might get on the train at a place where there *might* be a vacant seat!

So this is commuting from Long Island, I thought happily. *Now I am really a part of a throng of city people, all bumping, swaying, yawning, reading, sleeping, talking about what they did last night, and on their way to so many, many different kinds of work, occupations, jobs, positions, both creative and mundane.*

This is where Franz reads his Bible each day, while others sleep or read the morning paper or a book, talk, or stare at nothing. A half hour later we changed to a subway train with graffiti inside and out as if it were to be used in a film about New York and had been painted with an overexaggeration of graffiti. Not a spot was uncovered!

We walked through the crowded platform to first one stairway, then another. I would have been lost if I hadn't had someone to follow. Which exit? Which street? But soon we were out again, studying a cross section of early morning humanity, from actors studying script to businessmen trying to make a breakfast appointment, and tired-looking scrubwomen going home after their cleaning job. And who else? Impossible to know. The first stop was for breakfast. A Greek cafe smelled like coffee, toast and bacon; and the line-up of people ordering food to take to the office in paper bags left plenty of vacant tables. Never have I been served more rapidly. Within thirty seconds we had orange juice and coffee, and then our eggs and whole wheat toast appeared as if by magic. "Oh," remarked Franz, "they wouldn't have any business if they didn't serve rapidly. Everyone is so busy."

We wanted to get to the Steinway basement early for Franz's work day to begin and for my observation to include the whole day of changing scenes there. As again we hurried down the snowy, icy street, we didn't notice a man calling and running after us, not until we got to the end of the block. We then saw a waiter with his apron on, holding out something. My glasses! I had a surge of warm feeling about "leftover beauty." Here was beautiful thoughtfulness in a human being. *This* was New York, not a tiny Alpine village! I was not being mugged; I was being run after so my carelessness in leaving my glasses might not cause me a loss! A human being, being human, turned New York into a village.

We turned into the employees' entrance of Steinway and talked a moment to the night watchman, and then went on to the elevator where we shared space with a boy and his mop and pail of water plus cleaning fluid. "Hello—how much longer do you have?" "Oh just until about ten, I came on at three." He smiled and got off at the same spot. "Pleasant student, working his way through college," said Franz.

Every step of the way we stopped to say hello to someone. Franz introduced me to two secretaries in an office area. I lingered there to ask how long they had worked there, and how they liked it. Their replies were warm in praise of the Steinway company as a good place to work. They had worked a long time with the company. "And it really is just like a family. We have a good relationship with everyone. It is such a pleasant atmosphere to work in."

"Edith, look at this section of hall; it is a museum." I looked at trophies, pictures, and letters in glass cases, stopping to copy one as I remarked, "I love this one!"

From the Laboratory of:
Thomas A. Edison
Orange, New Jersey
June 2, 1890

Steinway & Son

Gents:

I have decided to keep your grand piano. For some reason unknown to me it gives better results than any so far tried. Please send bill with lowest price.

Yours,
Thomas A. Edison

We looked in several display rooms at pianos for sale, and at the oil paintings on the walls, and then made our way down to the basement again. Franz kept introducing me to people as we went, and also gave me a running explanation of all that surrounded us and of what goes on day by day.

We have fifty concert grands here in the basement to take care of the concert pianists. Often from Friday to Sunday night there are twenty-three, twenty-four, or twenty-five concerts for which we supply the pianos! The artists playing these come to the basement to pick out a piano. Each one is so different in his or her way of making a selection. One may decide on the first one. Another may play fifteen before then going back to the fifth or another one. Some artists come here to practice in the middle of the night, when the night watchman recognizes them and lets them in. There are always pianos being tuned and regulated and voiced after being chosen by an artist. Also there are always piano movers coming to wrap them in protective quilted material, and to carry them out to the trucks. This is a busy place, full of activity. All these pianos need the work of the four technicians in the Concert Department.

We were in the basement's main room now, where Ron Conners, Dan Jesse, Ludwig Tomescu, and Franz work together with an easy comradeship and harmony. An outstanding thing to me was the realization that each of them loves music. They also love these pianos almost as old personal friends whom they welcome back after concerts with a bit of anxiety to see whether any damage has been done in the journey.

"Hey, come over here and look at this," Ron and Ludwig called. We crossed over to look into a concert grand that had been played the night before. Something was pasted against a piece of wood. "Put there as a good luck talisman, I guess. Never saw that before," said Ron as he tore it off and rubbed off the sticky bit of adhesive with a forefinger. "What a lot of stories there are down here."

I walked back to Franz's corner to get out of the way as the men looked over their schedules and began the morning's work. I passed Ron's big workbench where he was carefully placing the insides of a piano which he had just lifted out of the concert grand he was working on. As the portion with the keys and action was arranged on his bench, he picked up tools to be ready for his next job—a silent one of working on the action. No sound here. Franz's bench was next to Ron's and I asked about the Perrier bottles standing in a row marked with numbers. "What is in the bottles?" "Oh," said Franz patiently, "number 1 is alcohol, number 2 is Afta—which is a cleaning fluid, actually alcohol and water—number 3 is benzene to take off finger marks from wood, and number 4 is the hammer juice, which we use to harden the felt on hammers to get a more brilliant tone, you know."

Franz Mohr applies his experienced touch to the tuning and regulating of a concert grand.

I settled down on the stool that was mine, and looked around with the same feeling one has when backstage looking up at pulleys and extra curtains, props and scenery. Here I was in *the basement*, the mecca of great pianists, and what was I seeing? Old desks and benches, workboxes with tools beloved by their owners, books of all sorts piled up with dog-eared telephone books on top, or in between. There were pictures over the workbenches of families, woods, lakes, Alps. There were an old refrigerator and a small old table near it with cans of coffee, paper filters, old piano legs, and stacks of yellowing newspapers.

And what was I hearing? "Bong, bong, bong, bong, bong, bong." A twist of a pin, a little bit to the left, a little bit to the right. "Bong, bong, bong." Another twist. "Bing, bing, bing, bing, bing." Another twist. And on and on and on—"bing, bing." Accuracy, precision, attempt for perfection, sensitivity to shades of difference.

"Did you see my new tuning hammer?" Franz asked Ron.

"Oh, I'm glad you got a good one with a good wooden handle. That plastic thing was a mess."

"That was just temporary—that plastic handle—it was because the other one—my good one—was lost. Now I am happy with this new one. The wood feels so great in my hand."

"Yes, don't you love the feel of good wood?"

The instrument called a tuning hammer really works like a wrench. It fits around the pin to turn it a tiny bit in one direction or another. The tuning hammer is made of metal, with a handle of another material, and both Franz and Ron agreed that the best material for a handle is a fine hardwood, smooth and pleasing to hold.

"Hey." Franz had a scrap of paper in his hand. "This says one of us has to be at the Met tomorrow to tune for the Beaux Arts Trio at 6 P.M. It's the evening concert at the Museum. Who'll do it?" "Jesse is busy, and I have to play in my church basketball game," says Ron, "but Ludwig has agreed. Right Ludwig?" "Yeah, yeah, I'll do it," says Ludwig, looking up from his work.

At this point six enormously tall and strong men came in carrying a grand piano wrapped in a green quilt. Placing it on its side, they proceeded to unwrap it, while another fellow put the legs back on. It was tilted up, and the technicians went over to look at it and to decide who would work on it and when. Jesse remarked that there is a new piano "over there," pointing, "that needs a *lot* of work."

Franz explained a bit more to me:

New pianos are *raw* and need breaking in. A new piano needs to become beautiful under your fingers. Each instrument is different in character. Woods are so different—not only is one kind of wood different from another, but no two trees are alike. So the woods are different from individual trees that differ from each other. This means that as pianos are different one must discover what they are good for. For instance, some pianos are good for Brahms, Tchaikovsky, Rachmaninoff—and others are not. You cannot make all instruments brilliant because they do not have it in them to be brilliant. To make a less capable piano too bright is to get something *harsh*. Your fingers must know how to tone to the best ability of your piano. You must really know your piano to bring out the best it is capable of.

This was Franz the master technician speaking with knowledge and understanding of his instruments and their varying capabilities. My mind went spinning around with some parallel thoughts—of pianos and people! When people put themselves in the hands of the Master Technician—that is, God their Savior and Creator—they may expect constant help. We go "out of tune," or become "harsh" so quickly. We need to come to the Master to be "tuned" with His strength put into us, substituted for our weakness. We are told in Zechariah 13:9 of being refined as silver is refined, and in Psalm 84:5, 7: "Blessed is the man whose strength is in You [the Lord],/ Whose heart is set on pilgrimage. . . . /They go from strength to strength;/ Every one of them appears before God in Zion."

Even as pianos need constant tuning and regulating—not only when young and raw, but all through their careers of being used for brilliant concerts—so people who are being used as "instruments of righteousness"—or, in other words, living creative, fruitful lives— need constant refreshing, "tuning." It came into my mind that receiving God's strength in our weakness as we call out to Him for help is very similar to a piano receiving new brilliance when the hammers are made harder with the proper juice or made softer and more mellow with some pricks of the needle-like instrument. Our "Master Technician," God, knows just what we need so that we are at times more "brilliant" for something we need to do, or more "mellow" or "soft" for other compositions we need to have come through us!

Jeremiah felt he had no "voice" with which to speak as God had asked him to speak. And God, in terms of piano technicians, "voiced" him for his difficult task of speaking with clarity.

"Ah, Lord God!
Behold, I cannot speak,
For I am a youth."
But the Lord said to me:
"Do not say, 'I am a youth,'
For you shall go to all to whom I send you,
And whatever I command you,
You shall speak.
Do not be afraid of their faces,
For I am with you to deliver you,"
Says the Lord.
Then the Lord put forth His hand and touched my mouth,
And the Lord said to me:
"Behold, I have put My words in your mouth." (Jer. 1:6-9)

God "voices" His children, His prophets, His creative people, to speak in various parts of history—even as a concert grand piano technician voices his instruments to bring forth compositions with clarity, according to the particular need.

In Ephesians 6:19-20, Paul asks for "voicing" in this respect:

[Pray] for me, that utterance may be given to me, that I may open my mouth boldly to make known the mystery of the gospel, for which I am an ambassador in chains; that in it I may speak boldly, as I ought to speak.

Paul did not act as if he had arrived at a finished state, with no need of help. He did not assume that because he had spoken well a day before, a week before, over and over again, that he would do well the next time. Our Master Technician must continually "tune" us, "tone regulate" us, "soften" us and remove some of the "harsh notes." We need "voicing" over and over again. We need to be cleansed of what is spoiling our beauty as instruments as well as being given the right work suited to our capacity as instruments. We are not to try to be prepared to bring forth that which we have not been made to do. As a flute, one can never be a piano; as a French horn, one can never be a harp. On the other hand, we are never finished products. Until the Messiah returns to change us in a twinkling of an eye to be perfect, we will always need the constant help of God our Helper and Master—even as a concert grand piano needs the constant, skillful help of the master technician. God alone really knows what our capabilities are, what is in us to be brought out.

As you sit listening to an orchestra, as the artists tune their own instruments, think of yourself being "tuned up" to be "in key," "in harmony," to be used in your place, wherever that is. Your part is important. Your coming in late, coming in early, hitting the wrong note, spoils the whole. You may think you are only an unimportant triangle in the percussion section, but the triangle is *important*. The portion that needs that triangle to blend in its voice is incomplete without the triangle being in tiptop readiness to make the composition complete!

There is an admonition in the book of Romans not to think of yourself more highly than you ought to think. It is a warning to be humble. However, a balance is needed. We are to *do* what God has for us to do with His special gift of "tuning" us for our part. Jeremiah was too quick to draw back and say, "I can't do it." But God pointed out that he could indeed do "it" with God's help. When Romans 12 goes on to speak of special gifts given us to really *do*, one is "the gift of encouragement."

What artist does not need someone to encourage him or her? This is an important gift. It needs to be well used. Artists, whether pianists, harpists, violinists, or painters, sculptors, film makers, architects, landscape gardeners, or curators of a museum, need someone to encourage them, as well as needing constant "using" of their "instruments." Another gift spoken of is contributing to the needs of others, which is an important thing indeed. You can contribute flowers or food, medical help or love expressed with a cup of orange juice or coffee or you can make a home that is an atmosphere for creativity. We need to be ready and enthusiastic to *do* what is given us to do, recognizing that our part of the symphony does not have to be the solo part to be important, significant, and essential to the satisfying completeness of the whole composition.

These thoughts were continuing as I watched Franz and Ron and Ludwig work with concentration. There was an endless repetition of chords in two keys and the soft swish of Scotch 3M on new strings. New strings? Yes, there was all that perfection in the factory, but now the strings needed polishing again before the final tuning and regulating. Ron looked up and pointed to a piano sitting in silence. "That one needs voicing. It is at a stage where it needs a *great* deal of expression." "Yes," replied Franz, not looking up from his work, "280 also needs tuning." Ludwig picked up a piece of paper with a notation on it. "This selection needs three pianos for a choice—that is, the selection for Corpus Christi, Texas."

They bent to their work again. The "insides" had been put back into the piano that Ron was working on and his "bing, bing, bing" was added to Franz's, and to Ludwig's oft repeated chords. Not many people could be patient with the monotony of those repeated notes—monotone, two-tone—over and over again. Impatient people without understanding would get irritated. "What is happening?" they would ask. "I can't stand the sharp staccato repetition. I want *music*."

The flow of beautiful music you hear at a concert, or on the record you play over and over again, or on the radio is a wonderful satisfaction *because* there has been sufficient preparation of the piano and other instruments, and a sufficient preparation of the performer. You are only hearing the results. The instrument itself and the tuner or technician have had to have patience not only to *do* the preparation, but to listen to the preparation!

In life people want a flow of *success* without having the harsh notes removed or the flaws corrected. The hammer-effect of unvaried repetitive notes as the piano is being prepared may affect your ears or your chest as a sounding board, but it is as *nothing* compared to you yourself being worked upon by the Master Technician! There is an important line to fit in here from James: "Count it all joy when you fall into various trials, knowing that the testing of your faith produces patience. But let patience have its perfect work, that you may be perfect and complete, lacking nothing" (James 1:2–4). What a hint of exciting results! There is something that might be lacking if impatience pushes every difficulty away, and ignores the rich possibility of results that are in store. There is something ahead of us which is similar to the opening night of a production, or the hush before the artist hits the first note of a piano concerto. There is something that will be so marvelous because of the preparation that we will have nothing in life to compare to it. All will be forgotten in that distant moment. After all the preparation is behind us, we will be put to a wonderful, fulfilling *use*.

We have something the piano doesn't have. We can talk to the Master and make requests of Him directly and He will respond, that is if we are His own—one of His people, one of His family in the same way Franz and Elizabeth became a part of His family. That freedom to make a request is also described in the book of James:

> If any of you lacks wisdom, let him ask of God, who gives to all liberally and without reproach, and it will be given to him. But let him ask in faith, with no doubting, for he who doubts is like a

wave of the sea driven and tossed by the wind. For let not that man suppose that he will receive anything from the Lord. (James 1:5–7)

This is a freedom given to ask for help during the "tunings" of life, and during times of confusion and need. But, as with any coming to God in prayer, there is a condition of coming. We must believe that He exists. In that same chapter in Hebrews where we found the sentence which tells the person honestly seeking for an explanation of the origin of the universe: "By faith we understand that the worlds were framed by the word of God, so that the things which are seen were not made of things which are visible" (Heb. 11:3), we find a few sentences later, "But without faith it is impossible to please Him, for he who comes to God must believe that He is, and that He is a rewarder of those who diligently seek Him" (Heb. 11:6).

We have amazingly more than our own talents, or capacities, or energies to count upon. We even have more than the "testings" and "tunings" can prepare us to do. We have the invitation to ask for help. The Creator of the universe can be called upon to give us His wisdom and strength—not in one huge whoosh like a waterfall, but a drop at a time like a transfusion. He says, "My strength is made perfect in weakness" (2 Cor. 12:9).

Ron and Ludwig sat at two shining concert grands placed very close together. The "bong bongs" were being synchronized, as were the repetitive chords, over and over again, with the twists of the tuning hammers—first one, then the other—then again, again, and again. Franz looked over from his work and then turned to where I was taking notes. "Edith, they are preparing two pianos for a concert. These must be tuned to play perfectly together. Carefully, shades of difference are being discovered, worked upon to be brought together to make them blend and be alike. *These* two must be blending as one! It will make such a difference in the concert."

It was time for lunch. "I'll bring in something," said Ron. "What'll it be? Soup or sandwich? Or both?" Suddenly the room became completely quiet as the fellows went out for food. Franz turned to wash his hands—then stopped to tell me about Dan Jesse. Dan grew up in a Chicago suburb. As a musician and tuner, he found his work upstairs at Steinway, which consisted of managing the rental of pianos, frustrating. Dan told Franz of his great desire to tune and that resulted in his becoming apprenticed to Franz to learn concert regulating and tuning. Now he is one of the top technicians. Franz went on speaking about pianos and his own feelings about the Steinway:

> To me there is nothing that is satisfying like the Steinway. Look, if you have five dollars, you cannot give six! So it is with a piano. It cannot give more than it has capacity to give. I say with great conviction that Steinway is satisfying because it gives me so much to work with. You know, I think if there are pianos in heaven, they will be Steinway! I really love them.

And he means it. As you look at the pictures of Franz, you cannot see him fairly because this man is so vivid and bursting with enthusiasm and excitement that you need a moving picture, not just a still, to see him as he is. It is amazing that after all he went through with the death of twenty-four thousand neighbors and almost everyone he knew personally, that the terrible bitterness is all gone. One's impression is of a very vivacious, dynamic, energetic personality who responds to beauty in music and people, and who has a love of his work, and an interest and admiration and appreciation for the artists for whom he so carefully regulates the pianos. How can it be? How could he care about anything after living through the horrors? And how did the hate which filled him depart and leave space for such a loving response to people and pianos?

Franz would say in reply, "Give the glory to God." He really loves God his Father and Jesus his Savior in a growing way—not in a static fashion. This is not "religion" to him, but a living, growing relationship with a personal God. To Franz, the Bible he read during his search as a boy is truly dependable and increasingly precious. To him it is the word of God, and trustworthy. He has always taught it, since first coming to believe. Therefore, he would attribute his own changed life and work to his continuity of communication with God in prayer, and the help of the communication of God to him through the written word, the Bible, as well as answers to his asking for help, in day-by-day living and working. It would be accurate to say that Franz, the master technician of Steinway, knows very well the daily tuning of his own life by the Master Tuner of people! That was an exciting discovery that I had not expected to make in the basement when I first thought about that famous place where the great artists expect to find a piano regulated precisely for their needs.

Ron had brought bean soup from the Greek restaurant, and I was soon eating it with a plastic spoon out of a paper cup, and enjoying it immensely! What a fun place to eat soup! I felt as if I really belonged. Ron Conners finished his first ten years as a Steinway technician in September, 1985. He is Franz Mohr's assistant and has a lovely home with two little boys who laugh from their pictures over their daddy's workbench. Ron's wife is the "curator of a museum of memories" for her children and husband, as she makes an exciting career of thinking of imaginative things for the family to do together which will be more valuable than a bank account! She also could be called an "ecologist who is interested in environment"—that is, the balanced environment of "family," the proper atmosphere for growing human beings!

As we were eating, Ron looked at the piano beside his bench and remarked, "It's amazing to think that there has been no real change in the piano for over a hundred years—and that it is still made by hand, and tuned by human hands, ears, brain, and skill." He went over to make a cup of coffee, patting the piano as he passed it, and I realized that all of this deep appreciation for the creativity of human beings was very real. The delight in being directly involved—with ears, brain, and skilled hands—brought a satisfaction of doing what human beings were created to have a capacity for doing. Since Ron was also a believer and in close communication with God, he expressed his appreciation and gratitude for this satisfying work to God—as well as to his colleagues.

As Ron and Franz went upstairs, Ludwig came over to the piano which Franz had been working on, and idly played it while saying, "It's getting so beautiful, this piano. The voice is so much better. I so like that piano. It grows." Then with a deep sigh, he said, "I cannot live without music, but being here is really contact with music all the time. Tuning comes fast to a good pianist. Then too, here I have contact with musicians, so it is good, good."

Ludwig went on to tell me something about himself. It was not a happy story, as it is always a torn feeling to have had to leave one's own roots or country. He had come out of Rumania where he was a concert pianist. A far-off look came in his eyes as he told about this—the look that people get when transporting themselves into another geographic spot, and back to another time. He had been at Steinway four years working under Franz Mohr. Franz had helped him to find a new meaning and purpose in life by introducing him to God, and to the base that gives understanding and help to life as it goes on in a new country, in the midst of a new work.

"Ludwig," I asked, "you were a concert pianist. Would you please play something for me during this last bit of the lunch break?"

"Oh, I am out of practice." (How familiar a remark!) "But..." And he began. Suddenly as the music burst forth from his strong, flexible fingers, I felt as if a mystical thing were happening. The Perrier bottles, the old newspapers, the workbenches, the tubular neon lighting, all seemed to fade away, and in their place I seemed to be in the front seat of a concert hall, listening to the opening bars of a marvelous program. Ludwig himself seemed to be touched by a wand so that his white work jacket and work-a-day clothing were changed into a formal suit, the tails out over the piano seat, and his white tie beneath his chin.

Just as I leaned back with shut eyes to revel in my concert, Ludwig broke the spell. "Aaaaa...I don't like this....Come over here." He jumped up, tried one piano after another for a few bars and remarked as to what he was looking for and not finding, until he suddenly hit upon one. "Here, this is it! Do you hear the difference? I will get a Mozart for you on this one." And he reached up to a shelf and brought down a pale grey-green Mozart book. Opening it, he began to play. "Americans—they don't play enough Mozart," he remarked as he went on.

I turned pages as he played and then Ron came to the doorway. "Your appointment with Mr. Gene Inman, the vice president, is *now*. After that, I want you to go over to Carnegie Hall with me. Franz will be taking you to Alice Tully Hall for you to watch him voice a piano for tonight's concert."

I waited for my private concert to come to its proper end and left the basement—looking forward to more!

When is forever music going to begin? Is it possible?

CHAPTER *11*

Form and Freedom for Diversity

We stood in the empty Carnegie Hall, listening to the Vienna Quintet as they practiced for their evening concert. It was overwhelming to hear such gorgeously beautiful sound in a totally empty hall with its wonderful acoustics. It seemed so much like a dream with the red velvet seats waiting for an audience to turn them down, and the chandeliers sparkling, and those artists playing away with such expression, that I almost felt I should stop breathing so I wouldn't break the spell! It was sheer magic to have a private concert in such a setting. Should I clap at the end?

Instead, we walked down the long empty aisle and thanked them verbally. Ron had brought me in the stage door, and I had been introduced to the manager. One of the benefits of being a concert technician is the "open sesame" effect from coming in and out of the great halls so constantly to tune and regulate pianos. The welcome is always immediate; here is someone who is always needed.

Always needed? Yes, there is a continuity in the need of a piano to be tuned and regulated. Although the concert grand has been tuned and regulated before being sent out of the factory, we have found that a new piano is too raw to be at its best! Much more work must be done on it in the basement. And even though the pianos are tuned and regulated in the basement before and after they are taken out to be used at concerts—chosen with great preciseness by the artists who are going to play them—yet *after* the pianos reach the concert halls they need further regulating and voicing.

Every instrument in a large symphony orchestra needs tuning just before the concert begins. Whether it is a small trio, a quintet, a chamber orchestra, or a very large symphony orchestra, you yourself have heard the tuning take place. The disadvantage of being a pianist is that it is impossible to carry one's own concert grand along to each place (except in very rare instances)! Therefore, the pianist is dependent upon the concert grand technician. That fine regulating must take place for every piano that is being played by an artist of the keyboards, whatever the program is to be, classical or jazz. This means that the men in the basement of Steinway do not stay there all the time. Each of them goes out to prepare a piano that is to be played that evening, in one hall or another. Sometimes that going out means going to another city or another country. It may be across the street to Carnegie Hall—or it may be across the sea to Japan!

However, since these human beings are finite, they can only tune and regulate and voice one piano at a time. It is a personal work, and *that* pair of hands and *that* brain and *those* ears are involved. If several pianos need to be cared for in one day, the technician must leave one to go to another! The staggering thing to realize about God, the Master Tuner of His people, is that He can be personally involved with the tuning and regulating of each one, standing beside each, doing a detailed regulating because of a harsh note, or a flat note just before each "performance." However *He* must be called upon, and utter dependence upon Him must be acknowledged. It doesn't happen automatically. The instrument itself—you or I—needs to call out for help. "Call to Me, and I will answer you, and show you," says the Lord.

> The Lord GOD has given Me
> The tongue of the learned,
> That I should know how to speak
> A word in season to him who is weary.
> He awakens Me morning by morning,
> He awakens my ear
> To hear as the learned. (Isa. 50:4)

Of course no illustration fits perfectly, but it is correct to see a parallel between a concert piano needing constant regulating, and believers, the children of the Heavenly Father, needing *constant* help to be rid of harsh notes, of ugly voices, of flat responses, of too sharp a blast. We each need individual attention and cleansing of secret faults, as well as God's strength given to us moment by moment if we are going to do what we have been prepared to do!

Are we talking about perfection being possible? No. Let me quote a short bit from an article entitled "Temperament":

> Temperament means an adjustment in tuning in order to get rid of gross inaccuracy in the intervals between certain notes—an adjustment by the distribution of the amount of this inaccuracy over the intervals in general (or some of them) so that small disturbance to the ear results.
>
> Any close discussion of the subject becomes inevitably highly mathematical....a glance at the pianoforte keyboard to include seven semitones if *really* a "perfect" one would include not an exact seven of our keyboard semitones but 7.019550008654 of them.[1]

It is fascinating to me to recognize that "perfection" is such a fine, *fine* point, that even in tuning an instrument it cannot be achieved down to the finest mathematical point. The skilled genius— genius in the area of hearing, as well as in working with sensitive fingers to regulate strings, or hammers, or keys—has a far greater capacity for recognizing both perfection and that which is slightly inaccurate. When you and I sit down to listen to a concert, we may feel it is all really "perfect"! But a person who is a top conductor, or a master technician, or anyone who is truly capable of highly trained listening, hears the tiny differences as if they were gross inaccuracies!

Now when you come to the standard set by God, it is perfection. It is even beyond that precise figure of 7.019550008654! It is perfection to the "nth" degree! God has an ear for the very slightest inaccuracy so that even the good things we do are tarnished with falseness in the motive, or give a flat note because of pride. But God does not say, "That's all right, I'll just let it go, and call it that which is the closest you can get." He has done something quite different for us, in that the substitutionary atonement of the Messiah, the Lamb of God, was the death of the One Person who had kept the law perfectly. The matter of substitution is a two-way thing—He died for us so that we might be given His perfection. That perfect life accrues to us. The standard hasn't been lowered or shifted to make allowances. The standard has been kept *for* us, to be given us as a gift! God, who knows the gross sin in each of our lives, has provided a way for us to be forgiven, or justified.

1. Scholes, *The Oxford Companion to Music*, 1012.

'hat about the "frequent tuning" then? Yes, the penalty for sin
:en cared for, but we need help to live "in tune" with God's
wuᵢu, and that takes frequent regulating, tuning, and voicing—
whatever we are, and whatever we are doing. In this age which
stresses being independent, we need to learn to be dependent on God.
We live in an environment that is not conducive to helping us stay in
tune. It is as if a piano were in the worst kind of atmospheric conditions to stay in tune. The drag on us is all the other way. We are
warned not to try to live without help.

The concert grand pianos and the leading artists who play them
depend on the skillful help of experienced technicians. And for important concerts, not only are pianos selected by the artists themselves from among the ones standing in the 57th Street basement, or
in some other supply location, but the chosen piano is then regulated
and voiced for that particular artist at the hall where it will be
played. It is not a general sort of preparation, but a specific preparation for the music that is to be played and for this particular artist's
style of playing. In other words, the master technician who is going
to accompany that piano to the concert hall and give it the final preparation needs to know both the piano *and* the artist.

Come with me to watch Franz Mohr regulating and voicing concert grand CD323. Ron has taken me back across the street to the
Steinway Hall, and Franz is ready now to go to Alice Tully Hall—"A
bit of a walk, but not really far enough to bother with a taxi. Do you
mind walking?" We stepped out into the chill February wind, pulling
our collars a bit farther up, and tugging at a scarf to shield the base of
the throat. The snow, in patches on the sidewalk, and a bit more
shoved against the curbs is all that is left of the storm that had made
Long Island like a fairyland on Sunday. As late afternoon will soon
blur into evening, the wet will soon become icy patches to be
avoided. We stop at curbs, hurry across streets before the light turns,
look at the beauty of Lincoln Center as we pass by. "There is the Met,
and we soon will be at the side door of Alice Tully....Over there is
Avery Fisher Hall. It will all look different tonight when all those
lights are on as we come back for the concert."

We walk in and quickly go around corners, through doors,
down and up. Franz, nodding at people, hurries to his place at the piano in the same way a doctor hurries to his last patient of the afternoon schedule. Having spent so many hours through the last years
with my husband as he was in and out of Mayo Clinic with his can-

cer, I am reminded of Dr. Petitt's compassionate concern as he would come to Fran's bed before going home for dinner—the last thing of the afternoon's schedule. Franz sat down, adjusted his stool, sat again, doctor-like with his proper lab jacket on, and doctor-like in his careful concern.

We were just behind the curtain shutting off the stage. The piano had not yet been moved out to its position. A tall man walked out of a control room, smiling a welcome. "This is Edith Schaeffer, a writer, and this is Selwyn Malin, the chief stage manager," Franz said as he introduced us. "Just call me the 'Head Stage Hand of Alice Tully,' " said Selwyn Malin laughingly as we shook hands. He moved a chair over so that I could sit and watch Franz work. "This 323," said Malin, "is the favorite of all the pianists; isn't that so, Franz?" "Yes, yes, it has a beautiful voice and is so responsive. It is the favorite of many," replied Franz as he opened his tool kit, much as a doctor would open his medical case. "I remember," reminisced Franz as he began to work, "that I once said to Rubinstein, 'Maestro, I want to explain this to you, you watch and I will tell you what I have to do.' And Rubinstein shook his head and backed away, 'Oh no, no, Franz,' he said, 'you are the doctor. You do your work, but I don't want to know about it. I only want to play the piano.'

"This young pianist, Cecile Licad, a girl from the Philippines, and the chamber music group from Marlboro who are playing tonight, will give us a great concert. I am glad you are going to hear it, Edith." This was Franz speaking, and then Mr. Malin went on to say with much feeling, "I really do think this girl is great. I was listening to her practice, and I had to go out to see who it was. Such strength, I thought, I wonder who it could be. It didn't seem possible! Really great."

As I watched Franz carefully twisting the tuning pin and listening with such concentration, I thought of the fact that this girl's notes depend on how expertly the piano is regulated. That idea of dependence swept over me in this setting in a very graphic and unforgettable way! "Her fingers cannot produce what is not there," Franz was saying. "In tune is in tune, flat is flat, in proper tone, in perfect voice—this is what I must do now for her." Yes, bright enough, soft enough, the just-rightness for *her* touch is *his* genius—behind *her* genius! How very necessary for human beings to learn graceful and grateful dependence rather than to push for awkward and ugly independence in the wrong areas of life. And what a lesson it becomes also for each believer who, like Abraham, has believed God and has become one of His children. Each believer must gracefully and gratefully ask for God's help and learn to depend upon it!

Selwyn Malin began talking to me again, and as we moved over to his room, he told me he used to be a bass player in an orchestra, but that he enjoys this present connection with music. "You know," he said, tossing his head in the direction of Franz, "that man is more than a technician. He really sees into the minds and feelings of the pianists. Some artists come in here—I have seen them—and put out their hands like this, with palms up, and say, 'There is something wrong with this piano, but I don't know what. There is something that doesn't suit me, but I can't tell you what. I don't know myself.' And you know what? Franz sits down and starts working, and he *knows*. I mean he really understands these artists, one by one, better than they understand themselves. He *feels* what is wrong. He realizes something and he goes on and adjusts it. He voices the piano and they are satisfied. They say, 'Oh Franz, this is right now. You have done it.' You know, that isn't something you can teach a man. It is something he has within himself. It is genius. That man is a genius. He's unique."

Selwyn then began to talk a bit about Mozart and Salieri. "You know, Beethoven thought Salieri was a first class composer. He was a composer in his own right. I personally think, however, that Salieri's blocking Mozart the way he did brought forth the music that Mozart wrote. I mean I really think Mozart did better in the midst of pressure and suffering. My own creative periods have come in the time of suffering."

That turned my mind to a very central ingredient or aspect of the history of music: music and affliction. It is true that much creative work has been done in the midst of affliction, suffering, and a deluge of difficulties. Not only is great music produced in the middle of the most impossible set of circumstances and physical weaknesses, but music can also be one of the greatest comforts and helps to people who are suffering, in illness, in sorrow, and even as death is approaching. Creativity is not cut off by affliction, nor are the results of creativity erased by affliction. Results can be lost or hidden for a long time. Recognition can come years later, but affliction itself is not that which blots out either creativity or the effect on other lives as a result of that creativity.

Take Franz Peter Schubert as a vivid example of this.

He was born in Vienna in 1797 and died there in 1828 at the age of only thirty-one. Schubert carried a torch at Beethoven's funeral and the next year was buried beside him. He left worldly property of the tiniest of value and a huge mass of lovely music— more perhaps than the world will ever have time to know.[2]

At the moment I am listening (as I write) to String Quintet in C Major, D.956 played by the Melos Quartet, Stuttgart, with Mstislav Rostropovich with his marvelous cello making the fifth. It happens to be a record that Fran and I often listened to in our Swiss chalet, and no matter what I was doing, in my cooking in the kitchen, talking to someone in front of the fire, making beds, or working in my office, when that part started—where the cello is plucked with its deep throaty tone—I would stop and sit on the stairs listening...with pain ...because it is almost too beautiful to bear. During Dr. Petitt's last visit to my husband, hours before he died, that music was on, and Dr. Petitt and I silently listened with appreciation of the poignant, excruciating beauty of that portion. This was the double reality of affliction and music. I was in the midst of the deepest affliction of my life, and Schubert had written this so close to his own death in the depths of a serious illness. The double reality struck me as the creativity which poured forth at that time in Schubert's life expressed what I was feeling. I was feeling deep abhorrence about the abomination of that enemy death, yet at the same time rejoicing in the beauty of hope—the hope of what is ahead, the certainty of "forever music" being a future reality. Pain and joy were mixed.

Let me quote John Warrack who has written on the record jacket:

> Schubert wrote his only String Quintet during the summer of 1828, probably in August and September. It was rehearsed in October; but he never heard a public performance of his work for he was already mortally ill. He died on November 19, and not until 1850 was anyone sufficiently interested to play what is now universally regarded as one of the greatest of all pieces of chamber music....(He used two violins, one viola, and two violincellos.) None of this accounts for the almost painful beauty of this music. In his last months Schubert was developing still deeper powers, and attempting to support his new ideas with greater technical resources....The final Allegretto has the ease of Schubert's sunniest

2. Ibid., 931.

music with its jogging rhythms and cheerful tone. However there are harmonic shadows crossing the music—the "doubt" of D flat—even in the last bars. The brightness of this music is the greater for its knowledge of the dark.

That description of this music is accurate to what one experiences in listening. How gorgeously it fits with the truth of the reality of darkness and light, the reality of the devastating horror of the Fall as death was being chosen, and the sublime magnificent choice on the part of the Messiah to die, that life might be chosen by anyone who came to believe. As volcanos roar, pouring their hot destructive lava down a mountainside, or as a flood treats houses like matchsticks, as fire rages through wooded lands of Florida or elsewhere, one longs for an ending of such dark shadows of the abnormal history. Understanding the dark results of the Fall brings the only possible true understanding of the marvelous wonder of the contrasting perfection of what has been made possible for the future. Being eternally safe can't be appreciated without some understanding of what the danger consisted.

As I stood in the office of Selwyn Malin, he continued to talk about how Schubert had not only a short but also a difficult life. "He was so poor that he hadn't paper on which to write his music, and used old envelopes and brown wrapping paper because he had to put it down somewhere, even though no one heard or saw it! I've made quite a study of his life and works. It has fascinated me to find that Arthur Sullivan (You probably know him as having written *H.M.S. Pinafore* in 1878 with Gilbert.) searched through Schubert's house some time after his death and discovered a stack of music in a cupboard on these scraps of paper—unsightly manuscripts, but wonderful music." It was, then, according to Selwyn Malin's information, Sullivan who published Schubert extensively.

Suddenly I needed to go back to my place beside Franz. He wanted to show me something of the finer points of voicing. The action portion of the piano was exposed as Franz bent over it. He hit a key and asked me to listen. Now listening consists of trying to hear with your own ears what someone else is hearing. As the key was touched softly and then more forcibly, I very well knew that what I was hearing was not what the exquisitely trained ears of Franz Mohr were hearing! "Do you hear that?" he asked me. "It is a bit harsh— not right—do you hear?" Did I? I am still not at all sure. I *thought* I heard something of that which he was describing, but had I? "Now I will fix it so that it will be right for her tonight." He picked up his instrument which had the fine needles coming out of it. He jabbed the hammer ever so gently and ever so precisely to make the felt more resilient and to change the sound in the direction he wanted to change it. He knew explicitly what he was listening for, as well as what these very exact jabs of the needles would produce. As far as the piano's preparation for a specific artist goes, Franz has "ears of understanding." It was a comfort to know that he really knew what he was producing as an end result, not simply working mechanically.

Asking for "ears of understanding" can be a prayer! I mean, we can ask, "Oh, Lord, give me ears of understanding to hear Your Word. Give me eyes of understanding to *really* see." We need understanding to discover and appreciate truth, and then to come to the God of all truth and place ourselves in His hands for continuous preparation for each performance.

We stepped to the front of the stage when Franz was satisfied with his results. We discussed the possibility of having a concert to present this book when it is finished, when it goes through the months of its preparation and is ready as a debutante to be presented. "Or would it be like a premiere of a film?" I asked. "Being presented for the first time?" "If you do it that way," said Selwyn Malin, "you must have a reception after the concert. Have it here and it would be just right—with cheese and drinks in the reception hall, and discussion. Who are you going to have?"

I shivered a little with anticipation and then shivered with the chill wind as we stepped outdoors again. This time we were headed for a Chinese restaurant, with a quick stop first to change and freshen up for the evening. A large round table was ready for us, and soon we were joined by Elizabeth, looking fresh and lovely in spite of having come straight from work, and Michael, the Mohrs' twenty-two-year-old son, and his wife Donna. "Michael, you look great," said his dad. "What suit is that?" "Don't you recognize your jacket, Dad? And this shirt? And this tie? You see, I came straight from work at the factory, and I had to borrow your clothes because your house was on the way. There was no time to go home first. Donna met me there." "Well, you look splendid," I said. "But," said his mother, "he wouldn't wear a coat. He's going to freeze."

Franz and Elizabeth's sons both work at Steinway, with much enthusiasm for carrying on in their father's footsteps. Michael was married to Donna a year earlier and is at present making soundboards for concert grand pianos. We had quite a chat together about Sitka spruce and the maple used for bridges. He is enthusiastic about wood and loves the rightness of the proper wood for each part of the piano as well as obviously enjoying the variety and beauty of wood. He will follow his father's thorough preparation in learning every stage of piano making before going on into the area of tuning. He wants a background of real understanding. Peter was not there that night, but he also works for Steinway in the engineering department. His work is in research and development. He and his Elizabeth have been married a couple of years. Peter is now twenty-four. It says something about a company to have sons so pleased to be at last involved—a continuity that gives stability.

The Mohrs' friends, Dr. and Mrs. Arthur Pellicane, came to be with us, too, and soon we were enjoying a variety of Chinese dishes, eating with chopsticks, ordering a special fried banana dish for dessert, talking about the wonder of a Creator who can be known, as well as about music, the making of instruments, wood—and the concert we were looking forward to. It seemed an appropriate celebration for the Chinese New Year!

We found our seats in the wood-paneled Alice Tully Hall and waited expectantly. Elizabeth was sitting next to me, and Franz and Michael were behind the stage, as Franz had made himself available in case of any sudden need. The Marlboro group was satisfyingly beautiful, and the young pianist, Cecile Licad, was really splendid. She gave us an excellent opportunity to hear concert grand 323 show much of its capabilities! Franz and Michael joined us during the intermission and then stayed with us, and it was a new experience to realize that as the piano was being played with skillful and talented hands, the person who could recognize just how right the notes were was sitting beside us, smiling in satisfaction over the fruits of his labor.

When we talk about bringing glory to God, perhaps this picture may come to your mind. Other people hear us, see us, and are aware of something of what we are doing, but since we are children of the living God, only God can have pleasure in our performance, being the One Who has given us His strength in our weakness and has answered our prayers for help to do what we are doing. In a very real way, He can have the satisfaction (if we do what He has prepared us to do) of a Master Technician whose people reflect Him in their performance. Oh yes, I know that so often we refer to the fact that "He is the Potter, and I am the clay," but as we have our minds and our ears, our emotions and our appreciation flooded with music, it is good to recognize in this context the reality of our being able to bring joy to the Creator of creativity.

There is a small book which tells what some artists say about pianos. The statistics show that although only a small percentage of pianos sold in America are Steinways, 95 percent of the classical artists prefer Steinway. So it is not surprising to find these comments in a Steinway publication called *Talking About Pianos*.[3] It is more interesting to read what the artists themselves say about pianos than to hear any report in someone else's words.

Rudolph Serkin

I like to play a piano that is beautiful all over, that has a singing quality and brilliance and evenness. If I'm playing a Brahms concerto, I try to find a piano with utmost power that is also tender and light. One should actually play a different piano for each composer on the program. But that's impossible, just as it's unthinkable to play a 100 percent good performance. If you can get 75 percent, I think that's great. I've played many pianos during my career, and for me, the Steinway has it all. Full richness of sound, delicacy, expressiveness—and volume and power.

Things happen in concerts each time that never happen again. I take certain liberties, small liberties with nuance. I try never to play the same. A good piano can contribute a lot. Sometimes it's hard to know whether one does it oneself or if it just happens.

I'm lucky because I've never felt that the music is not fresh. For me it's always like a first time. The piano I have now is very beautiful, one of the most beautiful I have ever played. We are still discovering each other.

Eugene List

Pianists are always talking about "singing instruments." Naturally I don't think of the piano as a singing instrument because once the sound is produced it begins to die. We cannot sustain a tone or swell on it; we always have to fight against tone decay. But with the use of the pedal, and a beautifully resonant instrument

---

3. Corby Kummer, ed., *Talking About Pianos* (New York: Steinway and Sons, 1982).

with a beautiful tone, we can create the illusion that it is a singing instrument. The greatest pianists would make you swear that the piano is singing.

I think we all have an ideal of a piano in our head. It conforms very closely to what our own idea about playing is, and we like to stress in our playing the features that most appeal to us. If you are a poetic player you want a piano with a beautifully modulated tone that has all degrees of brilliance and tenderness. If you're a brilliant player you want a piano that will really deliver the brilliant message. I think actually we're all a combination of the best elements. We all know what we like and which instruments we're most successful with because the instrument, when it's performed on, takes the coloration of the artist.

I like a piano with a beautiful sound that is not strident in *fortissimo*, and not so inaudible that the people out front won't hear it. We all like a different degree of resistance. I remember an article in which Benny Goodman's pianist said, "I like a piano that fights back a little bit." I know what he means. You don't want to just blow on the keys and have them go down. You like to have the feeling that you're controlling it.

I also like a piano that has balance. Some pianos are too strong in the bass, which is always a problem because the bass strings are so much longer, and have a lot more power with a lot less effort. You're constantly balancing the treble against the bass.

I think that universities and conservatories don't always protect their good pianos, which sit out where anybody can bang on them. It's incredible what people do to pianos. They use them as ashtrays, spill drinks in them, flick their cigar ashes and throw cigarette butts in them. You always see the sides of pianos burned where people left cigarettes, and rings where they left drinks sitting. It hurts me. I think of the piano as a living thing.

Horacio Gutierrez

It sounds funny, but I really feel like a doctor. They say that by just examining the patient briefly, by looking and feeling, a good doctor can tell what's wrong; by just touching and listening I can tell very soon how good a piano is. I have to play only two notes. Seldom have I been fooled. When you play a note it has a kind of blossoming after it's struck. Hearing and judging it is an acquired instinct. It's very personal in most cases, but I think that every great pianist will agree about a really great piano.

I think the kiss of death for any pianist is a dull piano. You can tone down even the most brilliant, awful piano if you have enough control and technique. But a dead piano is hopeless, especially if you're trying to be heard through an orchestra.

Paul Schenly

No instrument can project what you hear in your mind. The minute you think of a performance and of making people in the last row hear what you're playing at its softest, you're setting limits that don't exist in your mind....But every piano is different, and the music that comes out is like a ray of light that takes on the color of the glass through which it passes. The way I judge my favorite piano, after picking a beautiful sound and voicing, is by the pedals. To me they are the miracle of the piano, and that's what I love about a Steinway. You can do things with the pedals that you can't do with any other instrument. That's why a Steinway can adapt itself to more different types of composers and shadings than any other piano I've played.

Andre Watts

I view the piano as a friend. It's both an extension and a partner. The piano is there to be manipulated by the artist, but it also has its own personality that you can only alter to a certain degree. Some pianos are very aggressive, for instance, and not prone to smile. Some are like very old people whose faces show lines of a life that has been rough and beautiful: there's a wonderful aliveness beneath a battered surface. Then there is a brand-new piano that is like a person who is extremely competent but who has no soul. I could make a fool of myself with characterizations of pianos. But they are like people.

It's practically impossible to make a pianist genuinely happy with a piano. He always wants an escape hatch, a way to blame the piano for something he's unhappy with. Let's say you get these great pianists and put them down in front of an impossibly bad piano. One will say, "This piano is terrible, I can't play on it," and he will get no music out of it. Another will say, "Oh, well, bad piano, just another concert," and it won't sound so terrible, but it won't be very exciting, either. Someone else will say, "Bad piano, but you know right here is a beautiful place and if you trill here it sounds fantastic," and maybe in that person's recital there will be a moment of magic.

I don't like to practice on a wonderful piano because I'll get very happy and then die on the road. But I do like a good piano. You have to stretch your limits and explore what qualities you can get from certain passages. Sometimes when you come to an extraordinary piano you find that an effect you were aiming at, but not achieving, suddenly comes easily. You get other ideas because of the beauty, and every idea will help your conception of the piece, even if the next piano you play isn't as good. For example, before I was 16 the piano I played had 26 strings missing. I wouldn't recommend that to anyone—it's a terrible situation, there's a lot you can't hear. But when I started playing concerts and expected the pianos to be wonderful, I wasn't knocked flat when they weren't.

Ilana Vered

I don't think it's a good idea to sit at home and play one piano forever, learning how to manipulate it and make it respond to you. When you go out on tour it's like a jungle. I like to go down to the Steinway basement just to play other pianos so I won't get the response I'm used to. An artist has to play as often as he can on as many pianos as he can. No two pianos are ever alike.

Vladimir Horowitz

You can't play the piano in black and white, just as it is. The ideal artist knows how to produce the most colors. The piano is a tool. It's a dead instrument, a piece of wood. We have to extract something from it. The piano is my mouth, my ear, my heart, my head. It gives me freedom. I can talk through it to my audience. I look for continuity of tone, which is a matter of adjusting the dampers, and for proper adjustment of the pedal, which is the heart of the piano, like our heart beating. Before I traveled with my own piano I would play in small towns and a string would go out. That can happen any time. But once in the '40s the pedal went off in the middle of the concert. There was no technician, so they closed the curtain and my wife fixed it herself. Now I don't go to very small towns. I have my own piano—I am very attached to it, I know it. When I left Russia for Berlin in 1925, I went to all the makers and tried all the pianos. I struck on Steinway and I never changed. Never.

Perhaps you will be able to hear Horowitz as he plays in his own home, as that has been filmed. Franz Mohr was his tuner during that film making, adjusting the piano whenever it needed it.

Franz Mohr's work takes him to very distant places at times. When Horowitz gave concerts in Japan, Franz Mohr accompanied him in order to adjust the piano constantly. When Van Cliburn played in the White House during Ford's administration, it was Franz Mohr again who was there, to tune and voice the piano.

The occasion in the White House was a reception for the Japanese Emperor. Franz had rented a formal suit for the evening, and was hurrying to put it on in his hotel, after having prepared the piano. He discovered that there was no tie in the box. It was after closing time and so he could not get one from the supply place. He asked hotel waiters if he could borrow a tie, but no one had a white tie. Where could he get a white tie to be properly attired for that formal occasion?

Suddenly he thought of making one! Being a resourceful man, he searched for a drug store nearby, bought the best white men's handkerchief it had, and also got a needle and white thread. Anxiously looking at his watch, he hurried to fashion a white bow tie so that it could be arranged under the collar and fastened at the back. "Hurry, hurry...ahhhhhh...there it is, now to put it on and adjust it," he whispered to himself as he took the final stitch. A knock at the door—"The limousine has arrived"—precluded any more time to adjust his handiwork. A glance in the mirror showed the results. It was a bow tie all right, but it was double the usual size! It looked something like a clown's exaggerated bow. There was no time to do anything about it. He had to go off to the White House to stand for pictures with the Japanese Emperor, the President of the United States and the First Lady, Cliburn, and Henry Kissinger, among others. Franz can be found easily in pictures of the evening with the bow tie, like a signature with an extra flourish, under his chin!

Franz was chosen by Arthur Rubinstein to travel with him, to tune and tone-regulate his piano before concerts. Rubinstein claimed that pianos have such distinct personalities but that he could recognize one among a dozen. Actually once when his own concert grand

Van Cliburn performs at the White House reception for the Japanese Emperor. Franz Mohr, wearing a hastily fashioned white tie, is seen between Betty Ford and the Emperor.

was repaired in Hamburg, they lined it up with fifteen, and told him to try to find his. After trying six or seven, he stopped at one he had begun playing and said, "This is it"—like a mother knowing the personality of a twin!

Dependence on a good technician includes taking the technician with the piano or the pianist to many scattered places. For seven years Franz (and Elizabeth was included in these special trips) went on a concert cruise. A shipping company had special cruises in the Bahamas, through the Caribbean and to South America, with excellent musicians giving chamber music each evening on board and sometimes on shore. Franz tuned and adjusted the concert grand, and also a harpsichord in these unusual and exotic locations.

Once again we need to be reminded that human beings are finite. No human being—no matter how badly one is needed for special work or longed for because "no one else can supply what you can"— is able to be in two places at once. Finiteness is limiting, no matter what skills one has to contribute or how much welcome there is awaiting someone thousands of miles away! To be on a cruise for the sake of those particular artists and those specific instruments is to *not* be in New York in the Steinway basement. Choices are essential to each of us in using that precious commodity—time—as well as energy and skills.

That kind of choice does not have to be made by the *infinite* God. If indeed there is a Creator of creativity, a Creator of creative people, He then knows us as individual personalities—no two of us are alike. He knows us better than Rubinstein knew his own piano. He not only knows us, but being infinite, He is available without having to neglect someone else, and without having to leave a location to choose to come to us.

This is what Moses said to Joshua, and it is a promise down through the centuries: "Be strong and of good courage, do not fear nor be afraid of them; for the LORD your God, He is the One who goes with you. He will not leave you nor forsake you" (Deut. 31:6).

After Moses' death, the Lord spoke directly to Joshua with a forceful condition. God's being with His people is not automatic, but depends on the honesty and sincerity of our search for Him and our turning to Him and His word, rather than to false teaching and lies. A turning to God carries with it a turning away from false gods. There is no neutral "no man's land." God promised Joshua He would be with him as He was with Moses, but cautions him not to turn away from the law.

This Book of the Law [the Bible, Scriptures] shall not depart from your mouth, but you shall meditate in it day and night, that you may observe to do according to all that is written in it. For then you will make your way prosperous....Have I not commanded you? Be strong and of good courage; do not be afraid, nor be dismayed, for the LORD your God is with you wherever you go. (Josh. 1:8–9)

In the book of Hebrews (13:5–6) the promise recurs, "He Himself has said, 'I will never leave you nor forsake you.' So we may boldly say: 'The LORD is my helper; I will not fear. What can man do to me?' "

Yes, we are allowed to boldly claim that our Master Technician will go with us by land or by sea! He is able to care for our needs and respond to our cry without needing to choose to leave other people, or locations to do so!

Diversity is the marvel of the Creator's universe! We are constantly staggered, as well as enchanted, by the enormousness of diversity. A lifetime is far too short to discover the diversity that there is in *any* area of nature, science or the arts, whether by reading books about what other people have accomplished or found out, or by totally original search. From snowflakes to planets, from flowers to animals, from rock formations to oceans' depths of surprise, from pianos to people...there are so many examples of diversity! That certainly is true of music. What is touched upon in this book is only a scratch on the surface of what could be written, discovered, experienced, discussed, searched for about music during one's own lifetime, let alone through history.

Many books have been written about jazz and its place in history, as well as in the lives and affection of many people in many of the world's locations. What I am about to say cannot be fair because it will be too short. On the other hand, to write about Model S baby grand Steinway 281261, now about to have its fiftieth birthday, and not to mention jazz, would be unfair to that piano personally, as well as to all other pianos! Pianos *can* play a variety of jazz, rock, and country.

I was coming home from New York to Minneapolis. My notebook was crammed with notes taken by hand. My attention was on reading over my notes, thinking in sentences and paragraphs and chapters, when my ear caught snatches of words and sentences of a conversation just in front of me, hidden by the backs of the seats.

I couldn't see the speaker, and then I realized it was because he was so small that he took up very little space. His conversation was an involved one about real estate, descriptions of land and houses and prices. I was astonished at the vivid interest and strong involvement as well as the tone of authority coming from this very small person who must have some disability. *Shall I speak or not? Would it seem presumptuous on my part to speak of my admiration for someone who obviously was getting right on with a positive direction in life, rather than "giving up" because of a handicap? Oh no, I'd better not say anything.* Before landing, I could resist no longer. I simply had to say, "I do admire you."

Now if I had been my daughter Priscilla, I would have known who it was I was about to speak to, since she has studied jazz and rock music, has not only collections of records, but lectures on the subjects, and lives in Huemoz, Switzerland, where she is very near to Montreux and Claude Nobs's famous Montreux Jazz Festival. Actually, year by year there a few jazz musicians who make it up the winding mountain road to listen, discuss in Chalet Tzi No, or to give a concert at L'Abri just for the pleasure of being with a smaller responsive audience, and for the reality of a philosophic discussion a bit away from the festival! But Priscilla was not there to recognize this young man whom she had heard in Montreux. Instead, it was the very less knowledgeable me!

"Excuse me—but I just wanted to say that I do admire you." What should I say next? "I've just come from Steinway in New York and I am writing a book about pianos—and—well, it's called *Forever Music.*" The handsome girl beside him spoke up at that point, "This is Michel Petrucciani, and..." "I am a Steinway artist. I practice there and use Steinway pianos for my concerts," said Michel.

Thus began a rather amazing conversation with this young and remarkable French-born jazz pianist and his manager. It turned out that he was giving a concert in the Walker Museum that night in Minneapolis, and they invited me to come along, if possible. Anne and Suzie were meeting me and their interest in jazz and the fact that all three of us had no pressing reason to return immediately caused us to search for a place to eat, and then to line up for tickets, as the concert had been sold out. Just before it started, Michel himself, along with his manager, came into the lobby and greeted us warmly with smiles, and then with complimentary tickets. So we *did* have the treat of hearing him.

It was an amazing experience to hear such power come from this twenty-two-year-old man, only three feet tall, whose body has been hindered from growth and strength by a disease he was born with called "osteogenesis imperfecta," which had caused about 160 broken bones in his growing up years. He weighs only fifty pounds, but the power in his hands and arms with which he produces the music that comes from his brain—so that it can be heard in the audiences' brains through the ears—is incredible! However, it would be just as incredible if he were six feet tall and weighed four times that much. Let me quote from a jazz review by Leonard Feather.

> The biggest new talent in piano jazz this year will also turn out to have been the smallest. Big, because he brings to his keyboard artistry the harmonic subtlety of a Bill Evans melded with the rhythmic dynamism of a McCoy Tyner, and has created from these and other elements a style of his own. Small, because Michel Petrucciani...stands all of three feet tall and weighs fifty pounds. He is the embodiment of what is known in Latin as *multum in parvo....* "My father was born in France and now lives there in Toulon." But his father was Sicilian. He was a tailor and didn't like it, so he just took a walk, literally, all the way north to the border and into France. "I was born in Orange, France, but I lived for ten years in Montelimar, near Avignon. I studied classical music there for seven years, but we also had a family band with my father on piano, my brother on bass, and I played drums, just for fun. I finally decided to quit classical music....My father got really mad, but...people like Mozart and Beethoven and those guys, they were jazzmen in the sense that they improvised, so I just wanted to improvise too."[4]

For just a moment think of the discussion about "quality of life" and that decision which certain parents and medical people think of as being "compassionate"! Not only has Petrucciani taken part in jazz festivals in Vienna, Pori, the Hague, Copenhagen, Montreux, and Lugano—as well as New York and Japan, not only has he made LPs, not only is he married, but you should hear what he himself says about whether his life has sufficiently high "quality" to be glad he is alive! A lot of people in today's strange discussions about "medical ethics" would be very glad for his parents and his doctor who saw the great value of his life and fought for it.

4. Leonard Feather, "A Big Pianist in a Small Package," *The Los Angeles Times*, April 24, 1983, 63.

Petrucciani refuses to believe that his crippling condition will have much effect on his plans. "Oh, man I don't let that bother me. Erlinda [his wife] is a wonderful help, and she's really my road manager as well as my wife. In my case I just don't believe the condition is really all that bad. I mean, I've had it all my life, and I sure had it bad enough, but I know people who have died from it. Me, I'm not going to die."[5]

When I was talking to Dan Jesse on the phone the other day, I asked about Michel Petrucciani, and he said, "Oh yes, I tuned for him once and listened to his playing. He really is fabulous. We supply pianos for his concerts."

I don't think that meeting on the plane was accidental! It was another part of my education! You see, so often a plane turns out to be a specialized classroom in my traveling graduate school.

Monty Alexander is another jazz pianist who loves Steinway grands. Monty was born in Jamaica to a mother who recognized the value of giving him music lessons. He had started to play the piano at the age of five with lessons, and to play well. His background was all in classical music, and he took part in concerts at an early age. At the age of twelve he began to listen to jazz and fell in love with it. His mother recently told me that his admiration for Louis Armstrong and Oscar Peterson influenced him a great deal. She said that these and other great performers also encouraged him to go on in jazz. Monty organized a school band in Jamaica and was prominently active in jazz concerts. He was seventeen when they moved to Miami. If you haven't heard of Monty Alexander, there is an interesting fact to remember. Jazz is more well-known in Europe than in America, as Hans Rookmaaker could have told you. Dr. Hans Rookmaaker, in addition to being the head of the History of Art Department of the Free University of Amsterdam, also wrote jackets for jazz records as he was an expert on the history of jazz. For some reason people who are big in Europe are not as well-known in America. However Monty has not only played in the Montreux Jazz Festival and in various festivals in Holland, he had many LPs you could choose from. Monty Alexander was chosen as one of the top favorites of Oscar Peterson's School of Music.

So often the diversity of music is given to people by versatile performers, with a wide variety of surprises in their personalities as well

5. Ibid.

as in their abilities to be adaptable. It is delightful to listen to Claude Bolling, the French pianist, and Pinchas Zukerman, at present the conductor of the St. Paul Chamber Orchestra, as well as one of the world's great violinists, enjoying themselves as they play "Suite pour Violin et Piano-Jazz Trio" (the bass is played by Max Hedguer, the drums by Marcel Sabiani). I'll quote the jacket paragraph for you:

> This is not the first but the fourth time that Claude Bolling has featured two opposing styles. Here it is Pinchas Zukerman who has commissioned this suite for violin and jazz piano from Claude Bolling. This wizard of the violin and alto enchants us with the limpid beauty of his sonority. What a treasure trove! This suite for violin and jazz piano, of tremendous musical richness, is made up of quick witted dialogues in which the instruments converse with a rare mastery and elegance. Yet another gamble had paid off! Or in French: Encore un pari de gagne!

Music is needed to help us feel comforted, at home, in touch with that which is familiar to us. To recognize a piece of music we have heard in the past under happy circumstances is to feel a warmth and glow that we may not analyze, but which is helpful in comforting us if we happen to be homesick or lonely. To hear familiar snatches of a folk song, or ethnic tunes that belong to us in some way, brings a response that is deeper than the response to smells, colors and textures—though perhaps no deeper than response to a sudden view of familiar mountains, lakes, rivers or the sea if we have been away from these for long periods. To be swept with the crescendo of our favorite composer as played by our favorite chamber orchestra, or band, or symphony, or pianist, or recorder is to be carried along on a wave of reminiscence that is the closest thing to being able to relive past times. The blend with another moment of history comes with the music so that time itself is seemingly being stretched! We wait for a phrase, a series of notes, a silence, a burst of drums, a sweet flute solo, a plucking of strings, and when it comes we feel satisfaction that cannot take place in silence.

Forever music. Can it be? What is ahead? What does the Creator of the universe say about music in the future? We who have had nursery songs, lullabies, Hungarian dances, and psalms sung to us, minor music, major music, Israeli music, Chinese music, Scottish bagpipes, enormous organs, great cantatas, symphonies, jazz, rock, funeral music, circus music, Irish jigs, romantic ballets, operas, church music...is there only silence ahead?

Or, is there *greater* sound? Is there greater music than anyone has ever heard in his mind or ears on this planet, being prepared for a future beginning?

CHAPTER *12*

Forever Music

O ne day the clock will strike for me, for you. Will we be suddenly ushered into our place in the auditorium, a dazzling one with perfect acoustics where we will hear music greater than anything ears have ever heard before? That is a hope that has substance and foundation based not on some human being's lively imagination, but on information that is reliable, and on promises from One Who speaks truth. God makes it plain that there is something being prepared for people who love Him—something that is more wonderful to be seen than eyes have ever seen, and something more wonderful to be heard than ears have ever heard before. It will be more wonderful than anything that has ever entered the imagination of human beings. This is to be future reality. This promise does not refer to some vague, nebulous, spiritual happening, but to something we *need* eyes and ears to experience, something that needs to be experienced in our bodies.

Is creativity enough in itself to satisfy human beings? The temporary, fleeting aspect of life and work, which so rightly bothers Dustin Hoffman and others, gives rise to a huge question mark in the midst of this abnormal history. What are life and work worth?

Vincent van Gogh wrote to his brother:

Oh, my dear brother, sometimes I know so well what I want. I can very well do without God both in my life and in my painting, but I cannot, ill as I am, do without something which is greater than I, which is my life—the power to create. And if frustrated in physical power, a man tries to create thoughts instead of children, he is still part of humanity.[1]

Does the power to create equal humanity? What about the Creator without Whom there is no satisfying *source* for creativity? Is there something "greater than I"? What a feeble exchange, exchanging dependence upon God for independence, to go through life, and illness and death rejecting the God who is there, rejecting the Creator who created people in His image so that they could create. It is the clay revolting against the potter; it is the wax or the marble revolting against the sculptor; it is the paint revolting against the painter. It is independence rearing an ugly as well as illogical head to scream, "My head is bloody but unbowed" and to declare, "I will never, never bow. I would rather be lost than to bow as a creature before the Creator." You are invited to turn away from revolt and to come to a concert which is a part of forever music.

Who invites us to this concert which is so complete, so perfect, so specifically a part of the future?

Who can assure you of a ticket that will be honored with a reservation?

Who has the power to use the word *forever* as a promise with meaning, because truth exists?

The answer is *The Messiah*. That is Who is able to do all things well and His promises and invitation to forever life and forever music should be taken seriously indeed. He has paid a costly price for the validity of the invitation.

The fabulous oratorio, *Messiah,* is what comes to many people's minds when the word *Messiah* is mentioned. Let me quote from *The Home Book of Musical Knowledge* by David Ewen:

> Although universally acknowledged to be one of the greatest masterpieces in all musical literature, the Messiah was completed by the composer [Handel] in the astonishingly short time of twenty-four days. When Handel finished the triumphant climax to the second part of the work, the "Hallelujah Chorus," tears were streaming down his cheeks. "I did think I did see all Heaven before me and the Great God Himself!" he told his servant. And when the score was written he pointed to his bulky manuscript and said simply, "I think God has visited me."[2]

1. *The Complete Letters of Vincent van Gogh,* vols. 1–3 (Boston: Little Brown & Co., 1959).
2. David Ewen, *The Home Book of Musical Knowledge* (New York: Prentice Hall, 1954).

George Frederic Handel was born at Halle, a month before J.S. Bach, and was baptized on 24 February, 1685. He died on Saturday, 14 April, 1759, just over a week after a public performance of "The Messiah" at Covent Garden which he had directed. Handel had hoped to travel to Bath on 7 April but, as the *Whitehall Evening Post* announced, the visit was cancelled as he had "been for some time past in a bad state of health." He was buried in the evening of 20 April in Westminster Abbey, in the presence of some three thousand people.[3]

The first performance of the *Messiah* was on April 13, 1742, at William Neal's New Music-Hall, Fishamble Street, Dublin, with a public rehearsal four days earlier. It was announced that the money, a half guinea a ticket, would be "For Relief of the Prisoners in the several Gaols, and for the support of Mercer's Hospital in Stephen's Street, and of the Charitable Infirmary on the Inns Quay." It was requested that the ladies would come without hoops as it will "greatly increase the Charity, by making Room for more company." A similar request was made for the second performance that gentlemen were "to come without their swords."

There was opposition on the part of the High Church of England and other churches to this oratorio being performed as entertainment.

It is reported that during the first London performance the audience, carried away by the power of the "Hallelujah Chorus," arose to its feet as if by an arranged signal. Ever since then, audiences of all sorts and the world over express respect by rising at the beginning of this chorus and remaining standing until the conclusion of the section. That spontaneous reaction, it seems to me, has to do with the wonder of the music. But I also believe the words have a momentary impact.

To go over the words of the oratorio is stunning and awesome, even though words are pale in any attempt to state what is included in the entire work. When one contemplates how many thousands upon thousands of people have heard the *Messiah* sung from April 13, 1742, until *now*, words like "dazzling," "confounding," "staggering," don't seem strong enough. Statistics of how many people have heard one piece of music and one set of words is not any great

3. Charles Enderby, *Messiah and Handel: the Contemporary Background.*

thing in itself. It is *these words* that are dazzling, confounding, and staggering.

Who has really listened? And with what sort of ears or understanding?

After the first performance in London when Lord Kinnoul thanked the composer for "entertaining" the audience so completely, Handel replied, "I should be sorry, my lord, if I have only succeeded in entertaining them; I wished to make them better."

I am reminded of only one powerful description in the Bible, describing listening to God's Word, as a kind of listening to entertainment. Ezekiel the prophet had been told by God what to say to the people of Israel if they ask, "If our transgressions and our sins lie upon us, and we pine away in them, how can we then live?" "Say to them: 'As I live,' says the Lord GOD, 'I have no pleasure in the death of the wicked, but that the wicked turn from his way and live. Turn, turn from your evil ways! For why should you die, O house of Israel?' " This is in Ezekiel 33:10–11. At the end of the chapter comes this: "Indeed, you are to them as a very lovely song of one who has a pleasant voice and can play well on an instrument; for they hear your words, but they do not do them" (Ezek. 33:32).

God is pointing out that to listen to strong words from His Torah, Bible, Scriptures, as listening to instruments, and as listening to an entertaining song, is *not* enough. The content is to be listened to, considered in the mind, believed, and then acted upon.

Yes, the *Messiah* is a great piece of music, marvelous when sung with great voices accompanied by wonderful instruments. But although music is important to God the Creator of music, He gave the words to be *understood.*

Put the music on right now, if you can. I have it on as I write. Let us together really look at the words.

After the overture the tenor thrillingly begins with the fortieth chapter of Isaiah.

RECITATIVE, TENOR:

> *Comfort ye, comfort ye my people, saith your God. Speak ye comfortably to Jerusalem, and cry unto her, that her warfare is accomplished, that her iniquity is pardoned. The voice of him that crieth in the wilderness; Prepare ye the way of the Lord, make straight in the desert a highway for our God.*

How can iniquity be pardoned? When will warfare be finished? With what comfort can God's people be comforted in the midst of the pain and sorrows of life? When will all this be an accomplished fact? Whose voice will cry out in the wilderness calling for a straight highway for God to be made in the desert? Listen with deep satisfaction to the beauty of the music, but sit on the edge of your seat waiting for the answer to these questions so centrally important in each person's life.

TENOR ARIA:

> *Every valley shall be exalted, and every mountain and hill made low, the crooked straight, and the rough places plain.*

The repeated words emphasize and underline the longing in your very soul if you, or someone you love, is suffering pain in a hospital bed, or if you or someone you love is going through a rough time in some kind of storm, or slippery, rocky, uphill climb. How you wish for the beauty of the change that is described—the deep valleys lifted up, and the cliffs yet to be climbed brought gently down to be easily accessible, and the jagged thorns and sharp stones made smooth. How long, O Lord, until this takes place? Is something real being pointed to, or is it just poetic? When will this happen?

Listen to Matthew, Mark, and Luke tell it clearly.

> In those days John the Baptist came preaching in the wilderness of Judea, and saying, "Repent, for the kingdom of heaven is at hand!"
>
> For this is he who was spoken of by the prophet Isaiah, saying:
>
> > "The voice of one crying in the wilderness:
> > 'Prepare the way of the LORD,
> > Make His paths straight.' " (Matt. 3:1–3)

> The beginning of the gospel of Jesus Christ, the Son of God. As it is written in the Prophets:
>
> > "Behold, I send My messenger before Your face,
> > Who will prepare Your way before You."
> > "The voice of one crying in the wilderness:
> > 'Prepare the way of the LORD,
> > Make His paths straight.' "

John came baptizing in the wilderness and preaching a baptism of repentance for the remission of sins.

And all the land of Judea, and those from Jerusalem, went out to him and were all baptized by him in the Jordan River, confessing their sins. (Mark 1:1-5)

Annas and Caiaphas being high priests, the word of God came to John the son of Zacharias in the wilderness. And he went into all the region around the Jordan, preaching a baptism of repentance for the remission of sins, as it is written in the book of the words of Isaiah the prophet, saying:

"The voice of one crying in the wilderness:
'Prepare the way of the LORD,
Make His paths straight.
Every valley shall be filled
And every mountain and hill brought low;
And the crooked places shall be made straight
And the rough ways made smooth;
And all flesh shall see the salvation of God.' " (Luke 3:2-6)

God had given Matthew, Mark, and Luke a crystal clear account to write down for all who will carefully study the matter. Isaiah had been given a prophecy when he spoke to Israel looking ahead with encouragement to what would come in the future. Now the moment of fulfillment had arrived. John the Apostle was given the task of going one more step in unfolding what is taking place in that time. He wrote,

Now this is the testimony of John [the Baptist], when the Jews sent priests and Levites from Jerusalem to ask him, "Who are you?" He confessed, and did not deny, but confessed, "I am not the Christ." And they asked him, "What then? Are you Elijah?" He said, "I am not." "Are you the Prophet?" And he answered, "No." Then they said to him, "Who are you, that we may give an answer to those who sent us? What do you say about yourself?" He said: "I am 'The voice of one crying in the wilderness: "Make straight the way of the LORD," ' as the prophet Isaiah said." (John 1:19-23)

So it was answered. Up to this point it has been answered!

John the Baptist was the one Isaiah pointed to as God gave him the prophecy to announce to Israel seven hundred years before. History's stage was set for the next solo, but *not* simply the solo of an oratorio. No, it is space, time, and history that matters to each of us. We are affected by what took place. Handel took *these* words, these truths, and set them to music during three weeks! He did this believing the truth of what would be sung. The music goes on now to Haggai and Malachi, prophets who are speaking after the return from the Exile, and pointing to a future time also:

BASS:

> *Thus saith the Lord, the Lord of Hosts: Yet once a little while, and I will shake the heavens and the earth, the sea and the dry land; and I will shake all nations, and the desire of all nations shall come. The Lord whom ye seek shall suddenly come to His temple, even the messenger of the covenant, whom ye delight in; Behold he shall come, saith the Lord of Hosts. (Hag. 2:6–7 Mal. 3:1)*

Thrill to the depth of the bass voice, but much more to the depth of the words. Haggai is pointing beyond his present time when people were in danger of comparing Solomon's temple to the one then, which was so much less—even puny by comparison. He is pointing to a future completeness, when the Lord Himself shall come! Expectation is to be on the level of looking forward, believing that this is *true* and will happen.

Malachi is the last prophet in the Old Testament. His name seems to be a shortened form of Mal'ak ya, "Messenger of Yahweh." The next message spoken after the announcement that the Lord will suddenly come is a question that strikes hard.

BASS ARIA:

> *But who may abide the day of His coming? and who shall stand when He appeareth? For He is like a refiner's fire. (Mal. 3:2)*

Who indeed? Who can do anything but tremble at the thought of the Lord of Hosts coming—face to face with me, with you? How very much refining there is to be done! What impurities would float to the top of me in the refiner's fire? What to do? Would sackcloth and ashes be enough?

The long full version of the oratorio includes:

> *He will sit as a refiner and a purifier of silver;*
> *He will purify the sons of Levi,*

> *And refine them as gold and silver,*
> *That they may offer to the* LORD
> *An offering in righteousness. (Mal. 3:3)*

Ask the question with Malachi again, "Who can endure the day of His coming?" How can we stand such scrutiny? What will save us on that day? We need to cry with Paul, "O wretched man that I am! Who will deliver me?" (Rom. 7:24). We need to feel the mucky waters of a deep marshland with Pilgrim from *Pilgrim's Progress* in the Slough of Despond and *feel* the sinking, with rescue an urgent need.

With the background of such recognition, listen to this:

RECITATIVE ALTO:

> *Behold! A virgin shall conceive, and bear a son, and shall call his name Emmanuel: God with us. (Isa. 7:14)*

Isaiah, a prophet from a distinguished Jewish family, is the prophet who told at the beginning of his book of the judgment upon immoral and idolatrous people who, along with all people of the earth, have sinned. Isaiah also gives hope—great hope. All this, which was written between 740 and 680 B.C., needs to be a part of everyone's base of knowledge for finding the answer to Malachi's question, "Who may stand before the Lord?"

Read the entire quote from Isaiah itself: "Therefore the Lord Himself will give you a sign: Behold, the virgin shall conceive and bear a Son, and shall call His name Immanuel."

Matthew, in telling of how the angel appeared to Joseph in a dream to reassure him that his fiancée had not been unfaithful to him, quotes Isaiah in his explanation:

> "...for that which is conceived in her is of the Holy Spirit. And she will bring forth a Son, and you shall call His name JESUS, for He will save His people from their sins." Now all this was done that it might be fulfilled which was spoken by the Lord through the prophet, saying: "Behold, a virgin shall be with child, and bear a Son, and they shall call His name Immanuel," which is translated, "God with us." (Matt. 1:20–23)

Throughout the whole of the Old Testament there is a pointing ahead by the bringing of a lamb in worship. Abraham was instructed to substitute a ram as an atonement for Isaac. Isaac could not have had a stronger understanding than he was given. How to recognize the one Lamb or true Messiah was unfolded as time went on. Now Isaiah has given a sign to wait for and recognize. The Messiah had to be a virgin-born child. He had to be a *son*, not a daughter. This promised Person was to come in a specific moment of history, with a recognizable sign introducing Him to the waiting people.

The alto aria and the chorus immediately continue to unfold what will happen, what people could look forward to. These declarations are a marvel when we realize Isaiah wrote them seven hundred years before John the Baptist announced the Messiah was about to appear.

ALTO AND CHORUS:

> *O thou that tellest good tidings to Zion, get thee up into the high mountain! O thou that tellest good tidings to Jerusalem, lift up thy voice with strength! lift it up, be not afraid! Say unto the cities of Judah, Behold your God! O thou that tellest good tidings to Zion, arise, shine, for thy light is come, and the glory of the Lord is risen upon thee. O thou that tellest good tidings to Zion, good tidings to Jerusalem, arise, say unto the cities of Judah, Behold your God! Behold! The glory of the Lord is risen upon thee! (Isa. 40:9)*

What are the exciting tidings? What do these good tidings have to do with me? Is something being said that will *really* be a message, an answer, that affects you and me personally *now*?

The bass recitative now gives us in a deep bass which pounds through us the contrast of what is being talked about. There are good tidings, yes, but they are contrasted with an alternative.

BASS:

> *For behold, darkness shall cover the earth, and gross darkness the people: but the Lord shall arise upon thee, and his glory shall be seen upon thee. And the Gentiles shall come to Thy light, and kings to the brightness of Thy rising. (Isa. 60:2–3)*

While Isaiah is speaking to the Jews of the coming One whose arrival in history will bring light in the darkness, he is speaking not only to the Jews, but also to the Gentiles. This is to be the hope which is available to all people. You—whoever you are, stumbling in the "slough of despond" or wallowing in a marsh of despair—there is hope that is true. The quicksand that is just ahead of your feet can be removed. There is solid rock to be substituted upon which you can stand!

BASS:

> The people that walked in darkness have seen a great light. And they that dwell in the land of the shadow of death, upon them hath the the light shined. (Isa. 9:2)

Hope makes you turn the page in the chapter of your life to see what may come next. Hope is given in God's account of history past, present, and future—on the basis of *truth,* not fable. It is a solid rock upon which to stand during the typhoons of life. It is a light at the end of the tunnel. There are sunshine and green pasture ahead, with a pool of water for refreshment. Darkness can be left behind. As we find ourselves in the shadow of death, it is possible to discover the reality of the Light.

Now the lightness of joy comes with the chorus as the soprano voices soar with the good news!

CHORUS:

> For unto us a Child is born, unto us a Son is given, and the government shall be upon His shoulder, and his Name shall be called Wonderful, Counsellor, the mighty God, The Everlasting Father, The Prince of Peace. (Isa. 9:6)

Who can this be? Wonderful. Counselor. The Mighty God. The Everlasting Father. The Prince of Peace. *Who* can fulfill all our needs in this magnificent combination? Only the Messiah Himself. He is unique in the universe—in space, and time, and history—the only Son of God, the only promised Messiah. He is the only One Who is qualified to bring light and salvation, with a complete solution to darkness and lostness. This One alone can offer life in place of death.

Now we are ready for what is known as "The Christmas Story" from the book of Luke. How devastating is the trivial tinsel that speaks of a mere custom in the Western world. What the soprano is now singing is either truth—or a devastating lie. Were shepherds actually sitting there in the fields above Bethlehem that night? Did they really see and hear that fabulous series of announcements given by one angel's voice, and then a glorious chorus of information given by the music of an angel choir? Were humble Jewish shepherds the ones to whom God chose to announce the titanic event by which all history is dated—B.C. or A.D.?

What a strong, intense choice God made to mark the moment for which all nature has held its breath during the ages. Would there be a solution to the Fall? Would the abnormal history ever have a possibility of being changed? Could there be a restoration ahead? And when the moment for the beginning of the *event* of all events arrived, a group of human and down-to-earth shepherds, sitting on the ground, faithfully taking care of a field full of sheep were the audience for the great announcement! This was so far removed from the plastic replicas of the event; it was so much a part of the real world, the nitty-gritty life of people who think and act and feel, wonder and discuss and yet continue in a straight line to faithfully take care of their responsibilities, no matter how mundane.

RECITATIVE SOLO, SOPRANO:

> *There were shepherds abiding in the field, keeping watch over their flocks by night. (Luke 2:8)*

ACCOMPANIED SOPRANO:

> *And lo! the angel of the Lord came upon them, and the glory of the Lord shone around them, and they were sore afraid. (Luke 2:9)*

SOPRANO:

> *And the angel said unto them, Fear not: for behold, I bring you good tidings of great joy, which shall be to all people. For unto you is born this day in the city of David a Savior which is Christ the Lord. (Luke 2:10–11)*

ACCOMPANIED SOPRANO:

> *And suddenly there was with the angel a multitude of the heavenly host, praising God, and saying: (Luke 2:13)*

It takes a chorus, so Handel rightly decided, to bring something of the glory of the angels singing into the quiet night of those hills, splitting the air with a joyous declaration, and splitting the dark with brightness.

CHORUS:

> Glory to God in the highest, and peace on earth, good will towards men. (Luke 2:14)

This quotation is translated more accurately as "peace to men of good will." The Lord says He gives a peace that is different. It is an inward peace in the midst of a continuing battle. Evil has not yet been destroyed. The last enemy, death, has not yet been destroyed. One day the peace will be total...forever...glorious. The peace that is real now is real on the basis of the reality of God's promise, "I will never leave you nor forsake you," and on the basis of the true solution He has unfolded.

Turn back to the prophets and find what was prophesied concerning the Messiah's coming and concerning what He would do.

SOPRANO ARIA:

> Rejoice greatly, O daughter of Zion! Shout, O daughter of Jerusalem! Behold, thy King cometh unto thee! He is the righteous Savior, and he shall speak peace unto the heathen. (Zech. 9:9–10)

ALTO RECITATIVE:

> Then shall the eyes of the blind be opened and the ears of the deaf unstopped; then shall the lame man leap as an hart, and the tongue of the dumb shall sing. (Isa. 35:5–6)

ALTO ARIA:

> He shall feed His flock like a shepherd, and He shall gather the lambs with His arm and carry them in His bosom and gently lead those that are with young. (Isa. 40:11)

SOPRANO:

> Come unto Him, all ye that labour, ye that are heavy laden, and He will give you rest. Take His yoke upon you, and learn of Him, for He is meek and lowly of heart, and ye shall find rest unto your souls. (Matt. 11:28–29)

CHORUS:

> His yoke is easy, His burthen is light. (Matt. 11:30)

Give a deep sigh of wonder, a deep sigh of hope, and bow in response! All this is telling that the Messiah came in history, in a geographic space, there in the fields outside Bethlehem. He lived and walked in Judea and Jerusalem where you can walk and look up at the same sky. You can have your feet on the same soil in a different time, but in a time in history that is connected with Jesus by normal dating. If this is true, it needs serious consideration. We are not talking about two or three different political parties, nor of two or three different denominations, nor of two or three different football teams, nor of different tastes in music, art, interior decoration, architecture, or food. It matters a great deal whether this is true or not.

Handel has already discovered the reality of the truth of what this Lamb of God did for him. Handel has already discovered what "forever" is all about! His putting the following words to the penetrating music is his way of speaking truth into generations of ears. This music, which he meant to emphasize the words, is his legacy.

CHORUS:

> Behold the Lamb of God, that taketh away the sins of the world.
> (John 1:29)

HE HAS COME! He may really be seen, beheld! He is the promised One Who would give the solution to the broken spoiled world. The lambs used in worship by Abraham, Moses, and all through history, looked forward to *the* Lamb. And now—here He is. Shivers of fearful and delightful recognition should fill you and go up and down your spine. To take this with a flat, dry, dusty, theological kind of attitude, whether positive or negative, is horrible!

Behold the Lamb of God!

Then what? What does one do about that happening?

It is the Old Testament that must be turned to now. This is where the understanding comes from. This is what must be known in order to appreciate the perfectly awesome wonder of what has taken place. It is not an unprepared for, unexpected happening—God has revealed through His prophets what was to happen. Read *all* of Isaiah 53. And without previous ideas entering in (if you can open your mind in that way), think of who it is speaking. Then remember again that Isaiah was written 700 B.C. and that he spoke prophetically.

ALTO ARIA:

> *He was despised and rejected of men; a man of sorrows and acquainted with grief. (Isa. 53:3)*

CHORUS:

> *Surely He hath borne our griefs and carried our sorrows, He was wounded for our transgressions; He was bruised for our iniquities; the chastisement of our peace was upon Him. (Isa. 53:4–5)*

CHORUS:

> *And with His stripes we are healed. (Isa. 53:5b)*

CHORUS:

> *All we like sheep have gone astray; we have turned every one to his own way. And the Lord hath laid on Him the iniquity of us all. (Isa. 53:6)*

TENOR RECITATIVE:

> *All they that see Him, laugh Him to scorn, they shoot out their lips and shake their heads, saying: (Ps. 22:7)*

CHORUS:

> *He trusted in God that He would deliver Him; let him deliver him if he delight in him. (Ps. 22:8)*

TENOR RECITATIVE:

> *Thy rebuke hath broken His heart; He is full of heaviness; He looked for some to have pity on Him, but there was no man, neither found He any to comfort Him. (Ps. 69:20)*

The book of Romans in the New Testament quotes Psalm 69 as referring to Christ the Messiah: "For even Christ did not please Himself; but as it is written, 'The reproaches of those who reproached You fell on Me' " (Rom. 15:3 quoting from Ps. 69:9). The threads are intertwined throughout all of history to give the full tapestry of truth.

TENOR ARIA:

> Behold and see if there be any sorrow like unto His sorrow. (Lam. 1:12)

Certainly there has been no sorrow in all of history to compare with the sorrow of the suffering of the perfectly righteous Son of God as He took upon Himself the sins of the evil world. His suffering was not for anything wrong He had done, but for the choices made through all the ages by those who had chosen deliberately to do the wrong thing. We each have deliberately and specifically made choices and decisions knowing the wrongness of those choices, realizing to some extent the sin involved, no matter how low our ethical or moral standard is compared to some other standard. We are clearly told in Romans that no matter what standard people live by, they have broken their own standards and God will judge them on the basis of that: "Therefore you are inexcusable, O man, whoever you are who judge, for in whatever you judge another you condemn yourself; for you who judge practice the same things. . . . And do you think this, O man, you who judge those practicing such things, and doing the same, that you will escape the judgment of God?" (Rom. 2:1,3).

God makes known to us that perfection is beyond us, and that we are guilty of sin in a variety of areas. He then compassionately, lovingly, and with great suffering opens the way for us to His forgiveness, on the basis of His paying the price for us. It is a substitution. It is an atonement. He who sinned not became sin for us. The act of doing that brought sorrow like no other sorrow.

TENOR RECITATIVE:

> He was cut off out of the land of the living, for the transgression of Thy people was He stricken. (Isa. 53:8)

TENOR ARIA:

> But Thou didst not leave His soul in Hell nor didst Thou suffer Thy Holy One to see corruption. (Ps. 16:10)

What earthly good would it do us if the Messiah had died and stayed dead?

What a glorious prophecy and expectation is given in the psalmist's wonderful prayer, praise and thanksgiving to God in Psalm 16. Read the context of that tenor aria:

> Therefore my heart is glad,
> And my glory rejoices;
> My flesh also will rest in hope.
> For You will not leave my soul in Sheol,
> Nor will You allow Your Holy One to see corruption.
> You will show me the path of life;
> In Your presence is fullness of joy;
> At Your right hand are pleasures forevermore. (Ps. 16:9–11)

The aria is taken from this. It is right to apply it to the Messiah. Had He not risen from the dead, had He not stepped out of the grave, there would be *no* hope. *But it is exciting* to realize that the psalmist and those who sang the Psalms in expectation of the coming Messiah *trusted* in a restored future in which they would find a reality of a path of life, and of discovering that in God's presence there will be "fullness of joy," and "pleasures forevermore." Often people ask me, "Is there any mention of future life in the Old Testament?" Oh yes, YES!

CHORUS:

> Lift up your heads, O ye gates, and be ye lift up, ye everlasting doors, and the King of glory shall come in. Who is the King of Glory? The Lord, strong and mighty, the Lord mighty in battle. Lift up your heads, O ye gates, and be ye lift up, ye everlasting doors, and the King of glory shall come in. Who is the King of Glory? The Lord of Hosts, He is the King of Glory. (Ps. 24:7–10)

A note of triumph. Death did not defeat the King of Glory. Rather He has died to give victory.

Hebrews is speaking of how God has spoken to us through His Son, rather than just through the prophets. The time came to send His Son to speak, as well as to do what no other person could do.

"For to which of the angels did He ever say: 'You are My Son, Today I have begotten You'? And again: 'I will be to Him a Father, And He shall be to Me a Son'?" (Heb. 1:5, quoting 2 Sam. 7:14).

SOPRANO ARIA:

> How beautiful are the feet of them that preach the gospel of peace and bring glad tidings of good things. (This verse from Rom. 10:15 is a quote from Isa. 52:7.)

So you see, in *both* the Old and New Testaments there is a recognition of the importance and beauty of making truth known, and of giving the people of the earth a message, "tidings of good things," rather than leaving them in ignorance. Truth has always been meant to be relayed!

Another aria, sometimes omitted, repeats this theme:

Yes, indeed: "Their sound is gone out into all lands, and their words unto the ends of the world." (Rom. 10:18, quoting from Ps. 19:4.)

The bass aria thunders the question:

BASS ARIA:

> *Why do the nations so furiously rage together, and why do the people imagine a vain thing? The kings of the earth rise up, and the rulers take counsel together against the Lord and against His anointed. (Ps. 2:1–2)*

Why? Why? They do this for the same reason that Eve turned to Lucifer's lies in the first place. They prefer the lie of Lucifer and the temptation to be masters of their own destiny rather than to bow before the living God and Creator.

TENOR RECITATIVE:

> *He that dwelleth in Heaven shall laugh them to scorn; the Lord shall have them in derision. (Ps. 2:4)*

This tenor is singing words that might be placed in the book of Job as God speaks of the minimal length of time human beings have to discover the secrets of creation, and of the form and substance of the universe.

TENOR ARIA:

> *Thou shalt break them with a rod of iron. Thou shalt dash them in pieces like a potter's vessel. (Ps. 2:9)*

The trust placed in the false gods described as being "like a scarecrow in a melon patch" in the book of Jeremiah (10:5 NIV), and the turning away from the Judeo-Christian God, is trusting rotten planks which will very certainly break and "dash them in pieces like a potter's vessel."

But, the compassionate God has opened the way, so that does

not need to be the final reality! Being dashed on the rocks *is* a reality all right—and a final reality for whoever turns away with deliberateness—but it need not be!

How long is a lifetime? How does it compare with forever? How lasting is "the work of human hands"? How does that compare with the work of God's hands? Piano Model S baby grand 281261, made in the Steinway factory in Queens in 1935 by the hands of four hundred human beings, is having a longer life than the length of the marriage of Francis and Edith Schaeffer who were married that same year. "Death parted" that marriage long before that piano lost its "voice." The cellos, violas, and violins you hear in concerts, made by the hands of Amati, Guarneri, and Stradivari, were made in the 1600s and 1700s, and have far outlasted the hands that made them, as well as generations of hands that have played them!

How is it then that God the Creator has created the complicated instruments of the human being with the intricate combination of body and mind—which death can so suddenly wipe out, while the creative beings God created can make instruments which last so much longer, which have a longer "life-span" so to speak? And can become sweeter and more mellow for years?

Accepting the fact that Lucifer brought death into history, was Lucifer stronger than God? And is the word *forever* meaningless to the instrument of the human voice, or to the human being? Did God fail?

This is what the Messiah is all about! The Messiah came, lived, and died that there might be a complete restoration! Musical instruments are often "restored" by expert hands. God has made clear that there is a restoration which will give marvelous restored bodies to each one who comes to Him believing. In the end, God's "instruments," the human beings, will be restored to last forever. Forever does have meaning. Forever applies to the restoration, which is not a manner of "patching up"...but a completely fresh beginning—a beginning without ending. The Creator created the most lasting Creation after all!

It is overwhelming to have "The Hallelujah Chorus" be the very next portion of the oratorio. The response is so stunningly instinctive, so very spontaneous and unpremeditated on the part of many who hear it for the first time. The music is so gorgeous and satisfying to every bone in the body. It is such a declaration of victory and majesty in that future moment when indeed the Lord God will have put every enemy down. "The last enemy to be destroyed is death." We are told this specifically. That is a future moment, as we see death on every side of us from a terrific diversity of illnesses, accidents, floods, fires, typhoons, tidal waves, and hurricanes as well as wars and deliberate murders. Death will be over one day! And the singing of Hallelujah is gloriously appropriate! As a great choir sings and a splendid orchestra plays, one is almost carried through the roof of the concert hall! But have you ever stood and thrilled with only the thrill of great music? Have you ever heard the stirring words without believing any of the ideas set forth, or understanding that the history being recounted is true?

Hallelujah, Lord of Lords. Hallelujah, King of Kings. It is fabulous. But is He *your* King and *your* Lord? This is not exclusive for club members only but is available to all.

CHORUS:

> Hallelujah! For the Lord God Omnipotent reigneth. The kingdom of the world is become the kingdom of our Lord and of His Christ, and He shall reign forever and ever. King of Kings, and Lord of Lords. Hallelujah! (Rev. 19:6, 11:15; 19:16)

Who will have part in the forever and forever so strongly promised and pointed to here? Forever music is to be a part of the forever, but who will be there?

SOPRANO ARIA:

> I know that my Redeemer liveth, and that He shall stand at the latter day upon the earth. And though worms destroy this body, yet in my flesh shall I see God. For now is Christ risen from the dead, the firstfruits of them that sleep. (Job 19:25 and 1 Cor. 15:20)

The strong expectation and hope expressed in Job's unmistakable words show that Job believed in the resurrection. What did he know about it? He had an assurance that this life is not all there is. He expected restoration and he declared that he would in his flesh see God. A spiritual resurrection? No, Job is talking about a physical resurrection. Read the rest of that passage.

> Oh, that my words were written!
> Oh, that they were inscribed in a book!
> That they were engraved on a rock
> With an iron pen and lead, forever!
> For I know that my Redeemer lives,

> And He shall stand at last on the earth;
> And after my skin is destroyed, this I know,
> That in my flesh I shall see God,
> Whom I shall see for myself,
> And my eyes shall behold, and not another. (Job 19:23-27)

Job has had his words not only written in a book but sung by great choirs. The rest of the aria is taken from the New Testament, where in 1 Corinthians 15 the resurrection is so clearly unfolded. It gives us a comforting reassurance to add to Job's personal assurance and to David's certainty in Psalm 23. An aria taken from 1 Corinthians 15:22 speaks of death coming by man (Adam that is) and resurrection also coming by man (speaking of Christ the Messiah who is truly man as well as truly God).

BASS ARIA:

> *Behold, I tell you a mystery: we shall not all sleep, but we shall all be changed in a moment, in the twinkling of an eye, at the last trumpet. (1 Cor. 15:51–52)*

The forever music will be introduced by a trumpet solo!

There is coming a moment that will be a certain minute on clocks, whatever time it is in each part of the world, when a trumpet will sound. The broadcast trumpet solo will be more than music—it will be an announcement! The dead will rise at the clear note of that trumpet, and those who are living and are believers in the God of the Bible and in His Messiah, the Lord's Christ, will be changed in the twinkling of an eye. They will be changed to have bodies like the body Christ had when He rose from His death and spent forty days on earth talking to many, many people so that His resurrection would be the best attested fact in history.

BASS ARIA:

> *The trumpet shall sound, and the dead shall be raised incorruptible, and we shall be changed. (1 Cor. 15:52–53)*

WE, we…you and I.
Please be included in the "we."
The end of Handel's *Messiah* is fittingly a chorus again.

CHORUS:

> Worthy is the Lamb that was slain and hath redeemed us to God by His blood to receive power and riches, and wisdom and strength, and honor, and glory, and blessing. Blessing and honour, glory and power be unto Him that sitteth upon the throne and unto the Lamb, forever and ever. (Rev. 5:12–13)

CHORUS:

> Amen.

What a gorgeous ending to the oratorio. But it isn't just a gorgeous ending to an oratorio, it is the reality of what is open to you and to me in expectation. We *can* say "forever music" with meaning because the God of Creation, Who created music in the first place and Who created people in His image to be able to create music too, has opened up a possibility. There is not a shadow of a doubt that He can keep His promises. The prophecies of the coming of the Messiah to suffer and die in the place of human beings who would have no other way to be rid of sin have all been fulfilled.

Now there remain prophecies and promises for what is ahead of us. The last chorus comes from Revelation. Let me quote it in context.

> "For You were slain,
> And have redeemed us to God by Your blood
> Out of every tribe and tongue and people and nation,
> And have made us kings and priests to our God;
> And we shall reign on the earth."
> Then I looked, and I heard the voice of many angels around the throne, the living creatures, and the elders; and the number of them was ten thousand times ten thousand, and thousands of thousands, saying with a loud voice:
> "Worthy is the Lamb who was slain
> To receive power and riches and wisdom,
> And strength and honor and glory and blessing!"
> And every creature which is in heaven and on the earth and under the earth and such as are in the sea, and all that are in them, I heard saying:
> "Blessing and honor and glory and power
> Be to Him who sits on the throne,
> And to the Lamb, forever and ever!" (Rev. 5:9–13)

Forever and ever? Yes, there will be music such as we have never heard before. A choir composed of startling numbers of amazing creatures from all parts of the universe and of history. What an event to be a part of! And it will never end.

We won't have to go home because we will *be home.*

Does forever music make sense?

It makes the only sense there is to have. Death and rebellion make no sense at all. God has done everything that could be done to meet the requirements of justice, and love, and to open fairly the way to forever happiness.

And there shall be no tears there and no more curse, but the throne of God and of the Lamb will be there. There we will hear the song of Moses and the Lamb, a glorious tying together of history, a marvelous continuity.

> And they sing the song of Moses the Servant of God, and the song of the Lamb, saying:
> "Great and marvelous are Your works,
> Lord God Almighty!
> Just and true are Your ways,
> O King of the saints!
> Who shall not fear You, O Lord, and glorify Your name?
> For You alone are holy.
> For all nations shall come and worship before You,
> For your judgments have been manifested." (Rev. 15:3-4)

> And there shall be no night there: ... And they shall reign forever and forever. Then he said to me, 'These words are faithful and *true."* (Rev. 22:5-6)

It is true.
It is not a myth.

> "I, Jesus, have sent My angel to testify to you these things in the churches. I am the Root and the Offspring of David, the Bright and Morning Star." And the Spirit and the bride say, "Come!" And let him who hears say, "Come!" And let him who thirsts come. And whoever desires, let him take the water of life freely." (Rev. 22:16-17)

This is your invitation to the concert.

It is a valid one, and will be honored. If you are thirsty, take the water of life freely. The Messiah says, "Come."

Enjoy music *forever*!

Bibliography

Anderson, David. *The Piano Makers*. New York: Pantheon Books, 1982.

The Complete Letters of Vincent van Gogh. Vols. 1–3. Boston: Little Brown and Co., 1959.

Ewen, David. *The Home Book of Musical Knowledge*. New York: Prentice Hall, 1954.

Gaines, James R., ed. *The Lives of the Piano*. New York: Harper and Row, 1981.

Hill, W. Henry, Arthur F. Hill and Alfred E. Hill. *Antonio Stradivari: His Life and Work (1644–1737)*. New York: Dover Publications, 1963.

Kennedy, Michael. *The Concise Oxford Dictionary of Music*. 3d ed. New York: Oxford University Press, 1980.

Kummer, Corby, ed. *Talking About Pianos*. New York: Steinway and Sons, 1982.

Roberts, Ronald. *Making a Simple Violin and Viola*. North Pomfret, Vt.: David and Charles Inc., 1975.

Schaeffer, Francis A. and C. Everett Koop. *Whatever Happened to the Human Race?* Old Tappan, N.J.: Revell, 1979.

Schaeffer, Francis A. *He Is There and He Is Not Silent*. Wheaton, Ill.: Tyndale, 1972.

Schaeffer, Francis A. *How Should We Then Live?* Old Tappan, N.J.: Revell, 1976.

Scholes, Percy A. *The Oxford Companion to Music*. 10th ed. New York: Oxford University Press, 1970.

Smith, Jane Stuart and Betty Carlson. *A Gift of Music*. Westchester, Ill.: Good News Publishers, 1978.

Steinway, Theodore E. *People and Pianos*. 2d ed. New York: Steinway and Sons, 1961.

Sumner, William Leslie. *The Pianoforte*. 4th ed. London: Macdonald and James, 1978.

Tolkien, J.R.R. *The Silmarillion*. Boston: Houghton Mifflin Co., 1977.

Vasari, Giorgio. *Artists of the Renaissance*, trans. George Bull. London: Allen Lane, 1978.